Redeeming the Dial

Redeeming the

Dial

Radio, Religion, & Popular Culture in America

Tona J. Hangen

The University of North Carolina Press

Chapel Hill and London

© 2002 The University of North Carolina Press
All rights reserved
Manufactured in the United States of America
Designed by Richard Hendel
Set in Charter and Champion types
by Tseng Information Systems, Inc.
The paper in this book meets the guidelines for permanence
and durability of the Committee on Production Guidelines for
Book Longevity of the Council on Library Resources.
Frontispiece: Father Charles Coughlin preaching on the radio.
Prints and Photographs Division, Library of Congress.
Library of Congress Cataloging-in-Publication Data
Hangen, Tona J.
Redeeming the dial : radio, religion, and popular culture in
America / Tona J. Hangen.
    p. cm.
Includes bibliographical references (p.   ) and index.
ISBN 0-8078-2752-5 — ISBN 0-8078-5420-4
1. Radio in religion—United States—History—20th century.
2. Evangelicalism—United States—History—20th century.
3. Religious broadcasting—Christianity—History—20th
century.   I. Title.
BV656 .H36   2002
269'.26'0973—dc21   2002005543

cloth 06 05 04 03 02   5 4 3 2 1
paper 06 05 04 03 02   5 4 3 2 1

Contents

Illustrations

Acknowledgments

I am very grateful to the many archivists, colleagues, and friends who helped make this book possible. When I began to study religious radio programs, their audiences, and the coalitions that formed in American society either to advocate for or limit religious broadcasting on radio, I soon discovered that there was no single repository of sources, no comprehensive collection of documents or recordings, and no computer-searchable database of early-twentieth-century religious periodicals. What might have been the frustrating task of tracking down primary sources for religious radio from 1920 to the 1950s instead has turned out to be a delightful journey, given the help of many patient librarians and archivists across the country. Thanks to the staff and interlibrary loan administrators at Brandeis's Goldfarb and Farber libraries in Waltham, Massachusetts; the Goddard Library at Gordon-Conwell Theological Seminary in Hamilton, Massachusetts; and the Randall Library in Stow, Massachusetts. I am grateful for the on-site research assistance provided to me by Robert Shuster, Wayne Weber, and Janyce Nasgowitz at the Billy Graham Center Archives in Wheaton, Illinois; by Sarah Smith and Carl Stole at the National Religious Broadcasters in Manassas, Virginia; by Amy Roberts and the staff of the Department of History of the Presbyterian Church (U.S.A.) in Philadelphia, Pennsylvania, and for permission from Curtis Kearns, director of the National Ministries Division, Presbyterian Church (U.S.A.), to examine the records of the Board of National Missions there; by Kate McGinn at the David du Plessis Center at Fuller Theological Seminary in Pasadena, California; by Gerald Perschbacher of the Lutheran Laymen's League in St. Louis, Missouri; and by Marvin Huggins and Mark Loest at Concordia Historical Institute in St. Louis, Missouri. Long-distance research help was generously provided by Janet Simonsen, Heritage Department of the International Church of the Foursquare Gospel in Los Angeles, California; Bertha Ihnat of the Ohio State University Archives in Columbus, Ohio; Steve Staiger of the Palo Alto City Library in Palo Alto, California; staff of the Federal Records Commission at the Federal Records Center in Suitland, Maryland, and of the Library of Congress Photo Reproduction Department in Washington D.C.; and two enthusiastic private collectors of radio ephemera, Read Burgan and Mike Khanchalian, who graciously shared recordings.

Mentors and helpful colleagues have nurtured this project at various stages, and I would like to thank Joel A. Carpenter of Calvin College, Harry Stout and Jon Butler of the Institute for the Advanced Study of Religion at Yale University, Larry Eskridge of the Institute for the Study of American Evangelicals, Garth Rosell of the Ockenga Institute at Gordon-Conwell Theological Seminary, Jason Loviglio of the University of Maryland at Baltimore, Stewart Hoover and Lynn Schofield Clark of the Center for Mass Media Research at the University of Colorado at Boulder, and Barbara Bradley of National Public Radio. Thanks also for comments, writing support, and suggestions from Christine Edwards Allred, Edith Blumhofer, Joan Bolker, Joanna Brooks, Chad Cover, Peter D'Agostino, Thomas Doherty, Martha Gardner, Philip Goff, Jay Green, Matthew Hale, Marci McPhee, Jenny Pulsipher, Jenni Ratner, Jana Riess, Pamela Riney-Kehrberg, Jonathan Sarna, Ted Slutz, Rebecca Sullivan, Bill Svelmoe, Hillary Warren, and Bryan Waterman. I also want to thank the members of the American History Department at Brandeis who helped nourish my scholarship during my graduate studies: David Hackett Fischer, Jane Kamensky, Morton Keller, and especially James T. Kloppenberg on my dissertation committee and Jacqueline Jones, my adviser and friend. Invaluable financial assistance was provided through Brandeis's Crown Fellowship and a dissertation fellowship from the Graduate School of Arts and Sciences, in addition to a fellowship from the Pew Program of Religion and American History at Yale. I received helpful suggestions on improving this project from participants at sessions of the Popular Culture Association, the American Studies Association, the Society for the Scientific Study of Religion, the Pew Scholars Conference, the Berkshire Conference of Women Historians, the Boston Area Religious History Workshop, and the Association for Education in Journalism and Mass Communication, where portions of this work were presented. Many participants of the E-mail discussion lists H-AMREL, H-AMSTDY, and ANDERE-L have offered references, clarifications, and advice about my project. I am most grateful to the editors and staff at the University of North Carolina Press and to the readers, who included Michele Hilmes.

Without a supportive family, I could not have found the time to work on this book. I am grateful to my parents and my siblings for their encouragement and research assistance and to a wonderful series of caregivers for my children. Most of all, I need to acknowledge the eternal, unfailing support of my husband, Don; this book is his triumph as much as my own, and I love him all the more for it.

Introduction

Imagine a wind-scoured farmhouse and beside it a small barn, huddled together under an ashen gray Montana sky. It is 21 January, the dead of winter, so cold that a widow woman will not venture out for anything but to milk her cows—and even then, not too early, not until long after daybreak. She is sixty-seven years old, farming alone, tending her herd with stiffening hands that have known hard times. Grown and now living far away with homes of their own, her children know she faces the farm's chores without hired help. Inside the barn, the air is a little warmer; the cows breathe by snorting clouds of vapor, which hang in the air. The woman sings and prays as she milks, listening to a radio set on a shelf among the pails and coils of baling wire. She sings a familiar gospel song, adding her voice to the rippling chords of a piano and a jubilant-sounding choir in sunny Long Beach, California, thousands of miles away. They cannot hear her, of course, yet she sings. Only the cows hear; the cows, and God.

No photographer captured this scene; no journalist or diarist recorded it. Besides the farmer herself, Mrs. Phoebe Huffman of Richey, Montana, no one witnessed the occasion. The fact that Mrs. Huffman chose to listen to Charles Fuller's *Old Fashioned Revival Hour* during her morning milking sessions might never have been known had she not penned a letter in early 1954 to the program's preacher. A Christian of "several years," she appreciated being able to hear religious services at her own homestead—so much so that she folded into the letter a ten-dollar bill to help Reverend Fuller continue the broadcasts over the two local stations on which Mrs. Huffman found them. Fuller's sermons, she wrote, had given "comfort" to her family while her late husband was alive and helped pass the long winter days. She went on to explain, with idiosyncratic spelling and no punctuation:

> I live on a farm here in Montana ever since March 1910 I no what hard times was when we had drout and hail stormes to take our crops but the Lord always took care of us in Some way I raised 5 children and lost one baby at Birth I am 67 years old dont go to church much in winter it is Cold to go an I dont drive a Car eny more But I can listen to good sermons over the rido on Sunday an on weekdays to and I always pray for all the ministers ever day Well I will close for this day an may God bless an keep you all
>
> Your friend Mrs. Phoebe Huffman, R.I. Box 25, Richey Mont[ana][1]

But for faithful listeners like Mrs. Huffman, with their regular habit of tuning in, their gratitude and prayers, and their humble contributions, religious radio itself might have been a passing fad of the experimental early years of broadcasting. Instead, commercial religious broadcasting hung on through the consolidation of nationwide radio networks; changes in the regulatory structure of broadcast signal allocation; the lean years of the thirties, when donations thinned; and the "golden age" of American broadcasting, when many radio programs were thinly disguised commercials for cosmetics or automobiles—always remaining a genre apart and above all persisting on the air.

That Mrs. Phoebe Huffman listened to a religious radio program during milking suggests that radio permitted some changes in the devotional practices of ordinary Americans. The private uses to which radio programming could be put suggest, in turn, that media messages—and perhaps particularly religious messages—are always subject to reinterpretation by their consumers. It is important, then, not only to know what was said and sung in religious radio programming but also to try to understand what Mrs. Huffman and her contemporaries *heard.* The growth of a vital industry purveying religious messages, objects, and ideas can be explained only by understanding its appeal to the mil-

Radio listening in a farm home in Minnesota, March 1942. The poem on top of the radio is titled "Friendship Lane"; the woman tuning the radio has a Swedish-language newspaper on her lap. Photograph by Jack Delano, Office of War Information; Prints and Photographs Division, Library of Congress.

lions who listened. Media and cultural historians Jesús Martín-Barbero, Stewart Hoover, Justin Lewis, and Frederic Jameson have insisted that audiences make the meaning, that unintended messages are always possible, and that interpreting the mass media is a process of negotiation and historical contextualization.[2] Recognizing the power of "alternative readings" of cultural texts, Mark Hulsether argues that "postmodern cultural theory highlights how the residual power of religious traditions can be expressed and contested—not merely defeated and trivialized—within a society that communicates through commercial mass media."[3]

Looking at the narratives constructed through mass media, therefore, is only the starting point for understanding the role these media, and particularly radio, have played in building identity and constructing cultural boundaries. The next step is to explore the agency exercised by the audience for religious radio and the social frameworks within which listeners "read" radio as a cultural text.[4] To achieve a multidimensional analysis, I not only use traditional organizational, biographical, and rhetorical evidence but also rely on listener correspondence and other sources of information to get at the meaning of religious broadcasting for its audiences and for the nation as a whole. Very seldom can we access ways the media served as a bulwark against the co-optations and degradations it simultaneously effected. The story of religious radio broadcasting is one way to get at that "other" story. Mass media, after all, channeled messages that were conservative (orienting, placing) as well as transformative (disorienting, displacing). Typically radio services have been seen as a way to avoid attending church; an example that comes to mind is an Aberdeen, South Dakota, listener who sat through Sunday night sermons "until time to take up the collection when we got busy elsewhere."[5] But radio also made it possible to *begin* going to church or to rethink entirely what church was and where worship could take place.

I hope this book will represent another voice in the current secularization debate and offer a historical perspective to those who study the interconnections between media and religion in modern America.[6] Simply put, some historians and sociologists had assumed that with the growth of modern society and the separation of churches from the structures of political power, society in general would become more secular, religion would fade away, or it would become completely privatized. Whether that is true for Europe, on which many of the secularization arguments were based, is beyond the scope of this book. But clearly, in the United States, it was another story, and this book will help explain how that story unfolded. Religion, even the kind that bills itself as "traditional" or "old-fashioned," found a ready place in modern mass media, enhancing and strengthening certain forms of religious behavior and practice.

The recent scholarly notion of mass media as a new form of an older, human need for aurality/orality interlaces neatly with my observation that Protestant religion is a religion of the heard word.[7] Radio introduced new narratives and voices to the American public, piercing the mystique of places and people previously less accessible. Potentially, religious experience could have been watered down, marginalized, or supplanted by the public's engagement with new forms of mass entertainment. Walter Ong and Mircea Eliade have informed my thinking about the unexpected way religion was enhanced by the mass media's "desacralization" of the world and how the sound of radio fostered the "personalist loyalties, strong social or tribal feelings and responses, and special anxieties" of an older oral/aural tradition.[8] Radio served as a pulpit for evangelism on a scale impossible only decades before. Charles Fuller, for example, could reach in just four half-hour messages "more living people on this earth than the greatest evangelist of the nineteenth century, D. L. Moody, was able to reach, with long journeys, fatiguing travels, and sometimes three meetings a day, in his entire forty years of Christian service."[9] Neither Fuller nor anyone else trying to launch a worldwide media ministry ever forgot the vast scale of possibility.

Despite that vast scale, a radio sermon—unlike attendance at an enormous mass meeting—could be experienced by a single listener like a personal chat. Radio religion often made best use of the medium's ability to speak to listeners as if in a one-on-one conversation. Shouting to a large crowd had been the staple of revival religion since before Benjamin Franklin spent an afternoon in 1739 calculating the number of people who could hear the famously loud George Whitfield sermonizing on the Philadelphia Court House steps.[10] But when Father Coughlin practiced the same kind of vocal dynamics in the 1930s, it merely drew attention to his delivery, often to the detriment of his message. "He harangues the microphone," complained Raymond Gram Swing, editor of *The Nation,* in 1935. "And if you shout and orate at a man in a small room, he will not listen to you as he would if you speak to him quietly and personally. . . . The microphone is the doorhandle into a man's living-room."[11] Likewise, "radio is the only medium capable of delivering the natural, personal, powerful persuasive spoken word directly into the midst of the American family where it can be considered, discussed, and acted upon immediately," argued an ad for the promotional capability of radio station KGVL in Greenville, Texas.[12] People often mentioned in fan mail to radio preachers how they felt singled out for personal attention by a message and how close the experience of listening to radio was to having an actual religious adviser sitting by their side. Radio shrunk distances, collapsing time and space with unseen power. Today, of course, we take the simultaneity of the mass media for granted, even demand that it deliver an immediate, emotionally satisfying (i.e., "true" or "authentic") representation of a faraway reality. Until television, radio was the only means for the immediate experience of a remote event, and that experience—partly because of its sheer novelty in the early years—could be jarring, epiphanic, even life changing.

Part of the appeal of conservative Christian broadcasting— or, to critics, perhaps its most maddening feature—was its absolute self-certainty. As John Roach Straton, pastor of Manhattan's Calvary Baptist Church and an early entrant in religious radio, put it in 1931, "The people will not get any doubts or negations or question marks from the Calvary pulpit."[13] Effective and commercially successful religious broadcasting polarized issues into right and wrong with confidence, wrapping assertions in language claiming biblical authority and divine approbation.[14] To many, the radio was what Paul Rader called a "new witnessing medium," and it offered clear evidence not of the entrepreneurial streak in American Protestantism but rather of the hand of God, rolling forward his divine plans.[15] Fundamentalist radio broadcasters gave a national voice to the folk religion of their listeners—expressing their millennial hopes, their faith to be healed, and the cadences of their oral worship. They believed religion could, and *should,* speak to the everyday, concrete realities of life—sickness, trouble, the search for peace of mind. Conservative listeners' apparent delight in radio illustrated their eagerness not only for their beliefs to be heard by those outside the fold of believers but also for their internal and personal concerns to be addressed by a God who could be accessed, heard, and spoken to in a modern and technologically complex world. To them, he was a deity as close as the dial on a radio, hard at work for his faithful, who themselves were dedicated to furthering his righteous causes. Combative preachers encouraged radio audiences either to ally with or against their teachings. Fundamentalist broadcasting illustrated the dynamic tension in conservative Protestantism between turning inward and reaching outward.

That tension is far from new in American religion. Nathan Hatch, Harry Stout, R. Laurence Moore, and Frank Lambert all have written extensively about the promotion of religious ideas through mass meetings, print, and other means in colonial and early America.[16] Protestantism's position as the dominant religious mode in the nineteenth century and the de facto civil religion of the whole nation was owed to the popular marketing of revivalism, and so in that sense the embrace of the mass medium of radio in the early twentieth century should not be surprising.

However, in other ways, the twentieth century seemed barren ground for old-time religion to take root and thrive. The early years were, as Richard Fox and T. J. Jackson Lears have written, a time of doubt and "cultural consternation," when "the old religious sanctions for the moral life, a life of sacrifice and toil, had begun to disintegrate in the face of both Darwin and the liberalization of Protestantism itself."[17] As the United States became more modern and secular in the early twentieth century, Protestants found that religious institutions seemed to have less authority to articulate values embraced by the entire nation.[18] Revivalistic, doctrinally conservative Protestants in the 1910s sought both to reclaim the authority they perceived they'd lost and to uphold the core ("fundamental") doctrines of the Christian faith. Key among the doctrines conservatives emphatically defended were the inerrant and literal truth of the Bible and premillennialism—the imminent second coming of Jesus Christ prior to a prophesied millennium of peace.[19] They founded Bible institutes and colleges to train people in these essential doctrines, held conferences and retreats to celebrate and defend conservative Christianity, and published scores of periodicals to promote this reinvigorated orthodoxy, including an influential pamphlet series, *The Fundamentals,* which gave their movement a handy nickname.

The fundamentalist movement, over the course of the twentieth century, became a dense network of interwoven denominations, parachurch organizations, educational institutions, and publishing outlets.[20] Mass media bound the network together, permitted its growth, and, to some extent, reflected its image and values. Radio—paradoxically—prevented the decline of old-fashioned religious belief. As Bruce Lawrence has noted, historians today seldom invoke Max Weber's thesis of Protestant religion as a modernizing force.[21] Without resurrecting Weber's thesis entirely, it does seem high time we acknowledge that without the institutions of modern mass culture religious fundamentalism could not have taken its present shape—and that mass culture, in turn, owes something to religion's aggressive advance in the twentieth century.

For a moment in the mid-twenties, however, modern science seemed to have vanquished Bible-thumping religion. Symbolic of the moment was the live radio drama of the Scopes trial in Dayton, Tennessee, in the summer of 1925, convicting a high school teacher of teaching evolution contrary to state law. The trial's oral arguments and verdict were broadcast on radio as well as covered by hundreds of print journalists, and they sounded, in the opinion of some, the death knell to fundamentalist religion. Or, at least, the widely held view has been that after Scopes fundamentalists retreated in confused humiliation, reappearing suddenly and without precedent in the mid-1970s.[22] In contrast, new studies, such as those of Joel Carpenter and Jon R. Stone, revisit evangelical and fundamentalist institutions in the decades after

Scopes and portray fundamentalists and other evangelical Protestants as actively creating parachurch organizations and a thriving network of religious institutions—and engaging popular culture through the media as early as the thirties.[23] Although for several decades fundamentalism ceased to exist as a tightly organized movement, the ideas and practices, and the core doctrines, did not fade away. Rather, some became diffused throughout Protestantism—Robert Wuthnow estimates that as many as 10 million Americans in the late forties could be considered "fundamentalist" if the criteria were a person's beliefs in "the divinity of Jesus, the literal historical reality of miracles, and the verbal inerrancy of the scriptures."[24]

By portraying their radio heroes, exploring their letters, and examining institutions they founded, this book taps a vast, protean, and largely unstudied segment of the American population. These were people whose conservative Protestant religion served to mediate in their encounter with the increasingly urban, secular, and impersonal world in which they found themselves.[25] What came to be called by the 1940s "evangelicalism" provided (in Peter Berger's term) a "plausibility structure" to interpret the discontinuity between the "old human conditions for encounter and the new dehumanized context—telephone, phonograph, wireless, film—in which they were increasingly embedded."[26] Evangelicals were energized by their difference from the sinful world around them, filled with fervent hope for change and restoration that could come only from divine intervention. As one example, the words of a 1947 Bible lesson published in the *Christian Beacon* illustrate the perspective most fundamentalists took toward modern life. It held out little hope for human-made solutions to the great problems of the day: "Our nations are too full of pride, nationalism, politics, covetousness, and kindred sins to humble themselves before God, and so they all continue to wallow and toss in uncertainty, doubt, and often despair and distress, and threats of bloody war hover over the sinful world. But we as individuals can be revived by wholly surrendering ourselves to Jesus Christ our Lord. . . . The revival must begin with us, but there is no limit to its extent. . . . Pray for a revival to start in yourself—expect that it will come and then spread it on to others."[27]

Hopes for a revival infused evangelicalism throughout the period covered by this study—and have not been lost entirely, although twenty-first-century evangelicals place far more trust in political solutions to moral problems than they did in the 1940s. The key point here is that neither modernity nor scientific rationality extinguished old-time religion; rather, they established the only environment in which it could be clearly delineated.[28] Bruce Lawrence has called fundamentalists "moderns, but not modernists." He means that, in Marshall Berman's terms, moderns see their world as a maelstrom, without solidity or footing, but they do not find themselves at home in that world.[29] Bobby Alexander noted that "religious conservatives . . . feel the constant pull of their religion, which is their center of gravity."[30] Their insistence on a transcendent reality builds on their belief that reality is not to be found in their temporal surroundings. Antimodernism depends on modernism against which to define itself. "The context frames the text; fundamentalists are products of modernity."[31]

The "maelstrom" of modernity has been attached to the rise of media and consumer culture by many cultural historians of late, among them William Leach, T. J. Jackson Lears, Stuart Ewen, and Susan Strasser.[32] Advertising in the mass media carried and encoded new myths, messages, and images in all their ambiguity, thereby complicating cultural boundaries.[33] Emerging scholarship on radio and other broadcast media in America has begun to explore the media as contested sites, social locations that reflect, interpret, and magnify broader cultural struggles. Yet none of the major works in the field discusses religion at all, even though during the first decades of the twentieth century a person's religion (or avowed nonreligion) probably determined his or her place in the cultural contest as much as any other identifiable trait. Typically this historiography takes the form of a declension narrative: the media broke down gemeinschaft relationships, standardized longings for mass-produced items, and transcended the local in unpleasant and disruptive ways.[34] Rural life, especially, appeared besieged by the loss of community that mass media such as magazines, movies, and radio fostered, although urban communities could also be segmented by the mass-produced qualities of network radio, as Lizbeth Cohen has shown in her study of Chicago industrial workers.[35]

Religious radio resonated with this nostalgic longing for better times and used the language, inflection, and metaphor of rural life. Radio evangelists connected to audiences beyond the immediate locale, thus hastening the nationalization of American folk religion and the involvement of mass media in even those parts of life formerly seen as private and sacred. At the same time, with their relentless criticism of modern, sinful life, they drew attention to the "worldly" structures of contemporary media and entertainment outside of which they claimed to operate. In my view, the introduction of the mass medium of radio cannot be wholly a woeful tale of loss and community breakdown; I agree with those who place mid-twentieth-century rural communities not as the antithesis of but as situated within—even shoring up—consumer networks and the industrialized, corporate, consumer world.[36] Paula Nelson's poignant account of South Dakota farmers in the twenties and thirties has suggested that the mass media had a complicated impact on rural life, which was itself in a time of painful transition. She writes, "The collapse of the agricultural economy in the immediate aftermath of the boom years of World War I initiated a trend of regional decline amidst national prosperity and cultural change. The rise of radio and mass culture during this period increased rural folks' awareness of national trends and tastes, a development which paradoxically increased their sense of remoteness and isolation."[37] In their study of "modern American culture," in the paradigmatic small town of Muncie, Indiana, Robert and Helen Lynd listed the radio among the 1920s inventions that were remaking leisure and had given rise to "ingenious manipulative activity" through the active listening it promoted. Moreover, radios were commonplace in the homes of both wealthy residents and those in working-class neighborhoods.[38] Even rural homes without electricity had radios that ran on battery power; by 1931 more than half of all American households had at least one radio.[39] Ubiquity became the medium's hallmark. For example, in 1938 a survey of the rural radio audience in Kansas found that between 80 and 90 percent of families living in towns owned at least one radio, as well as 68 percent of families on farms, for an estimated total of 360,000 radio homes in that state alone. A similar survey in Iowa found even less of a gap between rural and town radio ownership: 83.8 percent of farm families owned a radio, as compared with 89.4 percent of families living in towns.[40]

The programs that each of those millions of radios could access fell into two categories useful for our discussion of religious radio: sustaining time and commercial. Programs aired on time donated as a public service—often by an entire network of stations—were "sustaining-time" programs.[41] Because religion was thought to provide a public benefit by its mere presence on the air, stations offered sustaining time slots to religious organizations (predictably, sometimes the least profitable time slots). In contrast, commercial radio programs, which constituted most of the fare on radio, were sponsored by a corporation or paid for by an organization that bought the time at market rate. There were successful religious radio programs in both categories but important differences between them that I hope this book will make clear. Programming that was dogmatic or controversial or that clearly promoted a single faith almost never received public-service sustaining time. Consequently, religious radio evangelists with a firm conviction to convert others to a particular faith became commercial broadcasters of necessity. Thus, exploring the level of rapprochement between sustaining time and commercial time reveals an important underlying cultural conflict in American religion between doctrinally and socially liberal churches and doctrinally and socially conservative ones. Religion in the mass media sorted itself into two opposing and distinct realms, the extremes of which represented diametrically opposed modes of religious thought and opposing ways of using the medium to influence ordinary Americans and achieve their organizations' goals. In the following chapters I explore the conservative end of the spectrum, with glimpses into how those conservatives were perceived, resisted, and accommodated by groups at the other end, represented primarily by the Federal Council of Churches (reformed in 1950 and renamed the National Council of Churches).

Along this spectrum, the ends of which I have labeled "lib-

A family group listening to the radio, Pickaway County, Ohio, February 1943. The photographer's notation on this image reads: "Mr. and Mrs. Samuel George and their daughter, Christine, who are living on Harry Linebaugh's dairy farm. Mr. George received farm labor training at the Ohio state university." Photograph by John Vachon, Office of War Information; Prints and Photographs Division, Library of Congress.

eral" and "conservative" for the sake of convenience, lie the many varieties of American Protestantism, called and self-described by many names. I recognize that fundamentalists were generally evangelicals but that not all evangelicals were fundamentalist, that "conservative" carries all sorts of political as well as theological connotations, and that the terms religious groups used to describe themselves were often quite different from those historians and sociologists like to assign. However, the nature of mass-syndicated religious radio, in which the listenership of the programs I write about far exceeded the number belonging to conservative Protestant congregations, suggests that this programming succeeded in surmounting denominational and perhaps even sociological boundaries between the many and contentious denominations of American religion.

How lasting, and how meaningful, these coalitions and connections were is a question I hope this study will begin to answer. Some might argue that the community engendered by radio was somehow less than authentic, a "hollow yowling" that was incapable of true interactivity or connection. "The new electric sensibility," as Catherine Covert articulated it, "would range far more widely, but less contemplatively. It would accommodate the discontinuous more easily, but concentrate less effectively. It would extend relationships, but pursue them in less depth."[42] Yet throughout this book we will encounter those who believed otherwise; they argue persuasively that radio made possible coalitions and personal relationships that permanently changed individual lives, shaped the cultural and political life of the latter half of the twentieth century, and revitalized a set of religious traditions that seemed on the verge of extinction.

This work is, at the core, a story of what Dan Morgan has called the "counterforces that are steadily at work against the processes of homogenization."[43] For all today's talk casting "the media" as the pervasive enemy of civil society and decency, I hope to remind readers that the broadcast media have always spoken with many voices—that, far from being a cultural monolith, the media have been as much a tool to build religion as to undermine it. This is because, as Denis McQuail put it, broadcasting was "a social innovation as much as a technological invention, and turning

points in media history are marked by, if not caused by, major social changes."[44] The invention of radio and its rapid development
into an international mass medium constituted just such a social
innovation, and if media historians have consistently overlooked
the way that religious broadcasting was involved in that development from the first, there is no reason to perpetuate that omission
any further.[45]

Religious radio broadcasting, as opposed to televangelism, has
received fairly light treatment by scholars. There are a number
of broad overviews of the history of religious radio broadcasting, as well as some biographies of individual radio preachers.[46]
Quentin Schultze, William Martin, and Dennis Voskuil have provided the most thoughtful scholarship on the subject, albeit in
article form.[47] Most of the published scholarship on radio preaching takes a very traditional approach, focusing exclusively on
the preachers themselves and their rhetorical strategies without
much attention to the broader cultural framework. Notable ex-
ceptions include Howard Dorgan's ethnographic study of Appala-
chian AM-radio evangelism in the 1970s, Alan Brinkley's account
of Father Coughlin and Huey Long during the Great Depression,
and the recent contemporary evaluation of Dr. James Dobson's
radio ministry by Paul Apostolidis.[48] My aim is to portray revivalistic radio and its listeners as embedded in a rich and rapidly
changing culture—illuminating their strategy of trying to provide
stability and certainty as itself a product of the age in which conservative Protestant radio began to flourish.

Chapter 1, "Broadcasting Discord," establishes the cultural and
regulatory context within which we can understand evangelical
radio ministries. Unlike print media, the finite spectrum of broadcast frequencies meant a limit to the number of possible outlets.
Scarcity, in turn, forced decisions about the relative priority given
to certain kinds of programming in the way the frequencies were
divided. National radio policy encouraged religious programming
on the radio but did not specify how it was to be aired. As it happened, liberal mainline churches tended to receive free airtime
for their programs, while most fundamentalists and evangelicals
bought airtime. Despite the apparent discrimination, doctrinally
conservative programming demonstrated genuine staying power

and generated financial support, surpassing mainline programs in popularity.

The second chapter, "So I Sow by Radio," examines Paul Rader as one of the first revivalists to utilize radio. He became a Chicago radio institution during the twenties and thirties and brought his folksy *Breakfast Brigade* program to a nationwide audience before his efforts were scuttled by the depression. His career illustrates the early enthusiasm of an independent venture, as well as the uncertainty inherent in purchasing time outside the networks. In Chapter 3, "The Live Wire of Los Angeles," I turn to Aimee Semple McPherson's radio ministry from 1923 until her death in 1944, looking not only at the paradoxes in her antimodernist stance and her Hollywood-style celebrity status but also at her urban celebration of rural values and embrace of midwestern migrants in her congregation. Owning her own radio station freed McPherson to develop her own innovative and distinctive programming without accommodating to "secular" station management. In Chapter 4, "Pastors of the Old-Fashioned Gospel," we examine the radio ministry of one of the most successful and widely heard evangelists of the twentieth century, Charles Fuller, who with his wife, Grace Payton Fuller, aired the *Old Fashioned Revival Hour* for decades across the nation and around the world. Their enduring success on radio legitimized their other ventures at midcentury, including establishing Fuller Theological Seminary, building an evangelical coalition, and helping to launch the career of Billy Graham.

In the last two chapters, "We Must Not be Muzzled" and "Mainstreaming the Good News," I explore the strategies that kept religious broadcasters on the air, including fund-raising and publicity structures within the growing evangelical subculture, the development of a religious radio advertising and marketing industry, and the centrality of media as a motivation for conservative Protestants to create formal organizations (the National Association for Evangelicals and the National Religious Broadcasters, for example) in the postwar period. With the advantage of hindsight, the biographies in the first half of the book represent the best of many possible strategies for sharing religious beliefs through mass media. Radio evangelists who achieved financial success and became cultural celebrities over the radio airwaves—as did Rader, McPherson, and the Fullers—represented a bastion of "old-time" religion in a world that increasingly celebrated the new and the modern. This makes their use of the thoroughly modern mass medium of radio all the more interesting. Many paths could lead to a financially solvent radio ministry— but outside the realm of this study lie as many or more paths, through shaky fiscal houses of cards or unfortunate scheduling, that pushed disappointed religious broadcasters out of radio almost as soon as they had gotten in.

As for their listeners, from whom we will hear throughout the book, the act of tuning in—like that of frequent Bible reading and other everyday "checks" against their religious worldview—kept evangelicals on the straight and narrow way. As David Morgan rightly stresses, the everyday has been undervalued as helping to shape personal and institutional identity but may play a more formative role than the rarer "hallowed rites and dramatic events."[49] What believers do over and over again not only reinforces their perceptions of reality but comes to constitute their reality as well.

At the outset of this journey, I propose three observations about the impact of religious radio on popular culture. First, the persistence and growth of evangelical radio during radio's golden age provide a good measure of the strength of conservatism in this period. Evangelical radio nourished, legitimated, and enlarged the boundaries of evangelical Protestantism throughout the period covered by this study. The relationship of fundamentalists to their audiences was a close one; broadcasters depended on voluntary donations to pay for increasingly expensive airtime, and listeners depended on radio evangelists to provide familiar and reassuring programming. By 1948, more than sixteen hundred fundamentalist programs were being aired each week.[50] One study concluded that while Baptist, Gospel Tabernacle, and Holiness/Pentecostal broadcasters bought two-thirds of their airtime in the forties and fifties, more mainstream denominations such as Methodists and Presbyterians purchased a mere third, and 70 percent of Roman Catholic airtime was free.[51] Evangelical broadcasting achieved remarkable prosperity despite receiving almost no free airtime. The national success of religious media programming, as Larry Eskridge has written, "lent the greater fundamentalist movement a measure of popular visibility and sense of accomplishment that was otherwise hard to come by in the lean years following the fiasco of the Scopes trial."[52] Quentin Schultze argues that religious radio served as a "means of creating a national evangelical identity, locating and promoting symbolic leaders, and legitimizing particular values and attitudes."[53] Evangelical radio buttressed the fundamentalist movement—or, more accurately, helped give it institutional and tangible, audible form.

One important and underutilized resource for information about evangelical self-identification through radio is listener correspondence, which I draw on throughout the book. Of course, fan mail as a historical source leaves much to be desired, being impossible to quantify and representative of such a small sample of listeners. Yet there are enough letters scattered through enough archives and published sources at least to suggest the ethos of a religious community, one with clear hopes and plans for America's future and for the role of believers in that future.

Second, religious radio not only proved important for evangelicals themselves but also played a "speaking part" in shaping the medium from its very first broadcasts. In particular, radio evangelism was part of the national identity forged by radio—as so many of these broadcasts went out overseas—and of the ambient sound of midcentury American life. Its echoes were heard in the spread of indigenous southern music through radio venues such as the *Grand Ole Opry;* in the call-and-response rhetoric of sixties civil rights leaders, which brought the sound of revival preaching (and its nascent liberation theology) to the wider culture; and in musical genres as varied and popular as bluegrass, rhythm and blues, country, and gospel.[54] The sheer number of popular musicians and public figures whose roots were in revival religion in itself suggests this point. I have always thought it more than coincidental, for example, that Aretha Franklin, one of the quintessential voices of American pop music, is the daughter of a south Georgia radio preacher and that country singer Dolly Parton is the granddaughter of a Pentecostal preacher who helped introduce rural mountain music into top-forty country radio.

Religious radio is a kind of American folk art, one that has nearly vanished from our national consciousness, if not from our airwaves. Although much radio religion went unrecorded, what remains preserves a collective memory of the sound, the cadence, the rhythm, the songs in four-part harmony with a vibrato organ underneath.[55] Letters from listeners to religious preachers describe the complex feelings evoked: nostalgia for an American Christian past that may or may not have ever existed; fear for the future of the nation and for the state of one's soul before God; longing for inclusion and meaning in an American present ever threatening, disorienting, and full of trouble; gratitude for a shared language of religious experience; and pride in a thriving evangelical Protestant subculture with access to the powerful channels of American media. All these impulses are important to the story of religious radio in American popular culture.

Finally, by bringing revival religion to the radio, evangelists accessed the cultural authority of the medium and gained a toehold back into their preferred role of guardian of the nation's values. In 1922, liberal Presbyterian Harry Emerson Fosdick, dismayed at the intolerant tactics employed by Christian conservatives in their efforts to purify church and society, asked in a famous sermon, "Shall the Fundamentalists Win?"[56] By 1944 fundamentalist Carl McIntire would declare a victory only the mass media had made possible: "The fundamentalists are coming back," he wrote, "organized, with their feet on solid ground. The arsenals of the historic faith are being freshly stocked, and with a full dependence on the King of kings, the Leader of the battle, they believe that their efforts shall not be in vain."[57] As Joel Carpenter has concluded, fundamentalists "turned failure into vindication, marginality into chosenness, survival into an opportunity for expansion, and a religious depression into a prelude for revival."[58] I suppose Fosdick's question is still an open one, judging by recent scholarship on liberals said to be "suicidal" or to have "missed their mission" and conservatives who are supposedly "embattled but thriving."[59] Deciding the future course and cultural place of radio religion epitomized the ongoing clash between liberal and conservative Protestantism, as I show in the following chapters, demonstrating the compatibility of religious worldviews with both modernity and postmodernity.[60] The evidence amassed here compels the conclusion that we can find in

American culture a vibrant juxtaposition of religion and secularism, not the gradual replacement of the former by the latter. On radio, revival religion and secular entertainment were yoked in dynamic and creative tension.

Fortunately, I have not attempted to tell the entire story here; there are many avenues of rich exploration best left to others. If this book evokes memories, provokes dialogue about media and religion in America, and inspires further research, I consider my job well done. *Redeeming the Dial* touches on multiple narratives of the early to mid-twentieth century and will, I hope, add to those stories while raising many new questions. Something of the migration of rural midwesterners and southerners to the California coast is here, and so is the slowly building groundswell of support for black civil rights—though no one yet has explored black radio evangelism and its role in that movement. The vulnerability of heartland family farmers is here, their struggles and dislocations. A rising tide of materialism, consumer culture, and loosening of social moorings is part of this story, as is the growth of some Christian denominations at the expense of others (for a movement that has been declared dead or dying on a regular basis since the early 1920s, evangelical Protestantism has shown remarkable, even dramatic, resilience). The exportation of "American" religion and values is here, as radio reached around the globe to speak to other countries and to American soldiers and missionaries serving there, paired with the strident impulse to protect society here at home from hidden dangers of ideology, doctrine, and behavior coded at the time as sinful.

My narrative ends when television became a thoroughly entrenched part of American culture, at the end of the "golden age" of radio. By then, a new generation of media evangelists was poised to move broadcast religion into the televisual age. Not until the 1980s would religious radio be reinvented as an indispensable means of informing and mobilizing religious conservatives as a force in U.S. politics, both local and national. What follows is a story—largely—of a revivalistic, *apolitical* religious right, but without which the subsequent growth of the political religious right would be unimaginable.

1 Broadcasting Discord
Religious Radio before 1939

A pair of strange guests joined the choir of Pittsburgh's Calvary Episcopal Church one frigid January morning in 1921. Donning choir robes to blend in, two engineers from Westinghouse monitored the "wireless telephone receiving apparatus" installed for the occasion of the nation's first religious radio broadcast. Calvary's Sunday service was sent out for a thousand miles over the jerry-rigged facilities of the first radio station in the United States, KDKA, which had been broadcasting since November to the handful of Pennsylvania folks with crystal receiving sets. The radio station received enough favorable response to its broadcast of Calvary's service that the weekly program became a regular feature of KDKA's schedule.[1] Thus radio and radio evangelism were born together. The Westinghouse engineers in choir robes— one Jewish and the other a Roman Catholic—provide an enduring image of the decentralized, even haphazard, entrance of religious organizations into the brave new world of radio in the early twenties.

There were those, such as fundamentalist Presbyterian Clarence Macartney, who worried that church services "sent indiscriminately abroad into all kinds of places" would be "grotesque and irreverent." Some Christian fundamentalists' distaste for every aspect of popular culture led them to reject radio altogether or to caution that the radio airwaves were the devil's own province with which good Christians should not tamper.[2] Such views might be expected but were surprisingly scarce. Within just a few years, religious groups almost universally acknowledged that the radio was just another—and particularly well suited—form for the spread of God's word.[3] Individuals and denominations scrambled to get in on the new market as the public appetite for radio broadcasting grew. By 1924, a church or religious organization held one out of every fourteen licenses; the number of stations operated by religious groups climbed from twenty-nine in 1924 to seventy-one in 1925.[4] In that year churches or other religious organizations controlled 10 percent of the more than six hundred radio stations in the United States.[5]

In the early 1920s most radio stations were locally owned by private individuals or corporations, such as churches, newspapers, or department stores. Broadcasting was a vibrant experiment. Hobbyists across the nation delighted in picking up the signal of distant stations, and broadcasters tried to be heard by installing larger or more powerful transmitters, broadcasting at unused frequencies, or even using those allocated to another station. William Ward Ayer, the first president of the National Religious Broadcasters, remembered his introduction to radio in 1922, when he was a young pastor in Valparaiso, Indiana: "While visiting the home of one of the officers of the church I was asked by a young son if I wanted to listen to the radio. He took me to his room, which was filled with radio gadgets, put a set of earphones over my head and worked with an old-fashioned crystal set. After the squeals and screeches died away, I heard a voice speaking and then some music being played. I was told it came from Chicago—fully fifty miles away—there were no wires to conduct it, just picked it out of the air. I thought it was marvellous, but I had no conception of the place that radio would occupy in the years ahead."[6]

By the middle of the decade, radio broadcasting was a chaotic industry, poorly regulated by the Department of Commerce.[7] Religious broadcasters had no clear or organized strategy in these years: some took time whenever it was offered from stations or bought it when they could afford to, while others started their own stations and tried to keep them financially afloat. A dual cultural struggle underlay the effort of churches to find a place on radio. First, religious people wanted to make their beliefs available to the American public; second, Protestants were engaged in a mortal battle for leadership of the American religious establishment, with both modernists and fundamentalists eager to use radio to put forward their own views.

The inauguration of networks and the passage of the Radio Act in 1927 limited some religious broadcasters in their efforts to preach on the air. The first radio network was launched in 1926 when the National Broadcasting Company (NBC), a subsidiary of the Radio Corporation of America (RCA), began broadcasting. Executives at NBC decided that their nationwide programming ought to include religion, and they made two decisions with long-reaching consequences. First, NBC chose not to sell airtime for religious broadcasts. Second, the network developed a policy of donating a block of time to representatives of the three major faith groups in the United States: Catholic, Jewish, and Protestant. For its Protestant group, NBC contacted the Federal Council of Churches of Christ in America, which represented twenty-five mostly liberal mainline Protestant denominations and whose New York Federation office was handy to the NBC studios. Network executives formed a twenty-member advisory council in the interest of fair and nondiscriminatory broadcasting and invited the general secretary of the Federal Council, Charles S. Macfarland, to serve on the board.[8] The relationship between the Federal Council and NBC was a cozy one; network executives made it their personal business to make sure, for instance, that Macfarland had a top-quality RCA radio in his home.[9] From its inception, the network sought meetings with and advice of Federal Council leaders to "determine clearly the attitude of the Protestant Churches to radio activities" and to address what General Secretary Macfarland called "the broader and larger problems of national nonsectarian services for the country as a whole."[10] Macfarland himself went on to act as chairman, at the same time, of the Federal Council's National Religious Radio Committee *and* of the religious activities of NBC itself.[11]

From this cooperation emerged several long-running standard Protestant services on NBC, produced by the Federal Council's Department of National Religious Radio and broadcast during time slots donated by NBC. The flagship program was the *National Radio Pulpit,* a suitably nonsectarian and widely heard forum for liberal Protestant preachers such as Dr. S. Parkes Cadman, the Reverend Ralph Sockman, and Harry Emerson Fosdick.[12] Catholics and Jews, the other members of the triumvirate of religious "insiders," had free time on network radio with programs such as *Catholic Hour* and *Message of Israel.*[13] The National Religious Radio Committee also sponsored programs of general religious boosterism—for example, a 1928 broadcast of President Calvin Coolidge's reflections on "religion as the basis of national life."[14]

While liberal Protestants were favored by the emerging national radio networks, conservatives found that their cause was not championed by the Federal Radio Commission (FRC), established by the Radio Acts of 1927 and 1934. The FRC (which became the Federal Communications Commission [FCC] in 1934) had authority to grant and renew station licenses and to allocate broadcast frequencies and transmission strengths, all according to a new legislative standard: "the public interest, convenience, and necessity."[15] To the FRC, religious broadcasting was one of seven categories of programming in the public interest, a beneficial "good" to be encouraged and fostered.[16] License renewal applications required broadcasters to account for religious programming in their schedules. But at the same time the commission also took steps to limit too much of a good thing, by reallocating broadcast frequencies in favor of stations with well-rounded programs over those broadcasting the ideas of a single denomination or group. Within a few years, many of the smaller radio ministries could not support time on the air. The number of religious stations dropped from sixty-three in 1927 to thirty in 1933.[17] Added to NBC's exclusive dealings with the Federal Council, the shuffling of stations and frequencies by the FRC had the net effect of limiting the access of fundamentalists and other "controversial" speakers to nationally heard airtime.

Getting time on NBC became nearly impossible for all but the Federal Council's speakers, and some religiously owned stations went under—but there were still venues for religious radio broadcasting in the twenties and thirties. On independent stations, or during times when stations had local discretion over programming, the situation was far more fluid. Some individual station owners sold or donated time to religious broadcasters. Other networks had their own policies, too. The Columbia Broadcasting System (CBS) began broadcasting in 1927, Mutual in 1934, and the American Broadcasting Company (ABC) was formed from the NBC Blue network in 1945. All three newer networks initially made some airtime available for sale to religious broadcasters, and this enabled those who could raise the funds to be heard on national network radio—most notably Father Charles Coughlin on CBS from 1926 to 1931, although he was certainly not alone.[18]

Nevertheless, most conservatives became firmly convinced that their version of broadcasting was an endangered species, being hunted to extinction by the Federal Council of Churches. In 1928, the Federal Council, with its prominent place on NBC's advisory council, moved to consolidate control over the sustaining time granted it, as a free public service, by the network. The advisory committee of the Federal Council drafted "five fundamental principles of religious broadcasting" to "assure the radio public of a constructive ministry of religion, unencumbered [by] sectarian considerations and free of all divisiveness." The five points, adopted without change by NBC, were:

1. The National Broadcasting Company will serve only the central [sic] of national agencies of great religious faiths, as for example the Roman Catholics, the Protestants and the Hebrews, as distinguished from individual churches or small group movements where the national membership is comparatively small.
2. The religious message broadcast should be non-sectarian and non-denominational in appeal.
3. The religious broadcast message should be of the widest appeal—presenting the broad claims of religion, which not only aid in building up the personal and social life of the individual but also aid in popularizing religion and the Church.
4. The religious message broadcast should interpret religion at its

highest and best so that as an educational factor it will bring the individual listener to realize his responsibility to the organizational Church.

5. The national religious messages should only be broadcast by the recognized outstanding leaders of the several faiths.

After this high-minded catalog were printed what can only be described as fighting words: "The Federal Council's Committee is pursuing an inquiry as to the local services conducted from the various centers of the country at the present time."[19] In other words, the Federal Council appeared not to be content to monopolize free airtime on NBC network stations but apparently was mounting an investigation into time on unaffiliated local stations —presumably, thought some fundamentalists, with the aim of cleansing the temple of those who bought and sold airtime for religious purposes.

The truth was, however, that an "inquiry" represented the outer limit of the Federal Council's ability to wrest control from the fundamentalist broadcasters who bought time on their unaffiliated locals, not the beginning of a powerful campaign of suppression. If anything, the threat was in the opposite direction. The familiar doctrines, old-time hymns, and folksy backwoods rhetorical style employed by most conservative radio preachers tapped deep nostalgic strains in American religion. Intellectuals and cynical eastern critics might dismiss the old-time religion so handily castigated in Sinclair Lewis's novel *Elmer Gantry,* but among the vast American laity and ordinary clergy, revival religion still stirred loyalty. As Thomas Reeves has put it, "Most Christians knew and cared little about such intellectual matters. Their faith survived in spite of the professors, and their penchant for fundamentalism remained powerful."[20] The mass audience for religious radio cut a broad swath through American society— people could easily demonstrate a lingering conservatism not by openly affiliating with fundamentalist churches but by integrating and assimilating diffuse cultural strands through their reading and listening habits.[21] The grand tones of the Federal Council's ecumenical five points suggested not a firm hold on the listening audience but their deep fear of losing it.

The debate among religious groups focused on whether religious programming should be broadcast as sustaining-time programs or as commercial broadcasts, sold at market value. The view of the Federal Radio Commission left the issue open to interpretation, recommending in its third annual report that "doctrines, creeds and beliefs must find their way into the market of ideas by the existing public-service stations."[22] Religious broadcasters could be forgiven their confusion at the FRC's juxtaposing "market of ideas" and "public-service stations" in the same sentence, for as long as religion was aired as a part of the overall broadcast schedule of radio stations, the FRC would not rule on what kind of religion or whether broadcasts should be sustaining time or commercial. The solution, in other words, had to come from religious organizations themselves.

But by the end of the twenties those religious organizations were no closer to consensus than at the decade's start. The Greater New York Federation of Churches, a Federal Council regional chapter, argued in 1931 that religious radio was a "public utility" entitled to sustaining time, pledging "every effort" by the council "to keep away from theological controversy and to offer a clear and understandable presentation of religious truth"—in other words, a truth that was generic rather than specific.[23] Since "frequent and persistent applications" were being made by various denominational and sectarian agencies "for the broadcasting of their own religious programs," the federation went on the record opposing any particular denomination's request, "however worthy," to keep from setting a "dangerous precedent."[24] General Secretary Macfarland, addressing the nation by radio, condemned any religious "iconoclast for vituperous and defamatory tearing down."[25]

For their part, fundamentalists rejected the Federal Council's claim to speak for all of Protestantism, citing what they called a damaging inclusivity that undermined the gospel message.[26] Their view was expressed by fundamentalist historian James DeForest Murch, who has praised the efforts of "aggressive exponents of Bible truth" such as radio preachers John Roach Straton and Robert ("Fighting Bob") Shuler.[27] According to Murch, radio attracted disgruntled members of mainline churches. He claimed that "thousands who had been denied Bible preaching by liberal ministers in their own churches rejoiced at the opportunity once again to hear the old Gospel."[28] Fundamentalists believed that the Federal Council had mounted an "organized, systematic campaign to monopolize religious broadcasting," against which conservatives, with no powerful organization of their own, needed to be constantly vigilant.[29]

Mainline churches had several articulate organizations promoting or producing sustaining-time religious broadcasting: the Federal Council had its own Department of Religious Radio and was well represented on NBC's advisory council, and some of the larger denominations within the Federal Council, such as the Presbyterian Church (U.S.A.), had their own committees on religious radio. In contrast, no single organization could speak for conservative Protestants. Fundamentalists were in organizational disarray in the twenties and thirties. At times they seemed united only in their opposition to the Federal Council, voiced in periodicals such as Carl McIntire's *Christian Beacon,* John R. Rice's *Sword of the Lord,* and the venerable *Sunday School Times.* All three papers had ties to radio programs — Carl McIntire, for instance, purchased time on WPEN in Pennsylvania for his broadcasts — or reported regularly on radio and published schedules of approved broadcasts.

The evidence fundamentalists marshaled to accuse the Federal Council of radio monopolization can nearly all be traced to a single, erroneous source: a press report from the 1929 Religious Publicity Conference at the Hotel Chalfonte in Atlantic City, at which Charles Macfarland was a keynote speaker. The general secretary of the Federal Council at the time, Macfarland gave a speech entitled "How Can Radio Be Incorporated into the Publicity Program of the Churches?" An unnamed "publicity man" in attendance made what he called a "mostly verbatim" abstract of Macfarland's remarks and sent it out as an official press release. Macfarland was reported in the press release as saying that the Federal Council was in the process of collecting stations' assurances to carry only Federal Council programs. The press release quoted Macfarland describing the mission of a Federal Council field agent, Frank R. Goodman, to tour the country stumping "all available stations" with the aim of signing them up to "iron-clad contracts obliging them to use the Federal Council religious programs and none other." During the question period following his remarks, the press release stated, Macfarland confirmed that the Federal Council was working to "control all religious broadcasting."[30]

Macfarland immediately set about trying to control the damage done by the press release. To the concerned president of the Lutheran-sponsored St. Olaf College in Minnesota, Macfarland stressed that his remarks at the conference had been confined to the Federal Council's efforts to recruit only additional NBC affiliate stations to carry programs sponsored by the council. He denied any widespread attempt to dominate or monopolize religious broadcasting on all radio stations as a whole. His address had concerned only the time NBC had decided to make available on Sundays for its free hookups.[31] Later in the same week, Macfarland further clarified his comments in a memo sent to all conference participants. It had only been his "general observation," he wrote, that radio stations found it easier to give free time to "central Protestant bodies like federations," lacking the staff to coordinate individually with denominations and churches. He said he had urged radio publicity representatives to "get religion, Christianity and the Church before the people" but that, as a matter of logistics, it could not be done "on free time as sectarian, denominational, or organizational propaganda but it must be done by a cooperative method."[32]

The Macfarland "press release," predictably, had a far wider circulation than his rebuttals, giving fodder to the conservative belief that there was a conspiracy against commercial religious broadcasting. Macfarland's sketch of the Federal Council's plans to be heard on every NBC station could easily be inflated into a campaign to monopolize all religious broadcasting. The idea of such a campaign was made more believable when, in the same year, a proposed code of broadcast standards called for an end to the sale of airtime for religion. The *Christian Century* called the new code "a threat to religious freedom," but the Federal Council strongly supported the policy, saying that if the radio airwaves were left open to every type of religious fanatic, "the result would be such a bedlam that we would soon find that religion would be ruled off the air entirely."[33]

One important subtext of the Protestant concern over radio in the late twenties and early thirties was the radio career of Catholic radio priest Father Charles Coughlin. Federal Council general secretary Samuel Cavert, as early as 1929, noted that Coughlin was "very much in the minds of those who are thinking of the problem of controversial issues over the radio." He reported that Coughlin and "a good many sectarian" broadcasters, such as the Jehovah's Witness Judge Rutherford, the Moody Bible Institute, and the Lutheran Church Missouri Synod, had been "bombarding the national broadcasting companies for time on the air." He admitted that between Protestant liberals and conservatives "there are battles to be fought, but I think we must fight them through some channel other than the radio or else none of our religious groups will be able to use the air."[34]

Father Charles Coughlin has been the subject of considerable historical treatment, but some brief background may be helpful to explain why he became the symbol of all that was wrong with commercial religious broadcasting.[35] Father Coughlin had begun his broadcasting career in 1926 with a program for children, carried over telephone hookup from his parish in Royal Oak, Michigan, to WJR in Detroit. A gifted radio orator, Coughlin developed his broadcasts into a national sensation. By the late 1920s he held the 3:00 P.M. Sunday afternoon time slot on CBS; *Fortune* magazine called him "the biggest thing that ever happened to radio."[36] His programs in the wake of the financial crash applied the Catholic call to social activism to the industrial heartland's economic distress. Coughlin was further blessed with the support of Bishop Michael Gallagher while his programs underwent a notable shift in rhetoric and strategy in 1930.[37] Coughlin formed the Radio League of the Little Flower, to which thousands of Americans mailed money and letters and which he was able to mobilize for his cause.[38] In April 1931 CBS decided not to renew his contract, as historian Alan Brinkley put it, "deceiving no one with its explanation that the decision had nothing to do with Coughlin himself, but simply reflected a new network 'policy' against selling air time to religious groups."[39] Father Coughlin then did

Father Charles Coughlin preaching on the radio. Prints and Photographs Division, Library of Congress.

what any number of religious broadcasters had done for years on a lesser scale: he set up his own network, stringing together time purchased simultaneously on twenty-six stations.[40]

Coughlin was at the height of his influence during the next five years. His weekly audience was estimated at 10 million steady listeners.[41] He easily drew in the fourteen thousand dollars a week —at the lowest point of the depression—to pay for his airtime and employed an office staff numbering more than a hundred to open the mail. Coughlin received more mail than anyone in America, including President Roosevelt.[42] In 1934, a typical week brought eighty thousand letters, enclosing a total of twenty thousand dollars.[43] The following year Coughlin established a political lobby, the National Union for Social Justice. His broadcasts and newsletters became critical of Roosevelt's New Deal, reflecting his increasingly nativistic and fascist views.[44] With Roosevelt's reelection, popular support for Coughlin's strident views began to diminish.

Media watch groups such as the annual Institute for Education by Radio at Ohio State University despised what one delegate called Coughlin's "dramatic harangues."[45] Their distaste for both Coughlin's message and his methods grew as the decade of the 1930s progressed—and as Coughlin's own broadcasting underwent a noticeable shift toward the political far right fringe. In 1935, a delegate could politely express a hope not to "cause anyone offense" by saying that the "creation of the type of man of which Father Coughlin is an example [was] a liability of the radio, not an asset."[46] When the conference met just four years later, the politeness was gone, and the excesses of Father Coughlin had begun to taint all of religious broadcasting in the minds of the institute delegates. Coughlin's threat to democracy and his unswerving and caustic attacks on non-Christians were understood to be well known by everyone. An executive of the Municipal Broadcasting System in New York declared that the problem with Coughlin was that there was no presentation on the air of the other side of the controversial issue. His "anti-democratic propaganda" was balanced by no opposing program. He hastened to add that he felt censoring Coughlin would be wrong but so was the policy of failing to present the other half of the debate by airing what amounted to an unanswered attack on the nation's freedoms. Coughlin was, in short, a "radio menace."[47] Members of the Institute for Education by Radio resented the abuse of freedom of the air, in other words, in the way Coughlin undermined the very right that granted him (as a *religious* broadcaster) radio access to the American public.

Likewise, Protestants condemned Coughlin for his un-Christian tone: "His powers of vituperation, of condemnation and of innuendo, are unequaled among radio orators," declared the *Christian Century*.[48] And evangelicals—who, like Coughlin, bought their airtime—noted Coughlin's meteoric fall and learned not to repeat the radio priest's mistake. His fatal error, as they saw it, was meddling in politics rather than presenting "eternal" and unchanging doctrines. A radio sermon by Lutheran fundamentalist broadcaster Walter Maier in 1936 articulated the views of many conservative Protestants about Father Coughlin. Maier spoke of "a priest with a commendable passion for the cause of the American workman, who made the fatal error of crossing the Scripturally imposed line separating Church from State and who entered the arena of political affairs as a partisan leader." This unwise clergyman, said Maier, although "publicized a few months ago as few other churchmen in our history[,] . . . is today deserted by the majority of his followers, attacked even by clerics in the Church to which he had dedicated his help."[49] Maier made Coughlin the prime example of the folly of trusting human leaders rather than putting faith in God.

By 1938 Coughlin, now openly anti-Semitic, was a "once-defeated demagogue trying for a comeback."[50] Religious programming now posed a special problem for the radio industry. H. A. Bellows, commissioner of the FCC (and later the vice president of CBS radio), saw two solutions: either stations and networks could "auction off time," or they could "pass the buck" to church councils and let them fill the time.[51] Either way, broadcasters needed a standard for religious programs on which they could all agree. Lawrence Fly, chairman of the FCC, for his part disapproved of "radio propagandists" and "looked to NAB self-regulatory action as the only alternative to FCC action."[52]

In July 1939, the National Association of Broadcasters (NAB) proposed an industrywide code of standards. Several revisions of the NAB code included a provision about offensive material and cautioned against derogatory statements, probably in response to both Coughlin and the outspoken Jehovah's Witness broadcaster Judge Rutherford.[53] The final version stated: "Radio, which reaches men of all creeds and races simultaneously, may not be used to convey attacks upon another's race or religion. Rather it should be the purpose of the religious broadcast to promote the spiritual harmony and understanding of mankind and to administer broadly to the varied religious needs of the community."[54]

Coughlin seems to have been a particular target of the code, which had "produced considerable discussion" at the annual conference of the NAB and was viewed as a provision spelling the end of "crusading clergymen who have stirred up controversy in recent months."[55] In that year's Institute for Education by Radio meeting, one session debated the proposed code; one New York delegate called for the conversation to talk "coolly" about standards that would apply to all, rather than focusing on the "merits of a particular program" and becoming mired in "all of the emotion that surrounds the controversy over Father Coughlin."[56]

The new code—although not adopted by a majority of station owners—went into effect just after the outbreak of war in Europe in 1940. *Broadcasting* magazine editors predicted that the code would mean revenue losses for small-market stations in particular and that it would affect the purchased airtime of "several well-known ecclesiastics."[57] Stations soon "began canceling Coughlin off the air."[58] When he could no longer broadcast as widely as he would have liked, he withdrew from radio entirely. In 1942 the Catholic hierarchy finally spoke out against Coughlin.[59] His newsletter was banned from the mail, and he never broadcast over the radio again.

Marshall Fishwick has called Father Coughlin "the rock on which the radio church was built."[60] It may be rather more accurate to think of Coughlin as the rock on which the optimistically launched radio church was very nearly shipwrecked. Religious broadcasting in the twenties and thirties was vulnerable: fundamentalists depended, like Coughlin, on piecemeal purchasing and listener financing, while liberals were at the mercy of network and station decisions for their time on the air. More important, by the late thirties all the radio networks had begun to associate religious broadcasting with controversy and to think of religious broadcasting less as a "public interest" to be fostered and allowed time for and more as a controversy to be contained and bounded. A CBS executive made this clear in 1939 when he declared at the Ohio State institute conference that not only did CBS not sell time to Coughlin "or anyone else" but that it was "gradually evolving a policy of not selling time for the discussion of controversial questions."[61] Within a very short period of time, the industry had come to view religion on radio as of questionable benefit—putting all religious broadcasters on the defensive.

Those with a potentially polarizing message unwittingly altered the entire industry, so that by the end of the thirties both commercial and sustaining-time religious broadcasters had learned to consider public opinion and good taste or be forced off the air. By making paid-time radio ministry profitable, conservatives and others discovered that all was not lost if they could not gain easy access to sustaining-time handouts. In fact, their very success, in retrospect, threatened the apparent security of the liberals' hold on sustaining time. In religious broadcasting, the radio industry and federal regulators confronted some of the most extreme cases of broad issues such as freedom of speech, the limits of censorship, and the role of private interests in broadcasting to the public.

The struggle, on both sides, to appear legitimate in perilous and risky times would surface again often in the next decades. In 1941, for example, liberal broadcaster Harry Emerson Fosdick protested an FCC ruling that, he asserted, made it less financially rewarding for networks to set aside time for unpaid religious broadcasts. In a statement on behalf of sixty-one other clergymen, Fosdick wrote, "In a time of crisis, when morale is vitally important and when a spiritual ministry of non-sectarian character is by common consent needed as never before, it seems to us deplorable thus to throw religious broadcasting into confusion."[62] By "confusion," of course, he meant forcing liberal and mainline beneficiaries of sustaining time to buy time like the rest of religious broadcasters.

Fosdick was mistaken in one thing: there was very little "common consent" indeed over radio in the twenties and thirties. The following chapters present three different paths taken by commercial broadcasters to deliver a salvation-oriented message that was uncompromising on key points of Protestant doctrine. Although I call them commercial broadcasters, in reality the paid-time ministries in the next three chapters all have a curious, liminal quality. Their niche lay somewhere between strictly commercial—corporate sponsorship in order to sell a product—and noncommercial broadcasting. Beginning with Paul Rader, a talented tent revivalist in Jazz Age Chicago, commercial religious broadcasters would try to walk the narrow line between doctrines palatable to conservatives and modes of religious expression acceptable on the mass medium of radio—thus shaping both their message and the medium of its delivery.

So I Sow by Radio
Paul Rader and the
Creation of a Radio
Revival Genre

Tucking his flute case under his arm, Dutch immigrant Andrew Wyzenbeek crossed the street where busy LaSalle Avenue met North Avenue in downtown Chicago. Joining a stream of people, including daytrippers who came by train from as far away as Hammond, Indiana, he heard the band warming up inside the wooden Moody Church tabernacle. And there on the doorstep, pumping visitors' hands and swabbing the back of his thick neck with his white handkerchief, stood Paul Rader. The year was 1920. Radio was hardly invented yet, but it would soon become a central part of this energetic man's ministry, lending to it new elements of fame—and risk.

Wyzenbeek remembered Billy Sunday, the legendary revivalist before whom he and a group of snuff-chewing Swedes had succumbed to the Lord in Ottumwa, Iowa, a decade earlier. Sunday's rapid-fire biblical preaching had left Wyzenbeek "very much puzzled," but over time he'd begun reading the Bible, given up his drinking and card playing in the saloon, and become a lay song leader at the local evangelical rescue mission. When business brought him to Chicago to live on the South Side, he discovered Moody Church, which in 1915 was searching for a permanent pastor. Wyzenbeek was not alone in approving the selection of the dynamic, athletic Rader to the post. Rader, recalled Wyzenbeek, had "the ability to make the Bible come alive" and in his tenure at Moody had quickly moved to make the Sunday revivals "unlike a church meeting as much as possible." For an hour before the service, for example, Wyzenbeek and the rest of the brass band and orchestra turned the church into a festive atmosphere, not unlike the baseball stadium across town. The chattering crowds packing by the thousands into the humble sawdust-floored interior seemed to confirm that Rader's enthusiastic style was drawing some who'd never felt comfortable in traditional churches.[1] Rader knew that feeling. He'd sat in lifeless meetings too long and resolved that Moody Church should never become just another desiccated shell of a church.[2] Rader would become one of the first fundamentalist radio preachers, pioneering and defining the genre for many to follow, using the medium to shore up and enlarge his Chicago-area nondenominational ministry.

Although Daniel Paul Rader was born in 1879 into a line of Methodist itinerant preachers stretching back four generations, his conversion nevertheless took most of his youth. The Rader household was suffused with pious evangelical sentiment, and the example of his father, known on the preaching circuit as "Cowcatcher Rader" (for riding on the front of locomotives on his rounds through Wyoming and Colorado), deeply impressed young Paul. He himself had some early successes as a young itinerant calling lapsed Methodists back to their faith. But he found his religious convictions swamped by modern biblical criticism and liberal theology encountered at college. After a brief unhappy stint as a minister in Boston, Rader left the ministry to become a prizefighter and a Wall Street oil speculator. In 1906 he married Mary Caughran, an Oregon member of his father's congregation. Mary suffered from tuberculosis early in their marriage, and Rader spent some years in New York apart from his wife, who required the gentler Pacific Northwest climate. Their marriage, whether because of Mary's poor health or as a factor in her illness, was not a close one.

In 1912, just as his business prospects were rising, Rader experienced a soul-shaking reconversion. He heard the voice of God calling him on Wall Street, promising him a "Message." He immediately went home and earnestly spent three days studying the Bible and praying. After this he committed himself to Christ's service, marched into his downtown office, quit his job, turned over his share in the company, and began preaching on the sidewalk corner outside his old office building.[3]

Within a few weeks, Rader met members of an evangelical organization, the Christian and Missionary Alliance (CMA), who served as his contact network as he tried to make his way west preaching without a steady income. The CMA, founded in 1881 by the New York City Presbyterian Dr. A. B. Simpson, proved a good match for the idealistic and eager young preacher. The interdenominational alliance supported foreign and home mission efforts and was sympathetic to premillennial and holiness doctrines. Simpson had formulated a "four-fold Gospel" that allied with Rader's own convictions, emphasizing Jesus as "Savior, Sanctifier, Healer, and Coming Lord."[4] Comfortable with both the CMA's mission and its theology, Rader accepted a post at a CMA tabernacle in Pittsburgh and sent for his wife and children.

The move to Pittsburgh was a trying time for the young family; Mary had given birth to two of their three daughters and was recovering from an operation on her glands. She struggled to understand the dramatic changes in her husband's life. Mary had not been "born again," and Paul's reconversion had happened apart from her. They lived in a "ten-dollar-a-month house in the district with coloured folk."[5] Remembering this period, the normally ebullient Paul revealed the worry and tension that permeated their household: "Mrs. Rader and the children [Pauline and Willamine] came to Pittsburgh. We lived in a little flat. It was not pleasant for her. Often we didn't have anything to eat, and she was very unhappy because she did not possess the joy that I had, but I just kept praying for her." The emotional distance between Paul and Mary was only partially closed on the day she too accepted Christ:

> I will never forget when she opened her heart and let Him in. I was preaching in the schoolhouse in a little town. She always came to the meetings with me and sat on the side. There were about twenty people present. I got through preaching and gave the invitation but nobody came. I began to sing, still nobody came, but I kept on. Then I looked over where my wife was sitting and there she was looking out the window and her chin

quivering. I sang the next verse, and oh, how I sang, and then I asked, "Will not one come before the meeting closes[?]" And she said, "Daddy, I'm coming!" I put my arm around her and we knelt at the altar together. I didn't know when the meeting broke up and I didn't care.[6]

Mary and Paul's daughters remembered their mother as introverted, private, and dignified; the daughter of a downwardly mobile shipbuilder, she had earned the nickname "Queen Mary."[7] A family friend described her as a woman of "reserve and resource."[8] The whirlwind of Paul's spiritual journey and his rapid career climb within fundamentalism must have tried her resources nearly to their limits.

By 1914 Rader, under Simpson's tutelage, had become "a more-or-less full-time traveling evangelist" and rotated through the visiting pastor slot at the Chicago fundamentalist stronghold, Moody Church, several times. He was named the pastor of Moody in 1915 and oversaw the church's growth out of its small building into a large, wooden, five-thousand-seat tabernacle. In 1919 Rader succeeded Simpson as the head of the CMA. Thus, just a few years after his conversion, Rader had become a powerfully influential figure at the helm of two central fundamentalist institutions, at the same time that the fundamentalist movement itself was reaching its peak of organizational power and social influence in America.[9]

During his tenure at Moody, Rader maintained a seemingly perpetual, full-fledged urban revival by bringing into the fold admirers such as Andrew Wyzenbeek, the Dutch immigrant convert who played in Rader's orchestra. The celebratory services at Moody attracted on average more than thirty-five hundred people on Sunday mornings. And Rader's memorable preaching kept them coming back for what one fellow called his "reckless abandonment to Christ in the Salvation of Men."[10] People seemed drawn to Rader's charismatic stage presence and his folksy, engaging rhetorical style; but he gained critics as well.

The board of the Moody Church resented Rader's time away from the pulpit overseeing CMA missionary efforts and disagreed over where the church's finances should go: some within the

Moody Church hoped for a new and more substantial building, while Rader thought the wooden hall was fine so long as missions were growing (which indeed they were).[11] The dissension in the church "greatly grieved" many of the parishioners.[12] The situation deteriorated, and in May 1921 Rader stepped down as the pastor of Moody Church and set out on a tent revival trip. Within a year he was back in Chicago, however, for a six-week summer revival in the heart of a North Side neighborhood of Scandinavian immigrants. Obtaining a set of steel girders, he put up a canvas-sided tent on a vacant lot.

What began as a summer revival lasted more than a decade, and the "Steel Tent"—its sides hastily converted to wood to shut out the Windy City's winter blasts—became the Chicago Gospel Tabernacle. Independent gospel tabernacles were becoming a familiar feature of the evangelical landscape, and Rader's was particularly successful.[13] Rader exuded a salesman's confidence: striding from one project to another, perpetually dressed in natty linen suits, a bow tie punctuating his moonlike round face. His style was almost exaggeratedly masculine. An account of the tabernacle's first year boasted that Rader had reinvigorated the religious interest of Chicago's men: "From the vantage ground of the platform of the Chicago Gospel Tabernacle, it is easy to analyze the crowd. Of whom does it consist? Largely, thank God, of men. That fact is explained by the manliness of the preacher. A strong, fearless, virile man, like Paul Rader, is sure to attract men, and he is heard to the very best advantage when he is addressing a congregation consisting entirely of men."[14]

Advertising images in Rader's periodicals, too, reinforced this gendered aspect of his ministry—a 1927 advertisement for a book titled *Modern Salesmanship* encouraged "ambitious men" to emulate the secrets of "nationally-known star salesmen."[15] In some ways similar to Bruce Barton's rejection of an effeminate Christ in the contemporaneous book *The Man Nobody Knows,* Rader cast Jesus as a rugged loner with his emotions well in check. In Rader's retelling, the Bible account of Jesus weeping with Mary and Martha over the death of their brother Lazarus portrayed "a God that could cry real tears with a couple of girls just because He cared."[16]

SAVE THEM!

100,000 SOULS A DAY
ARE PASSING INTO A
CHRISTLESS GRAVE!

TALK ABOUT a crime
wave! It will turn to a tornado
unless there is a great turning to God
in Chicago!

**WHILE OUR FINE BUSINESS MEN
ARE BOOSTING CHICAGO, LET'S ALL
US CHRISTIAN WORKERS TURN LOOSE
FOR A GREAT SOUL-SAVING CAM-
PAIGN THIS SUMMER.**

I'M GOING to open a big
new "steel tent" tabernacle
Sunday afternoon, June 18th,
at 2:30, and I'm going to preach
every night except Monday all
summer.

PAUL RADER

**❝MEET ME AT THE NEW "STEEL TENT" TABERNACLE,
WHERE HALSTED MEETS CLARK AT BARRY AVENUE,❞**
=========== 3100 Block North ============

EVERY SINNER AND SAINT IN CHICAGO INVITED

*Handbill for Paul Rader's "Steel Tent" revival in Chicago, June 1922.
Archives of the Billy Graham Center, Wheaton, Illinois.*

Radio was the natural outgrowth of Rader's "manly" style. The medium at the time existed in a masculine world, largely the province of engineers and tinkering boys who built their own wire-wrapped boxes; radio was several years away from becoming domesticated in lovely carved wood parlor cabinets marketed like furniture to middle-class housewives. And certainly Rader liked to use a variety of media to advertise his meetings and generate local enthusiasm for the church, drawing on his prior experience as a Wall Street promoter and a professional boxer. He plastered buildings with sensational posters, sent up fireworks, issued souvenir cards and programs, even inscribed messages on spare automobile tires. He was especially keen on music, writing special songs and selections and assembling an orchestra, band, and choir to add to the festivities.[17] When preparing to inaugurate the "Steel Tent" revival in the summer of 1922, Rader did likewise, adding the newfangled promotional tool of radio.

Mayor William H. ("Big Bill") Thompson, eager to get in on the radio fad, had built a transmitter and station on the roof of City Hall, with the call letters WBU. He was looking to supplement programs such as "Municipal Accounting" and "How Your Letter Is Delivered" with local talent. Rader and his musicians hatched a "gimmick" to promote their upcoming revival on radio and soon arranged for a nightly broadcast two weeks before the meetings opened. They had written several new hymns for the revival and printed them in a pamphlet sent out to interested people with receiving sets. The idea was for listeners to learn the new hymns while the brass quartet played them—a kind of sing-along to generate interest in the revival. As Clarence Jones, a horn player in the quartet, remembered, "Radio was so nebulous and fantastic an idea to most everyone in those days that few paid serious attention to its potentials."[18] The first of these broadcasts was in June 1922, from a small pegboard building on the roof of City Hall, and in it Rader proclaimed that "one hundred thousand sinners within the sound of [his] voice" had to be saved by the revival that day, for only "non-sectarian, unquibbling, undogmatic religion" would bring them peace.[19]

The gimmick convinced Rader that radio had real possibilities.[20] Over the next few years, he and his brass quartet played

Paul Rader preaching a sermon on Chicago station WBU. Chicago Daily News, *3 June 1922; DN-074493, Chicago Historical Society.*

whenever they could on area stations offering free time, but always with an eye toward something more permanent. In 1925 Mayor Thompson founded another station, bearing his own initials, WHT, and offered to sell Rader a block of Sunday time. Rader, in turn—and without consulting the tabernacle staff—offered to buy the whole broadcasting day every Sunday. He handed down the challenge to his musical staff to help him produce fourteen hours of weekly radio programming with only two weeks' notice and without any provision for paying the bill.[21] Telephone lines ran from the well-equipped studio in the Wrigley Building to the tabernacle, where a curtain-muffled studio (nicknamed the "Burlap Bungalow") was built, and on 26 April 1925, Rader's *National Radio Chapel* became the first regular fundamentalist radio program in Chicago—heard during daylight hours from Massachusetts to the Rocky Mountains.[22]

Chicago Gospel Tabernacle's programming over WHT, which ran every Sunday for two years for between ten and fourteen hours, was varied and lively. Two separate services were broadcast live from the interior of the tabernacle conveying Rader's sermons, the music of the brass band, and a two-hundred-voice choir. But there were innovative studio programs as well. Rader envisioned that radio could reach people of all ages and circumstances, and he planned his programming to appeal to different kinds of audiences. His was an early and vivid example of what today we might call segmented marketing. A Sunday morning *Sunshine Hour* was "dedicated especially to the shut-ins, the sick, the discouraged, the down-hearted; the invalids and those in prisons and hospitals." The *Shepherd Hour* was targeted at small children, featuring Bible stories and songs. Teenage girls had the *Aerial Girls' Hour,* and teenage boys could tune in the Morse code messages and rowdy chants of the *Radio Rangers.* Bessie Johnson, wife of a wealthy converted banker, had her own show designed to bring spiritual uplift to working single women, called the *Young Business Women's Council Hour.* There was a vespers organ concert to accompany Sunday supper and a live call-in request show of sacred music. Rader employed twenty-five operators to handle the calls for his *Request Hour,* sometimes audibly scrambling through big notebooks of lyrics and tunes to find the one the caller wanted to hear.[23] The last hour of the programming day was *Back Home Hour,* an informal (usually unscripted) chat Rader offered from a comfortable chair in the Burlap Bungalow.[24]

Revival themes suffused Rader's on-air preaching; take a radio sermon celebrating the "manifold grace of God," delivered in 1928. With a crackle of confident energy, Rader opened: "Here is the answer to your problems. Here is shown a way through the hard place." Exhorting listeners to give their lives to Jesus so that his grace could work through even the most mundane moments of their lives, Rader acted out a conversation with a skeptic to demonstrate that grace was similar to—and could also utilize— technology such as radio. The lively colloquial exchange echoed on-air advertising or the rapid patter of an entertainment routine. Rader began:

Here is someone else that says, "I am so lonely."

"Say, Buddy, wake up, don't you know there is such a thing as a radio? Some of your neighbors hear all the day long singing and preaching, stock reports and the like."

"Well, I did hear about that, but I don't know, I didn't pay enough attention to it. You know, I intend to some of these days, but I am just so lonesome and I don't hear anything."

"Stop your false tears. You could have had a radio and you didn't get it."

"I did not know whether it would work."

"What do you suppose all the rest of the folks did?"

There are some of you folks that have no radio in your heart. You could have heard glorious harmonies from heaven. In your bosom God's pipe organ of grace could have been playing. . . . He is going to judge you for not taking it. He is not going to let you stand there and bawl and cry, as an excuse, "Oh, Lord, I was so lonesome, so discouraged. The devil fought me so hard. Oh, Lord, it was so dark."

Won't you yield here and kneel here and say, "Lord, you are calling me to this deeper fellowship and I will come. . . ." He wants to put that Spirit in you, not your spirit of weakness, your spirit of fear, your spirit of drawing back, but His

Spirit that went to Calvary, into death, that went out against the devil.[25]

Rader told his listeners that, when filled with divine strength, they would respond with the same dumbfounded amazement he experienced when seeing his first Colorado canyon: "I will never forget . . . how I felt as I dismounted from my pony and looked into that chasm. (I did not know I had gotten off my horse, and I let him go and did not find him for two days.)" He promised great returns for the simple act of recognizing Christ as a Savior: "When you stand transfixed with this glory, you will 'rave.' It is more than emotion, it is a glorious joy." His questions turned personal, inviting soul-searching among his listeners: "Have you caught the vision of it? Have you enquired into this new creation?" asked Rader as the sermon reached fever pitch. Near the end of the sermon, Rader wondered why people were afraid to stand with their hands up, praising God and shouting—"it is because we are becoming so starchy to-day," and he encouraged people to shed their inhibitions and follow Jesus daily.[26]

Letters to the tabernacle indicate that people often did respond physically to Rader's radio sermons. A Sheboygan, Michigan, "lonely old lady, living all alone," wrote that she "clapped with the audience this evening when they clapped."[27] Another letter described, "I was alone when brother Rader gave the invitation to come forward. Oh, how I longed to be there to give myself to the Lord. I bowed my head and closed my eyes and prayed, and as I was praying, some one began to talk to me. . . . He was right there in the room with me."[28]

The way radio worked at a distance, somewhat mysteriously, without a visible mode of transmission, drew on fundamentalists' experience with another tool of evangelical outreach: prayer. The motto on the wall of the radio studio at the tabernacle was "Broadcasting without prayer is *only* entertainment." Tabernacle radio announcer Floyd Johnson pleaded for the prayers of faithful listeners that the message would reach the unchurched and, "by the divine power of God, grip hearts in a very mysterious way and bring mighty conviction to thousands of unconverted people who listen to our Sunday programs."[29] He wrote elsewhere, "If a man can pray [at the microphone] in Chicago, and through the ether, his voice may be heard by a great crowd in Little Rock, Ark., and this made possible by the ingenuity of finite man, how much more may man talk to God and through the radio of Faith be heard and receive an answer."[30] Historians should not underestimate the meaning of this act for religious conservatives. It is easy to overlook the importance attached to their prayer lists, but for many American Christians it represented both focused attention and a form of direct action. To those for whom prayer at a distance was already a familiar adjunct to home mission efforts, radio seemed a natural extension of the way God worked to touch potential converts, outside the traditional organizational structure of a church, pastor, and physically present congregation.

Tabernacle services were illuminated with jazzy band numbers and flashy billboards, broadcast into homes hour after hour on Sunday like White Sox games, but Rader delivered a strong fundamentalist punch once that audience tuned in.[31] As one commentator observed, presumably with the intent to praise, "In Mr. Rader's message there is not the slightest attempt to set forth the Gospel in terms of modern thought."[32] Rader himself put it this way: "I believe in advertising, but I am not here to advertise Rader. If my face will get you here, all right. But when I get you here I want you to see the face of Jesus."[33]

Elsewhere he explained, "There's nothing in the Bible that tells the world to come to the Church; but, there's everything in the Bible that tells the Church to go to the world! Radio takes the Gospel to the unchurched. That's why I'm using it!"[34] He did call the WHT programming a "National Radio Chapel," but he did not intend for it to function like a church. The Chicago Gospel Tabernacle did not have any membership; it was an "independent evangelistic outreach center," not a new denomination.[35] The home mission effort received enthusiastic support from Christians eager for revival and for the dispersion of the fundamentalist message into popular culture. A listener from rural Andrews, Indiana, reported: "I have a mite-box, and I am saving up my *small* coin for your work. I think it is the best home missionary work that I know of being done. My amount will not be much, as I have a number of societies to pay into, and we farm women are not burdened with cash."[36] A testimonial from Beloit, Wisconsin, confirmed her hopes: "I know several who have been saved over the air through your messages."[37] The tabernacle staff claimed, "Thousands of people pick up our services, who never darken the door of any kind of a church."[38]

Perhaps more important, however, Rader's WHT programming reminded fundamentalist listeners that they were part of a large, growing—and critically important—circle of chosen faithful. Shows such as the *Radio Rangers* reassured young believers that others shared their perspective, and they demonstrated (sometimes with somewhat forced joviality) that evangelical piety could be modern, up to date, and fun. The *National Radio Chapel Announcer,* Rader's monthly periodical, described the Aerial Girls as "wide-awake, jolly girls" who wanted listening teens "to be as happy" as they were.[39] The script for a *Radio Rangers* episode called for a would-be junior recruit to say of the Rangers, "Them fellers sure has got pep and ginger. . . . It beats all what makes 'em so happy."[40] From Syracuse, New York, a solitary listener congratulated Rader on the "homey atmosphere" of the *Back Home Hour,* adding, "I felt like one of your 'family.' That this should be carried through space by radio waves in such a way that I could 'feel' it at this end only demonstrates the wonder of this new science." A farmer in Saskatchewan, Canada, related that while listening, "the Spirit of God was so real that we could feel His very presence, through the air into our room, and my wife, my family, myself and the hired boy all got so blessed that we had a little revival meeting right here in our home. We cannot get out to church very often, but we can feel the Spirit of God moving through your meetings."[41]

Contributors to the station had their names read on the air as "Radio Relatives" and hung on a potted "Family Tree" in the studio.[42] This "club" aspect of Rader's WHT programming, I think, should alert us to a longing among fundamentalists for belonging—a longing that was growing in a social climate in which traditional religious mores could no longer be assumed in the wider culture. Nostalgia undoubtedly played a part in the feelings of a Graham, North Carolina, listener who said, "I am glad that there is a station where I can tune in and hear the old time religion, preached to a dying world."[43] Both the religious and the social realms (inasmuch as they could be parsed in the minds of fundamentalists) seemed increasingly fraught with danger, with fewer footholds. A St. Louis woman testified: "I do not know what I would do if it were not for my Radio, and the possibility of my listening in to your sermons at the Tabernacle. My husband is a heavy drinker, and life would be unbearable if I could not hear the old fashioned songs of the Gospel and the sermons."[44] Radio programming like Rader's stood in for the worship some Protestant Christians obviously—sometimes poignantly—missed.

Just as Rader seemed to have the radio ministry running smoothly, in the spring of 1927 the newly created Federal Radio Commission, in its reallocation of Chicago stations, reassigned WHT to a wavelength of 238 meters. On this low wavelength regular listeners could no longer tune in, and even those within the Chicago area were affected. The tabernacle's debts climbed for about two months while the audience dwindled. Letters of disappointment flooded the tabernacle; one declared the radio to be a "useless piece of furniture until we get you back," and another complained, "We can get enough jazz, etc., in six days."[45] Thankfully, WHT resumed broadcasting at a better frequency within a few weeks and could again be heard by folks like the Wisconsin family who wrote, "You are well-known here. We live on a farm so you know that your services are well appreciated."[46] Unfortunately, Rader was unable to procure the same number of hours he was accustomed to filling on Sunday under the new arrangement with WHT, and he began casting about for a new venue for the tabernacle radio ministry.

By September 1927, Rader had bought full-day Sunday airtime from Jim Boyd, secretary of the National Livestock Exchange, who owned a station sharing a wavelength with Chicago WBBM. In effect, Rader's contract created a new once-a-week station, which was assigned the call letters WJBT. A radio contest sponsored by the Chicago Gospel Tabernacle resulted in the new slogan "*Where Jesus Blesses Thousands.*" For a dollar a year, plus the costs of operating the station all day on Sundays, Rader utilized the studio, equipment, and powerful twenty-five-thousand-watt transmitter of WBBM, which was the local affiliate of the newly organized Columbia network (CBS).[47] The tabernacle's radio programming over WJBT shifted slightly in emphasis: it seems to have focused more on the surrounding rural districts and turned its attention to groups of believers rather than the unsaved. This subtle shift apparently worked, as the tabernacle broadcasts over WJBT were financially self-sustaining for the next three years.[48]

Rader's philosophy of missionization at the tabernacle changed around this time as well. The fundamentalist movement—which had seemed so hopeful about nationwide revival just a few years before—was losing cultural capital in the broader mainstream of American life. At the same time, although it may seem contradictory, fundamentalist institutions and organizations were becoming more entrenched and stronger in certain locales. Some of these institutions adopted an aggrieved, embattled stance in opposition to what they perceived as a rising tide of secularism. Rader's approach was to move from the bigger-is-better revival model to one based on the early Christian church, with small, home-based enclaves scattered throughout a hostile secular culture.

As evidence of this sea change, Rader formed Bible study groups made up of what he called "World-wide Christian Couriers" and encouraged them to study together and testify about God's truths among themselves. When a Courier class added more than twenty-five members, a new class would form. The movement was intended to evangelize through face-to-face contact and to remain localized and small scale. Rader's glossy monthly, the *National Radio Chapel Announcer,* became the newspaperlike *World Wide Christian Courier.* Although the many varied activities associated with the tabernacle continued and Rader added new projects, the mood at the tabernacle was changing with the times in the late twenties and early thirties. Rader spoke less about global revival and more about putting a Bible in every low-income rural midwestern home.[49] He said in a 1928 radio sermon that "the trick of the devil in the modern church is that he has gotten us to doing a thousand things that are good in our church work, a thousand things that do not contribute to the evangelization of the world,—all good things,—but they are not *the thing* that God called us to do."[50] Perhaps from this "good clutter" Rader hoped to thin out the thousand things and return to the basics. This scaled-back version of the gospel from the tabernacle was a much more intimate vision of evangelical outreach, one that in some ways was better suited to the privatized medium radio had become.

The new emphasis at the Chicago Gospel Tabernacle turned out to be a good match with WBBM. The station's audience was primarily rural; in his license application to the Federal Radio Commission, station owner J. S. Boyd had written that this station would "cater to a considerable extent to the people engaged in the live stock and farming industry," adding that the entertainment to be broadcast would be "of a high class only."[51] During the week programs targeted specifically at farm families were aired, including daily reports of the midwestern agricultural markets and shows such as *Farm Community Network, Rural Frolic, Farm Belt Headlines,* and short segments sponsored by the Poultry and Egg Association.[52] The time-sharing agreement with WBBM sometimes meant that the two stations alternated within the course of a single day. On Sunday, 22 June 1930, for example, WJBT carried tabernacle concerts and programs from noon until 2:30 P.M., when WBBM broadcast the Chicago Cubs baseball game against Boston. Then WJBT was back on for the *Vesper Organ Recital* and *Fireside Fellowship;* WBBM aired three hours of music and theater, WJBT aired the *Back Home Hour* until midnight, and WBBM ended the day with dance bands.[53]

Rader probably recognized that many new listeners who heard WBBM programming and stayed tuned in on Sundays to WJBT were part of this less urban audience, measured in part by letters from places such as Minot, North Dakota, "away out here away from all churches and services of any kind"; Bismarck, "out here on the prairie . . . too far away from church to attend very often except in the summer months"; Mission Ridge, South Dakota, "40 miles from a railroad," where "a radio is wonderful for us folks without churches"; from Kentucky mountains and New England country towns.[54] One listener from River Falls, Wisconsin, wrote: "How thankful I am for the Radio, for we are on a farm, and it is so wonderful to listen in to a service which is taken from God's own Word, and without the confusion and discord of doubts. Pray for us."[55]

Accordingly Rader shifted his programming to accommodate his new audience, as illustrated by two new programs. The first was a short-lived program called the *Healing Hour* in 1929, during which Rader delivered a message about healing and prayed for the sick. Although this wasn't strictly a fundamentalist program genre—since faith healing smacked of Pentecostal emotional excess to some hard-line fundamentalists—the *Healing Hour* was hardly a broadcast that would have been sent out with the general public in mind. It was directed rather to those who had "followed the course of preparation" to be healed by faith.[56]

The second new program was an early-morning broadcast airing daily, not just on Sunday; this was originally called the *Breakfast Brigade.* The title sounds as if the program called forth Christians with trumpets and hoofbeats, but in reality the show was a simple little homily spoken by Rader, with gospel songs performed on the organ, introduced by a jaunty jingle:

We'll be sugar in your coffee and honey on your bread.
We'll be any kind of sweetness to get you out of bed.
We'll be telling you a story and singing you a song,
And we'll be fellowshipping with you all day long.[57]

Like the original *Back Home Hour,* the *Breakfast Brigade* spoke to listeners one on one, in their homes, at their tables. Rader spoke directly in the second person—"Oh, do you have to go so soon?" he'd ask.[58] He and the tabernacle staff devised a card stock "knapsack" into which listeners could put various souvenirs ("rations") for which they'd write to the station. They included songs, messages, and poems like Rader's homey "Hello by Radio," which reads in part:

Every morning I say "Hello!"
To you dear friends by radio,
I say this through my microphone
While sometimes feeling I'm alone
Until I picture you at home,

Telling me that I may come
Like a friend, an old time chum,
Into breakfast.

I use His seed, I do not know
Where His saving truth will go.
In hearts of faith, the seed will grow.
There are open hearts I know, so I sow
By Radio.[59]

In April 1930, Rader had the opportunity to sow the *Break-fast Brigade* into a much bigger field. At that time, the Columbia network accepted paid religious broadcasting to expand its share against its more established competitor, NBC. Rader signed a contract to bring the *Breakfast Brigade* onto network radio every morning. He wrote that CBS was offering a "rate I could not refuse. My hands trembled as I signed the contract, but my heart was steady in faith towards God." His hands might well have trembled; he was contracting to provide a daily program to an initial chain hookup of ten cities (Buffalo, Syracuse, Pittsburgh, Philadelphia, Cincinnati, Cleveland, Toledo, Detroit, Kansas City, and St. Louis), at a probable cost of more than fifty thousand dollars a month, just as the Great Depression was beginning. He admitted he'd had "no resources back of this contract but God and His people," and as it turned out, this time "His people" were unable to provide.[60]

The tabernacle's longtime benefactor, A. M. Johnson, went bankrupt and dropped out of the group helping to fund the CBS broadcast, and in the summer of 1930 the program, which ran in an early-morning slot, could not generate the revenue to sustain itself at network rates. By August Rader was in debt to WBBM for more than forty thousand dollars, and he made his last broadcast over CBS and WJBT/WBBM on 17 August. For once his reach had exceeded his grasp. Network radio was not the answer for him — it would take another fundamentalist program, Charles Fuller's *Old Fashioned Revival Hour* (on a different network), to make that formula successful.

For the next three years, the radio programming from the Chicago Gospel Tabernacle resembled a patchwork quilt. There was usually a *Breakfast Brigade* (later the *Courier Reveille Hour*) broadcast for fifteen minutes or half an hour daily over WLS, tabernacle services broadcast Sunday evenings on WJJD, and the *Back Home Hour* late Sunday night over KYW.[61] Historian Larry Eskridge estimated that Rader paid between fourteen hundred and seventeen hundred dollars a week for airtime on these various stations. Rader remained popular. In 1930 the Chicago Gospel Tabernacle sent out a million pieces of free literature. In 1932 the 250,000 souvenirs and reprints requested by listeners would far exceed the 90,000 letters the mainline Protestant Council of Churches would receive in 1934 for all of its programming on the national NBC network.[62] But the introduction of the *Breakfast Brigade* show is telling—the audience for Rader's radio ministry may have been large and loyal (that in itself is worth noting), but it remained solidly within the fundamentalist subculture. Under the new format, the *Courier Reveille Hour* reported on the activities of Courier classes in and around Chicago and brought in various classes as the musical entertainment.[63] By the end of 1932, the tabernacle's weekly radio schedule varied widely according to the available funds, and it ended altogether in February 1933.

In one sense, the depression had sunk the buoyant tabernacle, which never regained its vitality or prominence within fundamentalism. This was a common scenario in the early 1930s for many other religious broadcasters (and independent tabernacles like Chicago's). Rader epitomized both the potential financial success of self-sustaining commercial radio evangelism on radio and its fatal weakness: dependency on a steady supply of voluntary donations. The trajectory of the radio programming from the Chicago Gospel Tabernacle was reproduced by many others who had enjoyed relative autonomy when radio was new and experimental but who by the early thirties could not muster the financial support for paid-time programs. It did not comfort Rader, however, to know he was not alone.

Deeply in debt, he left the Chicago Gospel Tabernacle and moved his family—and his World-wide Christian Courier organization—to the Gospel Temple in Fort Wayne, Indiana. Founder B. E. Rediger, like Rader, had been broadcasting a radio ministry since 1928 as an additional feature of his local gospel services. The music director and radio announcer, William Dillon, had played in the band at the Moody Tabernacle and for ten years was a trombonist at the Chicago Gospel Tabernacle.[64] From Fort Wayne Rader helped broadcast the *Back Home Hour* (by then billed as "famous") and the Sunday afternoon service over WOWO, as well as a morning *Radio Bible Class* four times weekly.[65] Fort Wayne was small potatoes compared with the Chicago Gospel Tabernacle in its heyday; the arrival of a mere ten dollars in the mail moved Rediger to write, "My it was grand! . . . I nearly fainted for I have not seen such for so long and how it helped us out right now." Yet the message was unchanged, trumpeting the church's mission to save souls in the face of the declension of society: "its rapid increase of crime, suicides, sensualism, and atheism."[66]

In 1936 Rader and his family moved to Hollywood, California, in search of relief from his ill health. The depression caught up with them; they sold Mary's Packard and lived on only $250 a month.[67] On 19 July 1938, Paul died at age fifty-eight of prostate cancer. He has been little remembered in the canon of evangelical history—contributing no great theological or institutional legacy—but as a motivating leader and as an originator of fundamentalist radio, his legacy is significant. He converted and trained many who went on to leadership in a variety of midcentury fundamentalist organizations, including Youth for Christ and the New England Fellowship. It was Rader's preaching that converted Charles Fuller—who, as described in Chapter 4, brought the evangelical message to a much broader audience and helped establish the evangelical organizations that still define the subculture today.[68] Rader's "seeds" sown by radio scattered widely and grew as fundamentalism entered decades of vitality and growth; his hope for revival remained evangelicals' defining theme in the first half of this century.[69]

3 The Live Wire of Los Angeles
Aimee Semple McPherson on Radio

On the streets of Hollywood in 1938, ragged clothing spoke of the ninth year of grinding urban poverty and of the cumulative movement of down-and-out rural Americans into the sunny embrace of southern California's cities. Passersby must have gawked at the line of people wrapping around a circular, domed auditorium located where West Sunset crossed Glendale Boulevard, the home of Angelus Temple and the largest private charitable relief organization in Los Angeles. Between two shining steel radio towers on the roof, a tall neon cross slowly revolved while spotlights played over the facade, sending shadows of the palm fronds dancing like flappers' fringe across the stone columns. But this was no movie theater, the occasion not the unveiling of the latest model of a big-ticket car: this was the forty-eighth birthday of one of California's most colorful religious performers, the Pentecostal evangelist Aimee Semple McPherson.

Inside the building McPherson had commissioned in 1923, uniformed ushers showed patrons to their red velvet seats, while the sounds of a large orchestra and choir echoed off the cloud-frescoed ceiling. A pair of round microphones carried the evening's songs and sermon to thousands of radios over powerful station KFSG, owned by the International Church of the Foursquare Gospel. The station was the third radio station to be licensed in Los Angeles and the first entirely owned by a religious organization. McPherson had set aside her usual garb, a flowing gown with a cross sequined on the bosom, for a red gingham dress and a sunbonnet. She appeared on the stage with a large metal milkpail, brimming with "a collar of real foam," out of which she poured milk into cups held by disconcerted guests; she then passed the empty bucket out into the auditorium to take up the collection. Each year on her birthday, McPherson dramatized her remarkable transition from Canadian farm girl to world-famous media evangelist, selectively telling the story of her life with an emphasis on the moments of religious struggle and triumph. Apparently she was not the only one whose rural roots informed her present connection with revival religion. "How many of you," she wondered aloud to the audience, "have ever lived on a farm?" The entire audience stood up.[1]

The jazzy performance, complete with costumes, props, and a dramatic storyline, was vintage McPherson. Behind the romanticized tale of the religious journey from "Milkpail to Pulpit," as she always titled her birthday sermon, was a complicated life in which the gospel message and fame, fortune, and show business were deeply intertwined.

She was born Aimee Elizabeth Kennedy to rural Canadian parents in 1890. James and Minnie Kennedy farmed a hundred acres, including three orchards, in the little town of Ingersoll, Ontario. Minnie was considerably the younger of the two; she had been taken in as a fifteen-year-old orphan to be a household helper for James Kennedy's first wife, who died in 1886. James married Minnie, a dedicated member of the Salvation Army, several months after his first wife's death, and Aimee was born four years later. Little Aimee demonstrated early talent for both religious fervor and leadership, warming to the Bible stories that she recalls were her earliest memories and conducting imaginary Salvation Army corps meetings with herself as the "Sergeant-Major." On one occasion she turned her schoolmates from teasing her for being the only Salvationist to joining a rousing parade around the schoolyard with a "Blood and Fire" banner made out of a tablecloth.[2] In high school she dallied with theater—even attended the movies—and horrified her mother by going through a period of "rebellion" and doubt after learning about evolution. But all this worldliness was swept aside in 1907 when she walked into the

Sister Aimee Semple McPherson. Used by permission of the Heritage Department, International Church of the Foursquare Gospel, Los Angeles, California.

town's small Pentecostal mission and heard the preaching of a young Irish itinerant, Robert Semple.

By the time Semple's Holy Ghost revival ended in Ingersoll, Aimee had been converted—"speaking in tongues and praising the Lord . . . what shouting and rejoicing! Oh, hallelujah!" she wrote later.[3] She threw herself into Bible study seeking the "baptism of the Spirit," felt herself called to preach Jesus to the world, and fell in love with the intense and handsome evangelist Semple. They were married in August 1908 and set off in 1910 to evangelize China. Just a few weeks after their arrival, both contracted dysentery and malaria. Robert died in a Hong Kong hospital, leaving Aimee a nineteen-year-old widow, sick, and eight months pregnant.

Six weeks after her daughter, Roberta Star Semple, was born, Aimee went to New York to join her mother, who was working at the Salvation Army headquarters in Manhattan. Lonely and discouraged, working as a money collector in a Broadway theater lobby, she met grocery salesman Harold McPherson in 1912. He proposed marriage; she told him she would consent if he would agree not to prevent her from preaching if she felt called in the future. After the birth of their son, Rolf Kennedy McPherson, Aimee—weakened by surgery and seriously depressed—suffered a nervous breakdown. On her "deathbed" she heard the voice of the Lord calling her again to evangelism, asking, "Now will you go?" She answered yes; taking her children and leaving in the middle of the night in June 1915, she set off into the unknown.[4]

Aimee spent the next several years working at Pentecostal camp meetings, spending summers in Canada and New England, winters in Florida. She was sometimes accompanied by Minnie ("Ma") Kennedy, who cared for Aimee's children and managed the money. People began to come to her meetings in droves; wherever she went she attracted attention and drew large crowds. Driving around the country in a battered black "Gospel Car" emblazoned with the slogans "Where will you spend eternity?" and "Judgment Day is coming: Get right with God," Aimee conducted revivals and faith-healing meetings on several wide-ranging tours. She preached to black and white migrant workers in Florida cotton and tobacco fields, among poor and working classes in large cities and mountain towns along the route, following an emerging Pentecostal grassroots network. During these years she lived meeting to meeting, never more than a few dollars ahead. She camped under her car, fished for dinner, and relied on the charity of others to feed herself and her family.[5]

In 1918 Aimee felt impressed to go to Los Angeles, which eventually became her home and the launching place for her revival tours. She established a local following and purchased property for an evangelistic temple. Her message and practice widened beyond denominational Pentecostalism, and she began to gain national notoriety for her faith-healing meetings ("stretcher days" she called them), which packed stadium-sized crowds in San Diego, San Jose, and Denver. In 1921 McPherson broke ground for Angelus Temple, and within a year of its 1923 dedication she added a Bible college to train evangelists. Within another year she had erected two steel towers over the dome at Angelus Temple to carry the broadcasts of radio station KFSG (Kall Four Square Gospel). By the mid-1920s McPherson was what one historian called a "North American sensation" and the self-proclaimed leader of her fast-growing organization, now called the International Church of the Foursquare Gospel.[6]

Her popularity came in spite of (or perhaps was enhanced by) a singularly dramatic private life. The most famous episode occurred when Sister Aimee disappeared from an Ocean Park, California, beach on 18 May 1926. She was presumed drowned, but in the midst of the swell of grief and mourning among her followers—and just days before her own memorial services were to take place—McPherson resurfaced in the Arizona desert near the Mexican border, claiming to have been kidnapped. She triumphantly returned to her ministry, but the press and the police raised suspicions about her story. When the shack in which she claimed to have been held could not be found, the district attorney accused her of inventing the kidnapping to cover up a romantic tryst with Kenneth Ormiston, a former radio engineer at KFSG. She was subpoenaed before a grand jury for perpetrating a public fraud. The official investigation ended when the grand jury ruled the evidence insufficient to issue indictments for the purported kidnapers, but Aimee's detractors and the seemingly insatiable public appetite for scandal fueled the story for months afterward. Although her organization continued to grow, controversy over the incident remained. Once all the salacious details—down to a description of the lingerie found in her suitcase—had been discussed at length on the newspaper pages, Sister Aimee never took the pulpit again without a keen awareness that she was notoriously famous for more than her preaching. And in some curious way, she played on the public's curiosity about her private life by peppering her sermons with personal details and by fulfilling cultural expectations about how celebrities dressed and traveled in style.[7] In the 1930s her personal life took several more unexpected and downward turns. She argued with and split from her mother and longtime business partner, Ma Kennedy, and became estranged from her daughter, Roberta, who had been groomed to succeed her. She was charged in multiple lawsuits over "failed business ventures and feuds with associates."[8] In 1931, Aimee married David Hutton, a singer in the temple choir; their brief and unhappy marriage ended in 1934 when a woman with whom he'd had a prior affair sued Hutton for breach of contract.[9]

Despite the problems that dogged her private life, McPherson continued to preach to capacity crowds at the temple, conduct revival tours across the nation (including a well-publicized 1933 debating tour with atheist Charles Lee Smith),[10] broadcast over the radio, and lead her growing new denomination through the thirties and early forties. During the lean depression years, when many smaller religious radio stations and programs went off the air for lack of funds, McPherson's media outlets did not falter. She even opened additional branches of her church in dozens of cities. Sister Aimee died in an Oakland hotel room on 27 September 1944, from an overdose of the sedative she was taking to treat a serious kidney ailment.[11] Characteristically, her funeral—which attracted some ten thousand mourners to Angelus Temple alone—was a true media pageant, an extravagant display of flowers, music, sentimentality, and pomp. She was buried on her fifty-fourth birthday.[12]

If there was a defining characteristic of Aimee Semple McPherson's evangelism, it was her ability to draw and hold a crowd. She seemed to possess an innate capacity for successful promotion, with no hesitation to use colorful and unorthodox techniques for reaching a broader audience. She utilized many media during her career. The slogan-plastered Gospel Car was one early example; another was the way she advertised a 1917 St. Petersburg, Florida, meeting. She arranged for a flatbed truck to join an ongoing parade through town, while she played stirring Christian hymns on a small organ tucked under a reproduction of her revival tent. She also scattered leaflets from an airplane over San Diego in 1920 and sold photographs of herself for a dollar along with subscriptions to her magazine, the *Bridal Call,* to raise money during campaigns. In addition, Sister Aimee regularly entered floats in the Pasadena Rose Parade, once winning Best in Show for a replica of Angelus Temple.[13] She recorded sermons on electrical transcription disks that were rebroadcast worldwide, and she published long-playing phonograph records of her sermons for sale and radio play elsewhere.

Her promotional machine was well oiled. In advance of her speaking engagements, she sent to host organizations stacks of material to use in media promotion, with headings such as "reception committee, program, auditorium dress, ushers or usherettes, newspaper ads, lobby display, paper, newspaper mats, publicity stills, and radio tie-ups, hotel cooperation, and book store tie-ups." She published several books of her sermons and stories from her life and in the early forties prepared a screenplay for a feature film about her life, in which she was to star, titled "Clay in the Potter's Hands." She was prepared to use the new medium of television, too: shortly before her death in 1944, McPherson received a license to construct an experimental television broadcasting station.[14]

McPherson's revival meetings were spectacles of entertainment, music, and emotion-rousing preaching. To the accompaniment of a huge organ, a fourteen-piece orchestra, brass band, and hundred-voice choir, she performed "illustrated sermons" every Sunday night for twenty years. Her illustrated sermons drew on popular culture for subject matter and were executed with elaborate costumes rented from Hollywood studios and huge sets with special effects, thanks to the help of her vaudeville-trained stage manager, Thompson Eade.[15] She appeared in the uniform of a motorcycle traffic cop to proclaim that her audience was speeding to hell, or she dressed up like a navy ensign to sail the "Good Ship Bounty." Sermons re-created the eruption of Vesuvius, the destruction of Sodom and Gomorrah, Humpty Dumpty's fall, and Revolutionary troops at Valley Forge with snow drifting down to the stage.[16] One 1925 sermon featured an "Eye of the Needle" through which she tried to lead a camel rented from the Barnes Zoo; another, a Garden of Eden complete with live macaw.[17]

In this context, Sister Aimee's embrace of the medium of radio is hardly surprising, since she was eagerly employing as many other outlets for her message as were available to her. She became involved with radio soon after making her home in Los Angeles and was, she maintained, the first woman to preach on the radio. During an Oakland revival, the Rockridge Radio Station offered her free airtime on a Sunday morning in April 1922.[18] The opportunity coincided with an ongoing blossom festival, which entertained fifty thousand visitors with open-air radio broadcasting. She remembered:

> All the way across the ferry, our hearts beat nervously as mother and I talked of the great possibilities and prayed for the words to speak. When facing the machinery and electrical apparatus of the sending station, our nervousness was increased, especially when we found a newspaper camera man there for a picture and a story, also neighbors assembled to hear the sermon. But, after putting them all out except the operator, I felt more at ease—that is, as much at ease as it is possible for one to feel facing the great horn and having only its dark, mysterious looking depths for a visible audience.
>
> But closing my eyes, I looked to the Lord for help and began to speak—taking my text from Luke 4:18, "The Spirit of the Lord is upon me, for He hath anointed me to preach the gospel to the poor; He hath sent me to heal the broken-hearted; to preach deliverance to the captives, and the recovering of sight to the blind; to set at liberty them that are bound and to preach the acceptable year of the Lord."
>
> In a moment I found myself talking into that great receiver —talking somehow as I had seldom talked before. The room

with its electrical apparatus was forgotten, and all I could think of was the thousands at the Blossom Festival, the sailor boys, mothers' boys on the ships at sea, the sick in the homes where receivers had been installed, and I prayed and preached and prayed again and did most everything but take up the collection.

When the doxology was pronounced and the beaming operator turned some little adjustment, shutting off the apparatus, and we dared speak again, the room filled with those who had been listening through receivers in the other room and the long distance 'phone began to ring as people, one after another, enthusiastically declared that they heard every word and had been thrilled and blessed by a message from the Lord coming through the air that Sunday morning.[19]

Following this introduction to the wonders of radio, McPherson preached occasional services over *Los Angeles Times* station KHJ (to which listeners as far away as Oregon responded with telegrams) and in other cities while traveling.[20] She realized the medium's importance as an evangelistic tool after numerous followers, who heard her first on radio, sought her out in person at revival meetings. She recalled "the joy of men and women grasping [her] hand and saying: 'Sister McPherson, I am a radio convert. I heard the story of Jesus Christ and His love coming over the air. I listened in and have now through those messages accepted Jesus Christ as my personal Saviour.'" She reported in her newsletter that these early forays into radio religion produced not only conversions in some listeners but also physical healing "because of words of faith and guidance."[21]

Within a year McPherson inaugurated a donation campaign on the pages of the *Bridal Call* magazine to raise funds for a radio station to be installed at Angelus Temple. Using metaphors of magic and fantasy, McPherson believed that radio's promise was "like some fantastic dream! Like a visionary tale from the Arabian Nights! Like an imaginary fairy tale is the Story of The Radio. . . . These are the days of invention! The days when the impossible has become possible! Days more favorable than any that have ever been known for the preaching of the blessed Gospel of our

Lord and Saviour, Jesus Christ! Now, the crowning blessing, the most golden opportunity, the most miraculous conveyance for the Message has come—The Radio!"[22]

Part of the previously "impossible" now made "possible," as McPherson saw it, was to draw together her followers from disparate parts of the country into one simultaneous community. Angelus Temple had been paid for primarily by established supporters in other parts of the country, rather than by the smaller following she was beginning to gather in Los Angeles itself. Had the ongoing revival campaign in the new Angelus Temple been broadcast over radio, it would have rewarded those whose contributions had made the construction of the temple possible and broadened the reach of her message. "Now," she rhapsodized, "the Radio solves the whole problem! If this station can be installed, and the Message sent across the continent, what a glorious opportunity is ours! . . . What a congregation!"

Sister Aimee's magazine campaign for funds to establish KFSG underscored the key role that the medium of print, and the experience gained in itinerant tent revivalism, played in launching the medium of radio within the evangelical subculture. Both revival and print networks paved the way for radio to unify the national community of like-minded Christians by creating and strengthening what we might today call "virtual communities": people sharing common interests and goals but physically separated over long distances. What radio would add to this already vibrant evangelical world—and what Sister Aimee found so exciting to contemplate—was simultaneity of experience. Radio opened the possibility that the words spoken in one place could affect listeners located far away, replicating and reinforcing with technology what McPherson previously believed only God, operating through the Holy Spirit, had been able to do.

In the *Bridal Call* pages throughout 1923, Sister Aimee laid out a series of advertisements trumpeting the potential of radio, each one capped with a line drawing of Angelus Temple. Flanking the dome were two obelisks of steel scaffolding, and the artist filled the space between them with enormous energetic zigzags in the air. Toward this building, which fairly quaked with the force of the waves shooting forth from the towers, a massive crowd of

Help Convert *the* World *by* Radio

Greatest Opportunity to Spread Gospel World Has Ever Known

Advertisement to raise funds for radio station KFSG, *Los Angeles, published in* Bridal Call *magazine, 1922. Used by permission of the Heritage Department, International Church of the Foursquare Gospel, Los Angeles, California.*

people pressed in a determined crush. The ad's copy roused a sense of Christian duty as well as evoking the fantastic dream fulfilled by radio technology. In the first of these ads, Sister Aimee reminded readers of the imminent second coming of Christ, before which faithful believers must preach to all the world. Asking, "Are we availing ourselves of every opportunity of getting the message out?" she cautioned that "the world" had captured the moving pictures. "Shall we let them have the Radio too? Or shall we say: 'No, this is Father's Air and Earth, and we will send the Message upon its breezes to spread the Gospel in this wholesale and miraculous manner.'"[23] She then offered readers a donation form with a preprinted reply (in increments from ten to five thousand dollars): "Rejoicing that the Lord has called Sister Aimee Semple McPherson to preach the Gospel, and having heard the message with exceeding joy myself, I wish to help others who are not able to gain admission or to attend to hear it also, and am happy to assist in the donating to a Radio Broadcasting Station at Angelus Temple to thus assist in sending out the Message."[24]

Through this campaign, over a period of about a year, McPherson raised twenty-five thousand dollars to construct a five-hundred-watt broadcasting facility inside Angelus Temple, and in 1924 KFSG became the third radio station in Los Angeles. With this she became the first woman to hold a station license, and since the station equipment was paid for with voluntary donations, she could claim that KFSG was the nation's first media station owned and operated by a church.[25] When KFSG went on the air, there were only two hundred thousand radio receiving sets within a hundred miles of Los Angeles; but this, of course, was to change within just a few short years, and Sister Aimee was to ride the crest of the radio airwaves.[26]

Radio station KFSG's initial broadcast went out during the Los Angeles Radio Exposition at the Biltmore Hotel, on 6 February 1924. Early radio manufacturers and investment corporations were showcasing experimental radio receivers; it may have been an especially auspicious night to launch a new station. McPherson remembered signing on for the first time. "A beautiful dedicatory ceremony was held in the gray studio, attended by many notables in civic and religious walks of life. The time drew near.

A button was pressed, a little green light flashed and all was in readiness. Then the evangelist, heart throbbing with the import of the moment, sent out these words—the first ever spoken into a microphone at KFSG: 'For God so loved the world, that he gave his only begotten Son, that whosoever believeth in him should not perish, but have everlasting life.'"[27]

McPherson's remarks were followed by words from a parade of local dignitaries, including John Stuart Daggett, manager at the *Los Angeles Times* radio station KHJ; Harry Chandler, *Times* publisher; Boyle Workman, the president of the City Council; Judge Hardy of the Superior Court (who was to have his own time slot in the station's programming schedule); and representatives from the Chamber of Commerce. Daggett welcomed KFSG to "Radioland"—interestingly—with images of *visual,* not aural, illumination: "You are bringing the sunlight of a new day into the homes of the world," he proclaimed. "Surely, but surely the daily influence of this woman and the strength of her precepts will find its way as a new light into thousands of darkened hearts and homes."[28] To Sister Aimee, KFSG's beneficial promise was confirmed within hours of the dedicatory service as a born-again listener found his way to the studio. She wrote a few weeks later:

An old man was listening in on the night of February 6. As he held the receiver to his ears K.F.S.G., Angelus Temple Radio Broadcasting Station was born to send the glad message of God so all might hear.

The old man listening in caught those happy words of salvation. The glory of God fell upon him and he was converted. He dressed and set out into the night.

At 1 A.M. he came to the Evangelist at Angelus Temple to tell her of his new found joy and salvation. K.F.S.G. in its first broadcasting of Christ's word brought one soul, wandering in darkness, home to God. Praise the Lord! God grant that it may bring many hearts to His fold![29]

Sister Aimee had spared no expense on the equipment for her facilities; KFSG was a Class A five-hundred-watt transmitting station with unlimited broadcast time and a daytime range of at least 150 miles. The sound quality was excellent; the station could be heard over much of the western United States and the Pacific even as far as Hawaii. Inside the Angelus Temple auditorium, microphones were placed on the pulpit to transmit McPherson's voice, above the choir loft to capture the sounds of singing and organ music, and in the baptistery to amplify the ambient sounds of the weekly baptismal service.[30] During illustrated sermons, Sister Aimee used the microphone to describe the scene, introduce performers, and narrate for the benefit of the radio audience.[31] Under her red velvet chair on the temple stage was a black telephone connecting her to the studio in the upper rooms of the temple, allowing almost instantaneous relay of information from listeners calling in to the studio and establishing communication about the progress of the service with the studio operators.[32]

Upstairs, KFSG also sent out broadcasts from the "Gray Studio," a comfortable room furnished with "sofas, easy chairs, lamps, and tables for a comfortable, homey effect" and draped in heavy curtains to deaden echoes.[33] The antenna for KFSG was suspended between the two massive steel towers on top of the temple dome. McPherson's lush account of their installation suggests some of the themes her radio ministry would emphasize: drama, devotional language and imagery that appealed to human sexuality, and sentimental hyperbole.

> On February 6, 1924, that sanctuary of devotion lifted two arms Heavenward, pointing upward, ever upward, to the Lord. Two hundred and fifty feet above the ground they stretch. In their hands they hold four throbbing cables—the antenna of KFSG, Radio Broadcast Station. Those four cables are the whispering harp strings of Angelus Temple, home of the Four Square Gospel. Those two arms, as if in supplication, tower in the sunlight gleaming shafts of white against an azure sky. Illuminated at night by huge floodlights, they glow with silvery radiance like vast tapers, ever burning, ever pointing starward.[34]

The technology of the medium, its novelty and sheer electrical physicality, became almost an object of worship in itself. What might appear a tangled collection of mundane wires and steel poles were, to Sister Aimee's fancy, "alive, tingling, pulsing spires of steel, mute witnesses that at Angelus Temple every moment of the day and night, a silent and invisible messenger awaits the command to carry, on the winged feet of the winds, the story of hope, the words of joy, of comfort, of salvation—dispatched from KFSG."[35]

Radio station KFSG inaugurated a round-the-clock bombardment of the local airwaves, with an exhaustive broadcast schedule in which there was little time off the air. The station offered a significant contrast to much of the rest of church-owned radio broadcasting of the period, in which smaller-scale preachers—such as Paul Rader—could only afford part-time or weekend broadcasting, often with substandard, used equipment or in borrowed studios. The programming at KFSG was extensive from the beginning, covering nearly every afternoon and evening throughout the week.

A typical week in 1925 began with Sunday morning and afternoon devotional services from the main auditorium in their entirety, followed by the *Children's Hour,* hosted by Ma Kennedy in the Gray Studio; a sacred music show; and the Sunday evening revival service simulcast from the temple. McPherson's "family altar call" and prayer ended the broadcast day at 10:10 P.M. On Monday KFSG was silent, following local custom that permitted radio listeners to tune in distant broadcasts without interference. A divine healing service was broadcast from the auditorium on Tuesday, Wednesday, and Saturday; at 8:00 P.M. on Tuesday, Superior Court judge Carlos Hardy had half an hour to "deliver a vital message discussing the mighty influence of religion as a crime eradicator," followed by McPherson preaching a revival sermon and then a live studio program—such as sacred songs by "the Negro Swanee Jubilee Singers." Thursday afternoon broadcasting included an organ recital from the auditorium; *Talks for Boys,* featuring a local Boy Scout commander; and an evening baptismal service. Program notes describe the last: "The waters of Jordan splash over radioland in the baptismal water-baptism service—from 50 to 100 buried with their Lord in the waters of baptism each Thursday evening"—clearly sent out from a microphone just inches from the font. On Friday there were additional musical programs and an evening revival service, the *Crusader's*

Rally.[36] Some services were rebroadcast in the wee hours after midnight to reach listeners in other time zones.[37]

Over the years new programs were added to this lively schedule. By 1929, McPherson signed on each weekday morning with a family altar hour at 7:00 A.M.; this was followed by the *Sunshine Hour,* directed at hospital patients and the homebound sick, and Sister Aimee's selective reading of the daily news from a scriptural perspective.[38] Other new features included the *Bethesda Hour,* the *Vesper Hour,* a weekly "Travelogue," and the *Foursquare Junior Hour,* in addition to a nightly "Scripture Drama."[39] Just as Sister Aimee's illustrated sermons gave Pentecostal world-shunning churchgoers "entertainment that didn't reach their conscience,"[40] her radio programming offered an acceptable religious counterpart to secular broadcasting of the time.

Perhaps more so than any other fundamentalist media preacher, McPherson duplicated the genres of commercial radio. In the twenties, when KFSG's offerings were surrounded on the dial by early network musical programs and variety shows creating what Michele Hilmes has called "national narratives," Sister Aimee developed programming to engage listeners in a narrative of religious transcendence. If programs such as the *Eveready Hour* were shaping the way Americans perceived themselves, reflecting back into the homes of urban immigrants aural images of bucolic rural life and classless, unified "American" national identity,[41] KFSG programming in the twenties stressed divine power available to anyone regardless of wealth or circumstances and urged people to look beyond the immediate world to a life of deeper meaning in which all could be united in Christ. Likewise, when live-actor studio serials became a mainstay of secular radio, KFSG responded to *Superman, The Green Hornet,* and *The Adventures of Sam Spade* with weekly dramas bearing titles such as *Useless, the Studio Janitor, The Red Comet,* and *The Adventures of Jim Trask—Lone Evangelist.*[42]

Sister McPherson could be heard outside the range of KFSG as well. She made guest appearances on radio stations in cities where her revival meetings were held. Promotional literature from her office staff urged her hosts to arrange for radio spots in advance of the local event and reminded them that her presence would be a draw beyond the immediate area: "It is not unusual for people to drive one or two hundred miles to hear her. Therefore, in using radio announcements, you should take into consideration a station and an hour that reaches not only the immediate city, but also the surrounding territory."[43]

Her rapid success did not protect her from the ordinary trials of early commercial radio operators. In the mid-twenties, entrepreneurs filled the available airwaves, often causing signal interference. A more powerful distant station might drown out a closer station broadcasting at the same frequency. Federal regulators tried to control the common practice of licensed broadcasters "wandering" the airwaves in search of clear air during their programs. In 1927, Secretary of Commerce Herbert Hoover admonished McPherson to keep to her assigned wavelength. In response, she fired off a telegram that read: "PLEASE ORDER YOUR MINIONS OF SATAN TO LEAVE MY STATION ALONE STOP YOU CANNOT EXPECT THE ALMIGHTY TO ABIDE BY YOUR WAVE LENGTH NONSENSE STOP WHEN I OFFER MY PRAYERS TO HIM I MUST FIT INTO HIS WAVE RECEPTION STOP OPEN THIS STATION AT ONCE."[44]

Eventually Sister Aimee learned to be more diplomatic in her dealings with the federal regulators. As a station licensee, she needed to demonstrate to the Federal Radio Commission that she was operating "in the public interest, convenience, or necessity." Her 1928 renewal application, for example, emphasized the station's "entertainment and musical impact" first and foremost, describing the temple's organ and musical programs as "the finest . . . presented by the most talented and favorite artists." She may have been trying to allay the ongoing concern of the FRC about stations that rebroadcast commercially available musical recordings instead of live musical performance.[45] Next she stressed that KFSG provided "educational advantages" to its listeners, with "world famous speakers [to] bring messages of national, civic, social, educational, and religious interest." Only then did Sister Aimee turn to the station's "religious and moral benefits," exemplified by the "Sunday services of Angelus Temple, the largest church in America with its noted choirs and world-renowned musicians and speakers [, which] provides spiritual comfort for many thousands in and around Southern California." Finally, she declared that the "great public" had demonstrated its appreciation for KFSG's services with "unfailing support and maintenance during the last four years."[46] Sister Aimee's license to operate KFSG was never denied.

Although Sister Aimee took pains to emphasize to the FRC points of common practice between KFSG and the finest commercial broadcast radio, she also mentioned one of KFSG's truly unique features: radio healing. She stated that KFSG had a "unique ministry to the sick and afflicted . . . of inestimable value, which is ardently attested to by people of all walks of life." She was among the first to use the mass media to effect faith healing without direct physical contact. She would have "listeners kneel by the radio and place their hands on it to receive long-distance cures."[47] Laying her hands on the transmitter, McPherson would pray: "As I lay my hands on this radio tonight, Lord Jesus, heal the sick, bridge the gap between and lay your nail-pierced hand on the sick in Radioland. Let the unbeliever be unbelieving no more; let the sinner be a sinner no more. Let a revival strike America and sweep through this land of ours."[48] Surely her words suggest that she believed that religious use of the medium could "heal" the nation's cultural ills as well as the bunions, backaches, and cancers of its Christians.

The radio station served as a national signpost of fundamentalist strength that transcended region, but it was first and foremost the jubilant expression of a local Pentecostal congregation—one that often received visits from journalists seeking to explain the McPherson mystique. In the absence of other trustworthy historical materials—the Foursquare Church conducted no radio audience research, and membership records are paltry—the sometimes sarcastic and dismissive words of popular journalists do offer valuable insights into the demographics of Sister Aimee's community of believers and, by extension, the listening radio audience. Some derided those drawn to Sister Aimee as "ignorant and credulous," "childlike," and inclined toward "lunatic dogma."[49] But more careful (though perhaps no less biased) writers offer more detail. Sarah Comstock described her neighbors at a 1927 Sunday service as "many a horny-handed son of the Iowa farm." In her *Harper's* article she elaborated:

> A glance about shows that they are largely represented by the Middle West farmer or small-townsman and his family who have come to form so large a proportion of Los Angeles' population. On every hand are old men and women, seamed, withered, shapeless, big jointed from a lifetime of hard labor with corn and pigs. The men wear what would be their Sunday-best in Iowa. The women are often gaudy in the short, tight, adolescent garb that some salesperson has foisted upon them, and their gray hair is bobbed. The couples drag tired old bones to the Temple and listen as if at the gates of Heaven itself. Often the young people are quite as zealous. One sees earnestness, admiration, even exaltation now and then.[50]

Most of Los Angeles's new migrants were rural Americans retiring with modest means or displaced from their land by economic circumstances. Close to a million and a half midwesterners came to California during the 1920s alone.[51] The population of Los Angeles increased twenty-five-fold between 1890 and 1930.[52] The total population of southern California increased 1,101 percent between 1900 and 1940; the increase was 1,535 percent for the city of Los Angeles in those years, peaking in 1923, the same year Sister Aimee dedicated Angelus Temple and started constructing KFSG's radio tower.[53] Fundamentalist churches in the area drew close to 80 percent of their membership from people who had lived in Los Angeles for less than ten years.[54] California historian Carey McWilliams described the "social fluidity" generated by their relocation as an important component of Foursquare members' willingness to embrace Sister Aimee's colorful, energetic fundamentalism. He estimated that "nine out of ten of Aimee's followers were converts from the orthodox Protestant creeds, migrants from small-town and farming areas in the Middle West. Full of nostalgia for the corn belt but mightily intrigued by sunny California, aching with loneliness and the feeling of 'wanting to know someone,' they found their heart's desire in Angelus Temple, Sister Aimee, and the Shared Happiness of Kindred Souls."[55] An acerbic *New Republic* commentator agreed. Writing in 1929, Murrow Mayo observed:

> The great majority of people that move to California are not sinners. They have been saved for years. Most of them have been going to churches all their lives. . . . [McPherson] was a magnet, drawing to her the moronic, the bucolic, the sick, the aged—and a whole army of former back-East Christians who, growing mellowed in the warm sunshine of Paradise, were turning against the Hell-fire religion under which they had quaked all their lives. . . . From holy Kansas ten years ago, Mrs. McPherson surveyed Southern California. She saw a glorified carnival, with thousands of released Puritans, bewildered farmers, elderly folk, mental and physical incurables dallying along the gorgeous Midway.[56]

McPherson's most famous literary critic was surely H. L. Mencken, who despised her audience and made no attempt to hide his scorn when writing about the Foursquare Church in 1928:

> She was attracted to Los Angeles, it appears, by the climate. The Bible Belt was sending a steady stream of its rheumatic mortgage-sharks in that direction, and she simply followed. The rest, as everybody knows, was a swift and roaring success. The town had more morons in it than the whole State of Mississippi, and thousands of them have nothing to do save gape at the movie dignitaries and go to revivals. . . . There is comfort here [in her theology] for poor and wormy folk. They swarm in Los Angeles as they swarm nowhere else on earth. They come in from the farms and cow towns with their lumbago, their shortness of breath, their broken ribs, their ringing in the ears, their souvenirs of bad medicine, bad surgery, bad obstetrics, and Aimee cheers them up. In a little while they vanish into Heaven, but more are always on the way. If all the forlorn pilgrims she baptizes every year remained on her rolls, her Angelus Temple would swell to the proportions of a county, and shove Los Angeles into the Pacific. But they come and they go, each leaving a mite.[57]

Mencken correctly guessed that Sister Aimee indeed baptized many. By 1930 she counted about twelve thousand followers in Los Angeles alone and thirty thousand in the entire region.[58] Defending the station's license in 1937, Sister Aimee claimed that KFSG constituted a "church of the air" with a registered membership exceeding fifty thousand.[59] Her audience came largely from the urban white lower middle class of "small shopkeepers, barbers, beauty-parlor operators, small-fry realtors, and the owners of hamburger joints."[60] Sister Aimee claimed to "bring spiritual consolation to the middle class, leaving those above to themselves and those below to the Salvation Army."[61]

Although her followers, like McPherson herself, remained suspicious that the moral climate of their society was on its way to hell, they eagerly snapped up the latest trappings of modern consumerism. This is critical to understanding both McPherson and her audience; they were savvy to the "new" and the modern without also taking on a cynical contempt for old religious doctrines. Living an old-time religion did not necessarily mean being surrounded by yesterday's appliances. The irony of this was not lost at the time to commentator Bruce Bliven: "It is an audience which combines mental mediaevalism with an astonishing up-to-dateness in the physical realm. Its homes are full of electric refrigerators, washing-machines and new-type phonographs, its garages contain 1927 automobiles. It utilizes the breath-taking new marvels of the radio in order to hear rigid doctrines . . . and sees nothing incongruous in joining (over the radio) in a moment of silent prayer—silent, that is, except for the hum of the B-battery eliminator."[62]

If Sister Aimee's throaty, warm, exuberant voice was the background for thousands of Sunday chicken dinners, it was no mere accident. She possessed a storyteller's sensibility, both in her rhetorical style and in the way she became the lead character in a life lived on a grand scale. The narrative she created from her life was a rags-to-riches tale fit for a Hollywood film. She issued an irresistible clarion call to religious conservatives, reassuring them that the mass media could express their moral worldview without compromising their antiworldly stance. As John Hood has pointed out, she played a key role within the subculture of denominational Pentecostals, without which their subsequent involvement in the mass media—from Oral Roberts to Jimmy Swaggart—would have been unimaginable. "Indeed, much of what the movement knows of itself is a reflection of its media image. Of all the shadows, the longest was cast by Aimee Semple McPherson."[63]

Her celebration of the rural past in her own life, and in the lives of many of her migrant followers, also was deliberately constructed. Sister Aimee romanticized "rural-agrarian culture" in its apparent twilight.[64] Hers was "the old-time religion given a new buoyancy, vitality and bounce because of Aimee's exuberant, joyous expression of it."[65] But McPherson's embrace of rural religion and its communitarian values cut two ways. On the one hand, she helped legitimize the Bible-based evangelical way of thinking by bringing its discourse into the mass media and contributed to the growth of a vital subculture that perceived itself as the last bastion of American morality. On the other hand, she introduced into this insular community aspects of the secular media. She was at once a voice against and—with her silk stockings and her marcelled, bobbed hair—a representation of "the world" as evangelicals in the twenties and thirties saw it.[66] With Sister Aimee's Angelus ministry and its counterpart on the radio, conservative Christians might join in the outcry against the modern world; but they encountered it through her as well, and the two countervailing influences cannot be separated. She remains a fascinating example of the way religion functions as a form of popular culture entertainment in America and how faithful believers—religion's spokespeople—become transformed through their relationship with the media into objects of intense interest ranging from ridicule to reverence.

It seems only fair to let the last word on McPherson's media ministry be her own, as she was reinvented by others so many times during her life and in the decades since her death. A reporter once asked Sister Aimee what was her greatest wish in life. She considered the question and then replied from each of the two perspectives that were always in creative tension in her life. "As a woman," she began, "I would wish that I might have a happy Christian home, a devoted husband and family." Given the sad litany of personal disappointments she encountered, it is safe to say that the desires of her womanly heart went largely unfulfilled. But perhaps she had come close to achieving the great wish of her "other" self: "As an evangelist," she continued, "I would wish that I might have a pulpit and a public address system mighty enough to reach every person in the whole world with the message that God so loved the world."[67] With thousands of watts behind her every time she opened her mouth to preach and the outlet of a successful radio station that was never stilled, Sister Aimee amplified the audience for her cheerful version of Pentecostal Christianity.

4 Pastors of the Old-Fashioned Gospel
Charles Fuller, Evangelist to the World

The winter of 1963, coming near the end of his forty-year career as a radio evangelist, found Charles Edward Fuller mindful of the signs to which the troubled times pointed. To his good friend and colleague, Harold Ockenga, Fuller penned:

> I hope that these terrible storms in the East, Middle-West and South may soon be over and that we can get some rain out here. It is tinder dry and crops frozen. It seems the whole world is upset and that the Lord must be coming soon. I personally have no confidence in the Kennedy administration and feel they may well damage our economy. I personally feel a burning desire to send the Gospel out in power and am very glad for the keen interest of the radio listeners to pray and do their best financially. I could not ask for more loyal listeners and helpers, and I pray for strength to carry on in these darkening days.[1]

The part of him that lived in the shadow of "darkening days" was a side of Fuller that few saw. He was known to most of his fans as the "Heavenly Sunshine" man, who with his wife, Grace Payton Fuller, had created the highest-rated religious broadcast of all time, the *Old Fashioned Revival Hour*. On the air, Charles was cheerful and reassuring. But what he was seeing as the century unfolded disturbed and unsettled him. In his mind, his radio ministry and associated evangelistic career built a fragile bridge over a yawning chasm of godlessness and despair, across which ordinary Americans might grope their way toward the light of God—but under which Satan and his minions were ever searching for places to undermine the structure. Fuller was certain God would "undertake," as he so often said. But his task—to evangelize the world through radio—felt no less challenging.

Charles Fuller, more than any other evangelical Protestant of his time, achieved long-lasting success as a radio broadcaster. He preached thousands of sermons a year, most of which were broadcast in one form or another, for more than thirty years. He and his wife exemplified evangelicalism's genteel ambitions at midcentury, and the Fullers' efforts—especially in fund-raising and in packaging an image of fundamentalists as mainstream Americans —helped build a more centrist Protestant coalition that would solidify in the late forties and fifties.

Charles's parents, Henry and Helen Day Fuller, were Methodists from upstate New York who believed deeply in missionary work. A furniture merchant and an orange grove owner who had resettled in California, Henry headed a family of rising fortunes, and he channeled some of his spare earnings into a small trust fund for evangelism. In 1887, the Fullers' fourth and youngest son, Charles, was born in Los Angeles. Not long after, Henry and Helen built a tall, gingerbread-trimmed Victorian in the midst of their Redlands orange grove, where they raised their children. Henry was a distant father; an otherwise hagiographic account of Charles's childhood contrasts his parents: "[Henry] never gave personal attention to his sons. He never played with them, seldom joked with them, and never tried to be on intimate terms with them. [Helen] was a saint who knew how to keep peace in the home . . . faithful to a husband who at times might be difficult, and bringing her boys to the throne of grace every day in prayer."[2] Young Charles combined his parents' New England reserve with a California zest for activity; the lanky, hardworking student played football in high school and for Pomona College.[3] He graduated from Pomona in 1910 with a degree in chemistry (after the requisite grappling with the theory of evolution), having been voted president of his senior class and the Debating Society. The college yearbook captioned his photograph "Physically the biggest man in school, mentally a fine student, morally every inch a man."[4]

During these years he met and courted Grace Payton; the daughter of a prosperous physician, she was born in Oregon and raised in Redlands. After high school, Grace studied diction, public speaking, and dramatics at the Los Angeles Cumnock School of Expression and at Western College for Women in Ohio. When her father died in 1909, Grace cut short her schooling to be with her mother. Under the influence of a devout evangelical friend of the family, Mrs. Leonora Barnhill, Grace became converted from her spiritual dalliance with Unitarianism to evangelical Christianity. Grace and Charles were married in 1911, and the young couple bought a small orange grove but suffered heavy losses in freezes in the mid-1910s.[5] Around 1913, when they moved to Placentia and Charles became a packinghouse manager, Charles began to study his wife's tracts and books (including her recently purchased Scofield Bible) with increasing interest.[6]

Grace suffered from tuberculosis following a stillbirth; she was confined to bed with daily fevers for more than three years. During one of her periods of convalescence in the San Bernardino Mountains in 1916, Charles went to hear Paul Rader—whom Fuller knew only as a former professional boxer—when Rader preached at the Church of the Open Door in Los Angeles.[7] Rader's sermon moved Charles to accept Christ; as he wrote to Grace, "Now my whole life aims and ambitions are changed. I feel now that I want to serve God if He can use me instead of making the goal of my life the making of money."[8] Within a year Charles and Grace had joined the Presbyterian Church in Placentia, California, and Charles left business to prepare for the ministry, enrolling at the Bible Institute of Los Angeles (BIOLA) and studying under Reuben A. Torrey. After graduating from BIOLA in 1921, he began teaching a Sunday school class that ultimately grew into a Baptist congregation, called Calvary Church.

Calvary's statement of faith and the evidence from Placentia Presbyterian's records suggest that there was some tension among Placentia Protestants over doctrine and practice. The local paper, the *Placentia Courier,* reported that the new Calvary Church fulfilled the "urgent need felt and expressed from many sources for a church organization where only and all fundamental doctrines of the Bible are upheld by those wishing to lend their united influence against the worldwide trend toward modernism and materialism." Charles was ordained a Baptist minister in May 1925 and assumed Calvary Church's leadership; in sermons such as "Unity, Christian Science, New Thought, Theosophy, Spiritualism . . . and Unitarianism," "Bloodless Religion," and "Satanic Counterfeits," he took up the topic of false religion.[9] Although his strident fundamentalism would be tempered when Fuller became the most widely heard and popular religious radio personality in America, his determination to map the boundary line between true and false religion informed his every stand at the pulpit and his lifelong ministry on radio.

Charles Fuller had, in his high school years, been an enthusiastic amateur wireless operator. He bought his first equipment through the mail, earning the money a dime at a time by trapping gophers in the family orchard.[10] So he had some interest in and experience with radio when the opportunity arose to begin broadcasting in the early 1920s. His initial experience preaching over the radio was over the BIOLA station KTBI in 1924, giving Bible lessons twice a week, but the real inspiration came when he substituted for a regular radio preacher during a ten-day Defenders of the Christian Faith Conference at the Cadle Tabernacle in Indianapolis.[11] He later recalled that while riding the train back west in February 1929, he became convinced he was called to preach on radio.[12]

He launched a radio ministry, broadcasting occasional Sunday evening services from Calvary Church over KREG Los Angeles ("The Voice of the Orange Empire") from February 1930 to March 1933.[13] As he explained to his congregates and friends in a letter when the programs were first launched, "To broadcast requires financial assistance. We need your help. . . . Your investments will pay large dividends for time and eternity. Help to bring cheer, inspiration, and heavenly manna to thousands."[14] His letter seeking the $180 per month that his contract with KREG stipulated, as it turned out, set the tone for the rest of his life—a life, ironically, that was concerned after all with the goal of making money. Broadcasting was expensive, and it would take someone single minded in pursuit of funds to make a career out of broadcasting. Charles Fuller was indeed that man.

By the end of May 1930, the services simulcast on KREG were delivered to standing-room-only crowds in the Calvary meeting-house. But Fuller was disappointed with the station's range—only about twenty-five miles outside Santa Ana—and with its technical difficulties, which included a fishing pole strung from the studio window to the roof aerial that, in its contact with the building, grounded seventy-five of the station's one hundred watts.[15] So Fuller contracted with KGER Long Beach, a thousand-watt station, to carry Calvary's services starting in September 1930; his program could then be heard as far away as Washington, Idaho, and Iowa, judging by the letters he began to receive from some of the estimated fifteen thousand listeners.[16] By 1933 it was clear to both Fuller and the board of Calvary Church that his heart was in the radio ministry, which by then included a Bible study class aimed at Sunday school teachers and a program called the *Pilgrim Hour* that had even had a short stint on the CBS network. Charles Fuller had gained a vocation; but Calvary had lost its pastor. In March, he resigned as pastor to pursue radio full-time.[17]

Given what we have seen so far about the effect of the new networks, the nascent FRC rulings, and the depression's toll on fundamentalist radio broadcasting, embarking on a career as a radio preacher in 1933 would seem to be singularly bad timing. Fuller might easily have followed Paul Rader into debt and obscurity just as he had followed Rader into Christianity and evangelism. His move out of the relative security of an established pastorate was a risky, perhaps even a foolhardy, decision. By this time he and Grace had a young son, Daniel (born in 1925), whose health had never been strong. Daniel had nearly died in early 1932 of a serious bronchial infection; at the same time the Fullers' home and properties were attached by the banks, with little prospect of even applying the money from their crops toward their own mounting bills.[18] Nevertheless, Charles formed a nonprofit corporation, the Gospel Broadcasting Association (GBA), and went forward with bravado in his plans to develop radio programs for 15 million potential listeners in the western United States and Canada. "Put your dollars to work for God now," he stressed in a fund-raising letter, "The time is short. Occupy till He come. Pray Pray Pray." In his biography of his father, Dan Fuller commented:

"They took God at His Word and believed that He would see them through their financial difficulties. The scriptural teaching that people are lost unless they repent and believe in Christ so controlled Charles Fuller's thinking that all he could do was bend every effort to get the Gospel out. He assumed that other Christians felt the same sense of urgency and laid down the specific steps they could follow in helping him evangelize by radio."[19]

Fuller's first program over KFI, the *Sunday School Hour,* brought a Bible study course to a large portion of the United States over this single, powerful fifty-thousand-watt station. He also continued his *Radio Bible Class* over KGER Long Beach and other southern California stations that fall, hoping to move it to the Columbia network (CBS). But because of CBS's new policy of rejecting paid religious broadcasting, Fuller had to look elsewhere. He signed on with the independent station KNX for his half-hour *Heart to Heart Hour.* By the end of 1934, then, Fuller was buying four time slots on three stations for his radio programs, including the KNX *Revival Hour,* an hour-long live program of preaching and choir music first sent out from the Hollywood Women's Club.

Charles was also enlisting volunteers—one hundred by May 1934—whom he called "Prayer Warriors" whose prayers would, he felt, combat the opposition he expected would come from Satan.[20] He gathered strength from his sense that he was participating in a growing movement of fundamentalists. Grace edited a monthly newsletter, called the *Heart to Heart Talk,* which addressed readers in second person and read like a personal letter, "just as though you were sitting in my study and we were chatting together," as the first issue put it.[21] By 1940 the Fullers were sending the free, two-page *Talk* to sixty-five thousand people.[22] While the "Prayer Warriors" connected the movement vertically to divine power, the letters he was sending and receiving connected the movement laterally among diverse members of his radio audience with Fuller at the hub.[23] He enlisted more than five hundred prayer warriors by the fall of 1936, when the *Radio Revival Hour* made a quantum leap onto network radio. In time, the smaller group of loyal regulars in the *Pilgrim Hour* studio audience came to function for the Fuller family as their own church. They were the core of his financial supporters and of his "Prayer

Warrior" rolls; the Fullers and the *Pilgrim Hour* followers held a monthly communion service together, with sermons covering the "deeper Bible truths, given for the feeding of the flock of God" and preparing Fuller to reach out through the *Revival Hour* broadcasts to the unsaved.[24]

In 1936, KNX was acquired by CBS, which prohibited paid-time religious programming; Fuller had anticipated this and began making "electrical transcriptions" on phonograph records for re-broadcast. By mailing them to independent stations, he actually increased his coverage, although it was difficult work in a hot studio once a week recording the program, sometimes with several takes. Transcriptions were rare in 1930s broadcasting, and no other program had used them to such an extent. Charles and Grace could even, as they did one Easter vacation, listen to their own program parked by the roadside enjoying the outdoors. "It was indeed a strange and thrilling experience, and caused us to marvel at modern invention," recalled Charles.[25] However thrilling transcriptions may have been, they were certainly expensive. He went on tour, stumping on weekdays for the program in cities —Portland, Seattle, Boise, Salt Lake, Albuquerque—where he had bought Sunday time.

In late 1936, a new network was launched, the Mutual Broadcasting System. Mutual was open to Charles Fuller's advances; although the network considered religious programming policies similar to those of NBC and CBS, revenue from the *Radio Revival Hour* and other commercial religious broadcasts—such as the *Lutheran Hour,* which Mutual also carried—was too lucrative for a struggling new network to pass up. To make his program more attractive to the prospective network, Fuller changed the format of the *Radio Revival Hour,* making it, as he described, "more varied, interesting and more spiritual—but continuing our policy of singing the *old songs* and giving only the *old Gospel.* We are not called to discuss politics or plans for fixing up the world," he explained, in an unmistakable reference to Father Coughlin, who was then actively criticizing the Roosevelt administration.[26] Instead, Fuller stressed his evangelical goals: "We are called to preach *Christ* and men and women are hungering to hear."[27] However, Mutual's rules prohibited Fuller from asking directly for contributions, and even the initial station lineup cost twice as much as he had been paying out for KNX and the independent transcription stations.[28]

In the fall of 1937, after a summer of tight finances and bare scrapes to pay the weekly fees on sixteen Mutual stations, the network received another offer on Fuller's time slot from a tobacco company willing to sign with all Mutual's affiliates nationwide. Rudy Alber, Fuller's agent, broke the news to him in person. To Alber's surprise Fuller replied, "Rudy, you tell the Mutual Broadcasting System that the *Radio Revival Hour* will sign a contract today to go coast-to-coast on their network." This meant signing on with ninety stations rather than sixteen, a more than fivefold increase in weekly costs. In his negotiations with Mutual, Fuller gave up his prime 7:30–8:30 West Coast time slot to the new sponsor in return for a guaranteed slot at 6:00 PST (a time more amenable to East Coast listeners), provided he sign on with all of Mutual's affiliates in a short period of time. The first coast-to-coast broadcast of the newly renamed *Old Fashioned Revival Hour* was on 3 October 1937. Joining Fuller at the microphone and providing the "old-time" gospel hymns that became such a distinctive feature of the program was the male "Goose Creek" quartet and pianist Rudy Atwood, who also played on broadcasts of the Country Church of Hollywood.[29]

Within six weeks, forty Mutual stations opened up their time slots, requiring Fuller to go from raising fifteen hundred dollars to forty-five hundred dollars each week. He perceived this as a series of crises inspired by satanic opposition to the program's survival. He wrote in apocalyptic tones for the *Heart to Heart Talk* for October 1937: "In our weariness we have asked God for a respite—but He has shown us that as the days darken and the end of this dispensation approaches, the battle with Satan and his forces will grow even more fierce, so we must be good soldiers, putting on the whole armor and going forward with much prayer, hoping for no rest except as we rest in Him. We can expect only the most bitter opposition from Satan because this message of redemption is going right through his realm—the air. We must, in the future, meet all his thrusts with spiritual weapons, as we have done in the past."[30] When faced with the prospect of failure, as he was several times in the early days on Mutual, Fuller typically called his radio audience and his *Heart to Heart Talk* readers to specified days of prayer for the program. On the 15 November designated day of prayer, for example, he wrote in the *Heart to Heart Talk,* "As Mrs. Fuller and I knelt in prayer this morning we were thrilled with the knowledge that our prayers were just a little part of a great wave of prayer from all over the land, and Canada and Hawaii."[31] Fuller also stepped up his tour schedule, filling civic auditoriums and stadiums such as Soldier's Field in Chicago. The momentum was building as Fuller's tours worked to "consolidate a firm basis of support" for the program's listeners on Mutual.[32] By the end of 1938, Fuller had his Sunday evening time slot on each of Mutual's 128 stations, preaching each Sunday to an audience of 5 million people.[33] In addition, the program was favorably featured in the evangelical paper the *Sunday School Times* by the paper's influential editor, Charles Trumbull; the paper's readership numbered around a hundred thousand at the time.[34] As Mutual signed on additional stations, the *Old Fashioned Revival Hour* kept pace and expanded accordingly, with Fuller traveling to cities all over the country during the week to drum up support for the broadcast.

Hearing recordings of the *Old Fashioned Revival Hour*—of which hundreds are still extant—twenty-first-century listeners might be hard pressed to identify just what made the program so popular. The format simply replicated a revival meeting. To be more precise, the broadcasts usually *were* revival meetings with a live audience, after which "convicted" audience members might come forward to declare their decisions for Christ. But the program was truly aimed at the invisible and not-present audience rather than the physical one gathered in the auditorium. It inverted the traditional conventions of a religious meeting—after all, to whom else could a revival be directed than the folks on the benches? But on radio, the "real" audience could be not the "real" live people in numbered theater seats but instead uncounted millions listening in a variety of settings elsewhere. In effect, the revival supposedly being carried on for the benefit of the physically present audience—to which the radio listeners would be mere eavesdroppers—was in reality a program crafted to reach the invisible "Radioland" audience and to which the auditorium crowds were the eavesdroppers.

A "service within a service," like a play within a play, the hour was framed by Fuller leading the theater audience, his staff, and the musicians in a short rehearsal of the hymns the congregation would sing and then in prayer before the microphones started recording and after they cut off at the end.[35] At the signal of a green light, the broadcast portion opened with a choir rendition of a rousing hymn ("Jesus Saves"): there were no dirge-like selections on the *Revival Hour.* The program's signature song was a version of the hymn "Heavenly Sunshine," a simple, cheerful ditty that by the mid-1940s was sung during each broadcast. As many as eleven or twelve gospel hymns followed, with florid piano or organ accompaniment, sung alternately by the choir and the quartet—the latter had a distinctive barbershop style of vocal harmony. Between musical numbers, Fuller would plug the *Heart to Heart Talk,* identify the program for the benefit of those tuning in late, and enunciate the unforgettable address of the Gospel Broadcasting Association (Post Office Box 123, Los Angeles). Depending on the network and the rules of the air at the time, he might be permitted to request financial help to continue to deliver the *Revival Hour* over the air. The entire first half of the program was generally given over to music, with about five minutes for Grace to read excerpts from listeners' letters. Charles always introduced this part of the program by saying to his wife, "Go right ahead, honey." Grace chose three or four letters each week and read segments without naming the authors but giving some indication where they'd been sent from or what some of the writers' circumstances were. She'd sign off with a regretful "And that's all I shall have time for today, dear friends."

In the second half of the hour, Charles would deliver a sermon based on a short Bible text. He spoke simply, without flowery language or much sentimentality.[36] He addressed the listeners directly, calling them "Beloved" or "Fellow strangers and pilgrims": "Notice this verse," he would say, or, "Will you pray with me?" His sermon themes stayed rather narrowly focused around the necessity of salvation and of the individual sinner's responsibility to accept the gospel of Jesus—although he spoke little of hell or its horrors. Instead he tended to emphasize God's mercies, blessings on the righteous, and promises that their regenerated

The Old Fashioned Revival Hour *quartet, circa 1940.* From left to right: *Bill MacDougall, Herman Hosier, Al Harlan, and Art Jaissle, at the Mutual microphone. Fuller Theological Seminary Archive, Pasadena, California.*

lives would buoy men and women up to endure their everyday troubles. Every sermon led up to an altar call in inexorable, predictable progression. Writing of Fuller's homiletic style, professor Wilbur Smith has said: "There is nothing here that we would call oratory, there are no tricks, there is nothing of a sensational nature, and there are no prizes offered. Controversial questions are seldom discussed. . . . His thinking is in simple terms, and that is the way he preaches. . . . People can understand what he is saying, and of course that is a tremendous asset."[37] At the conclusion of his sermon as the choir softly sang in the background, Charles would urge listeners—first the invisible radio listeners and then the congregation in the auditorium—to save their otherwise lost souls. This example comes from a broadcast in the late forties:

> Let us bow our heads in prayer while the choir sings an invitation number. . . . Pray as they sing. And friends of radioland, as we are bringing the Old Fashioned Revival Hour to a close, will you take God at His word and come? He says, "Come, let us reason together." Will you take God at his word? God bless you. Kneel right down in your room, or by your bed, wherever you may be, look up into the Father's face through Jesus Christ, and say "God be merciful to me a sinner, and save me." While heads are bowed in this fine audience at Long Beach, put your hand up just before we leave the air, and say "Pray for me." God bless you. God bless you. There is no middle ground.[38]

The *Revival Hour* drew millions of listeners with this simple format. It was the second most popular show in its time slot.[39] By the mid-1940s Fuller's worldwide audience was estimated to be 20 million people each Sunday.[40] A syndicated columnist from Washington, D.C., praised the program's straightforward message: "Coming out of California every Sunday evening, this gospel hour of the radio breaks through the din and clamor of swing-whoopee, croonings, and news broadcasts to almost startle a weary world with its unretouched truths. This earnest, pleading Baptist preacher . . . exhorts a bizarre world in a manner simple and devoid of sophism."[41] It passed lightly over controversial subjects, not surprising given the Fullers' imperative to avoid offending large segments of the potential audience. Fundamentalists were notoriously contentious over sometimes minute points of doctrine, and Charles felt this was both unseemly and damaging to the movement at large.

Take, as the most obvious example, the ongoing controversy within fundamentalism over premillennialism, the doctrine that Christ's return would precede a millennium of peace foretold in the Bible. The many varieties of belief about the second coming of Christ can be reduced to two major categories: pre- and post-millennialism. Fundamentalists of the early twentieth century generally believed in dispensational premillennialism, versions of which were preached in Bible conferences and institutes and explicated in Cyrus Scofield's Bible annotations.[42] According to this mode of interpreting the Bible's prophecies, the earth's history could be divided into identifiable time periods, or "dispensations," the last of which would be inaugurated by a series of apocalpytic conflicts and events (the "tribulation"). Dispensationalists thus placed great emphasis on personal conversion—as nothing people could do to improve the world would thwart its eventual destruction—and on searching for one-to-one correlations between prophecies in the Bible and events or people in contemporary life. In contrast to dispensational premillennialism, postmillennialism holds that it is the work of Christian believers to conform their surroundings to the will of God, thus ushering in a thousand years of peace, after which Christ would return to judge all people. Within dispensationalism, there could be further divisions, too: for example, over whether the believers would be gathered out secretly—or "raptured"—prior to the tribulation of the churches (pre-trib dispensationalism), or if true Christians should prepare to suffer through these dark years (post-trib dispensationalism). Fuller himself started out his ministry as a strident dispensationalist at Calvary Church, and when he founded Fuller Seminary, the faculty had to pass a litmus test of belief in premillennialism.[43] His views became more tolerant over the years, partly through his involvement as chairman of the board of Fuller Theological Seminary and his ground-level perspective on the acrimonious disagreements over dispensationalism at the school. He backed the publication of antidispensational scholarly works from Fuller

Seminary by George Ladd (*Blessed Hope*) and Edward Carnell (*The Case for Orthodox Theology*), even though he took the heat from dispensationalists such as John R. Rice for not holding the line.[44]

By 1955, he was urging all "born-again believers" to have Christian tolerance, regardless of whether they held pre-trib or post-trib beliefs.[45] Privately he told fellow fundamentalist Harold Ockenga, "So many Fundies believe that Post-trib teaching is heretical. They need to be educated. This critical attitude hurts our financial support."[46] He could not go as far as some on the Fuller faculty who were "amillennial," but Charles did agree—without publicity—that the premillennial requirement could be removed from the seminary's statement of faith after his death and that there should be some latitude at the seminary on the issue. Ockenga congratulated him for his "broadness, when [he had] been committed to the dispensational view for so long."[47] Charles therefore was a prominent point on the crest of the neo-evangelical wave, legitimating younger voices calling for a more tempered view on dispensationalism and other formerly untouchable fundamentalist doctrines.[48] His stance did cost him some listeners —the dispensationalist Wilbur Smith in 1963 claimed (with probable exaggeration) that Fuller had lost 40 percent of the support for the *Old Fashioned Revival Hour* because of the seminary's policies.[49]

But the Fullers' strategy broadened their audience in the long run. In ways similar to Grace's practice of omitting the names of denominations when she read letters on the program, softening on-air dispensational theology plastered over differences and celebrated the common thread of revivalism that was at the core of all the fundamentalist churches. On the air, the Fullers seemed to assume that their listeners were members of a large and happy family—among whom private correspondence could be shared and religious doctrine agreed on—and this familiarity attracted people to tune in week after week to what might seem to be stultifying repetition of a narrow range of topics and old hymns.[50]

By the 1950s, when the program had been on the air continuously for some fifteen years, people were responding to the familiarity of the program itself and its consistent "cast" of speakers and musicians. If at first they were stirred by the familiar revival-meeting tone and music, as time went on the program's appeal became self-referential, and people kept listening not so much for what the *Revival Hour* reminded them of but for what it had come to stand for in their own lives. As one listener put it: "It just seems like you are real brother and sister, blood relation."[51]

The *Revival Hour* was also a "family business" in a very real sense. The Fullers' radio ministry involved both partners—and their son—on the air and behind the scenes. Charles Trumbull reported to his *Sunday School Times* readers that Charles attributed "the greater part of the success of the O.F.R.H. to Mrs. Fuller—to her prayers, her guidance, her wisdom."[52] It was true that Grace was a much more visible—or audible—spouse than that of any other radio evangelist. Although her time slot was brief during the *Old Fashioned Revival Hour* compared with the length of Charles's sermons, Grace was really more of a cohost in her role on the show. Both she and Charles were born radio personalities, with appealing broadcast voices. Charles exuded confidence and concern; Grace had a precise and well-trained voice. When she read snippets from listener letters each week, it sounded as if she was casually rifling through a pile in front of her and sharing favorite tidbits on impulse. In reality, the letters segments were carefully scripted—Grace changed words or sentences to make the letters sound better on the air, and she usually typed out her comments in advance, even down to the patter—"Now here's a real gem from the Midwest," and so on.

People writing to the Fullers often addressed Grace as "Honey Fuller," since Charles called her "Honey" on the program. Being called by a pet diminutive put Grace in her place, a clue to listeners that, though Grace might be involved and vocally participating in the ministry, she was still subordinate. She worked at the GBA office, and her task of managing the ministry's correspondence was a herculean one requiring a whole host of interpersonal skills that Charles apparently lacked, but little of her authoritative persona emerged during the broadcasts. Rather, Charles and Grace complemented each other well on the air, with an ease in their verbal exchanges that conveyed tender affection. In other words, they were the ideal postwar couple. In an era of a zealous return to normalcy after the Second World War, a booming marriage rate, and national middle-class plunge into home ownership, there was a generalized renewed interest in the home and the family in the late 1940s and the 1950s. The Fullers, whether they intended this or not, cast themselves as the fundamentalist mirror image of Ozzie and Harriet, and people looked to them as exemplars of marital stability and devotion. "To us you are the Abraham and Sarah of our time," wrote Mrs. Joseph Penicaro to the Fullers.[53] One man who taped the program each week so he could listen to it again wrote, "Sunday or two ago, was real cute, when Bro. Fuller and you were having a little family conversation over the program and Bro. Fuller laughed so freely, Ha! I still have that on tape and get a real kik [sic] out of that."[54] "Are you people always congenial like that in your home? Could such bliss really exist??" wondered another listener about the way Charles and Grace addressed each other on the air.[55]

Certainly "bliss" was the impression given by the effusively sentimental portrait of the Fullers' suburban home by J. Elwin Wright in the early 1940s—in which Pasadena became a Garden of Eden. He wrote this account in a book mailed out to fans and contributors:

> Driving along an avenue of oaks and tropical verdure, with the towering, wide-branched trees providing a lovely green canopy for the street, we come almost abruptly to a driveway leading to an attractive English, washed-brick home, the residence of Rev. and Mrs. Charles E. Fuller. Sycamores shade the lawn and a lovely flower bed at the farther end holds our attention for a moment of real pleasure.
>
> The inside of this attractive but unpretentious home is furnished in good taste, in keeping with the exterior. We are warmly welcomed by our most charming hostess, who takes her place on a low seat by the fireplace while we are made comfortable in chairs beside the library table.
>
> The house has a homey, used appearance, as though those who live here love to slip away from a busy world and find rest and refreshment within its walls, as though love and understanding too, are found here.[56]

The Fullers played up their happy home image in many of their marketing materials throughout the 1940s and 1950s. During the war, because their travel was restricted, the Fullers assembled a traveling package of two short films, sent out to churches agreeing to sponsor a "Revival Hour Night"—with proceeds from the night's collection to be divided between the host church and the *Old Fashioned Revival Hour.* The first film took viewers behind the scenes at the radio studio and profiled the musicians who performed on the *Revival Hour.* The second, billed as "a 14 minute motion picture" titled "Life with the Fullers," depicted the family's home life.[57] Charles prepared a sermon in his study, son Dan played tennis, and Grace in the kitchen prepared strawberry shortcake: a domestic arrangement fit for a fifties sitcom. In a 1953 interview with the *Christian Herald,* Grace was portrayed as Christian helpmeet and homemaker. She was quoted as saying— with almost disingenuous modesty—"I thank God for such a husband and for permitting me to have even a small part in his great ministry."[58] The truth was that the ministry was as much hers as Charles's. But her public image squared with the widely accepted and popular portrayals of women in the postwar period, as apron-wearing goddesses of domestic life, self-sacrificing, intuitive, and sentimental.[59]

The years during and immediately after the Second World War were ones of financial boon for the *Old Fashioned Revival Hour.* In 1947 alone, Fuller was drawing in forty thousand dollars a week from voluntary donations to pay for airtime.[60] Fuller added stations overseas to carry the program to soldiers in Europe—including Radio Luxembourg after the war—and the Pacific, and through reading letters on the air he served as another way for Americans separated by war to draw closer through mass media.[61] The show's nostalgic elements made it popular among soldiers, and the income generated in the war years allowed Fuller not only to secure its prime time slot on all of Mutual's stations and many overseas ones but even to purchase as many as four hour-long time slots on Sundays in major urban markets. Fuller reminded his *Heart to Heart Talk* readers that the war's "rubber shortage and gasoline rationing mean that more people are at home now with ears to the radio, *listening.*"[62] The *Old Fashioned*

Charles and Grace Fuller reading fan mail, 10 June 1955.
Fuller Theological Seminary Archive, Pasadena, California.

Revival Hour, accordingly, could be heard live or prerecorded several times a day in some cities, including times selected so that war factory swing-shift workers could tune in after punching out for the night.[63]

Busy times brought often unendurable stress—"Satanic" pressure, according to Grace. After a particularly tiring trip and a bout of severe sinusitis in 1948, for example, Charles collapsed, saying he could not go on the air to preach. Wilbur Smith substituted that week while Grace supervised Charles's treatment: shots of B vitamins in the arm, a vacation in Palm Springs, and the services of a good Swedish masseuse. "How he longs for a real vacation," she wrote. "There has been this constant pressure for 23 years—never a day free of it. . . . The years have been rewarding and joyful but have taken their toll. I personally—so close to Charles—do not feel he has had a nervous break . . . but the warrior is weary."[64] Charles himself wrote to Ockenga a few weeks later, "Sometimes I feel that I can hardly attempt the broadcast but when I get on my feet at the mike the Lord enables me for which I thank Him."[65] His mood in the June 1948 *Heart to Heart Talk* remained subdued, referring to his "time of utter exhaustion and weakness" and asking for both prayers and financial contributions to continue apace.[66] The weight of self-imposed expectations and of public scrutiny was a real challenge for the whole family. In 1953, Charles impulsively sold his Cadillac one day, apparently out of guilt. His self-denial puzzled Grace. "But darlin' you don't play golf," she remembered telling him, "or spend much on yourself—that's your *hobby*—you polish your car and brush it out and love the mechanical precision and you have so much fun and relaxation with it." Charles asked Grace to pray with him and, weeping, confessed his worldliness and resolved to put more of his own funds into evangelistic work.[67]

So much of the Fullers' life was consumed with being "on stage" that there remains little in the way of private reflection for historians to examine. Charles's and Grace's personal letters to Ockenga, from which these two episodes are taken, offer a realistic glimpse into a household in which fame and prosperity brought their own intense conflicts and of a couple whose emotions were stretched taut over their spiritual responsibilities. The more sanitized version of these private battles went out in the *Heart to Heart Talk* and in *Revival Hour* sermons in words such as these penned by Charles in 1963: "Though these have been discouraging days because of Satanic attacks, yet I firmly believe that it is God's will and plan that we survive these difficulties and go on, continuing to carry to this sorrowful and fearful world the message of God's love, and of His provision for forgiveness of sin through Christ Jesus."[68] If one's family business was felt to carry this much cosmic weight, the notion of failure was simply too much even to entertain.

Like the other radio evangelists in this study, the Fullers had two overlapping audiences: those who attended the services, and those who listened to them by radio.[69] Holding the *Revival Hour* broadcasts in a large theater, as did Aimee Semple McPherson, made attending the program an event worth the time spent traveling and waiting in line. Charles would informally canvass the audience prior to each broadcast to see where people were from. Grace estimated that of their weekly audience in the Long Beach Auditorium from 1943 to 1958, which averaged thirty-five hundred people, 80 percent were "first-timers."[70] Seeing a live show drew religious tourists, too; in 1945 Los Angeles was leading the nation in commercial religious broadcasting.[71]

A far greater and more diverse group than the auditorium crowd in Long Beach tuned in the *Revival Hour* by radio. Fuller's listeners have been characterized, even by recent historians, simply as "rural, limited-education listeners who adhered to traditional values and enjoyed the old-fashioned elements of the Fuller ministry."[72] Fuller himself said that when he began preaching on radio, he envisioned people "living in some out-of-the-way place. When I'm speaking over the radio, I'm not thinking of those in apartment houses or in the thriving cities, but my heart goes out to those who are up in the canyon creeks and the mining gulches and in the remote places."[73] Between 1945 and 1952, a clipping service employed by the Gospel Broadcasting Association found ads, articles, and mentions in radio logs across the country with no clear regional stronghold.[74] A study of religious radio listening and television viewing habits in New Haven, Connecticut, in 1952 turned up more than eight hundred households of regular *Revi-*

val Hour listeners, two-thirds of which were forty-five or older, concentrated among the semiskilled or unskilled laborer occupations.[75] A radio log from the early 1960s shows that independent stations broadcast the *Revival Hour* in every state in the nation.[76]

Ultimately, listener letters—of which a large but partial collection is extant—are all we have by which to know Fuller's listeners. Besides those at the Fuller Seminary archives, two inexpensive books about the *Revival Hour,* one published in 1940 and the other in 1949, devoted considerable space to reprinting letters.[77] In addition, Grace selected and compiled a third book devoted entirely to letters, shorn of their dates and names and interspersed with her faith-promoting commentary.[78]

Farm and rural folk did write to the Fullers with regularity.[79] A Eugene, Oregon, farmer put a radio in his dairy barn when the program came on at milking time.[80] One ten-year-old girl confessed, "We hardly ever get to c[h]urch. We live fifteen miles from it. The roads are muddy and bad. Please pray for us."[81] A lonely widower wrote that Sundays were the hardest, isolated on his Montana farm without a car: "I walk back and forth from one window to the other. I know no one is ever coming but out of nervissness [sic] I look just the same. In the forenoon it is not quite so bad as I can listen to all the Sermons over the Radio."[82] Some farmers were quite prosperous, such as the couple from Leamington, Ontario, who raised thirty acres of potatoes, four types of orchard fruits, and close to a thousand chickens.[83] Others were much closer to the margin of subsistence: "Like so many others, the flood took the crop on our small farm, and as it is the only source of income I have, won't have a tithe much longer, So I am sending you this small offering of what I have on hands," wrote a woman from Freedom, Indiana.[84]

Rural letter writers described their struggles making a living from the land and their efforts to make do and shared not only their frustrations but also their meager bounties. One anonymous listener mentioned with pride his or her "fine watermelon," a Montana woman sent home-canned elk meat, and a woman in nearby Anaheim who had "more chickens than money right now" offered the Fullers a Cornish game hen ("either a roast or fryer whichever you prefer") the next time they were driving near her home.[85] Grace reprinted the following letter in her book, as a typical response from those who enjoyed the gospel in, as she put it, "the midst of poverty's corroding cares":

> We are just poor folks, trying to raise enough on our little farm to feed the family, and to get the place paid for. We work hard, but never seem to get ahead, likely because the soil is poor and we are so far out in the country and have to haul so far. We don't have much to do with, and it is lonesome, and would be discouraging if we did not know the Lord.
>
> Two years ago our oldest son worked for a farmer near town, and bought us a good radio. He is away in the service of his country now, and my, what that radio means to us no one will ever know! . . . I have never been in a fine church, with a big organ, but I don't have to, because we have the finest organ music in the country right here in our little home on Sundays. And, Mr. Fuller, when you preach, you make God so real to us, and the Bible so plain.[86]

Letters from rural listeners made up a significant but not overwhelming proportion of the Fullers' mail. Many more drew no attention to their particular circumstances, and some were clearly from urban listeners.[87] Correspondence and donations arrived from laborers of the class the New Haven study identified: a Boston chambermaid who sent her tips; a Washington, D.C., cab driver; and an "uneducated" Swedish day laborer from Glendale, California, just to name a few.[88] One 1942 letter arrived scribbled on the reverse side of packer's invoice slips from the Chevrolet plant in Flint, Michigan.[89] Others came from soldiers and short-wave listeners overseas (missionaries in particular).[90] Several were sent on prison letterhead from penitentiary inmates—even one from an American imprisoned in a Korean war camp.[91] Examining the letters, one is struck by both the geographic and denominational diversity they reveal. No region of the country predominates; none is absent. Fuller heard from Methodists, Baptists, Presbyterians, Wesleyans, Brethren evangelicals, graduates of BIOLA, Wheaton College, and Moody Institute, and members of the Christian and Missionary Alliance and Foursquare churches—in other words, a broad swath of Protestant America. Even Anglicans and Catholics listened and responded with letters, in both North America and the British Isles.[92] What united them were two interlocking concerns: the state of their souls before God, and the moral and spiritual health of the nation.

If region or level of urbanization turned out to be a poor way to identify the audience of the *Old Fashioned Revival Hour* as different from the rest of the population, another—less quantifiable—measure suggests itself. Above and beyond identification with the program's fundamentalist theology and its hosts' down-home public image, correspondents to the *Revival Hour* seemed intent on cementing a personal relationship with the Fullers themselves. Many asked for pictures of Charles and Grace or of the studio, as if wanting to make the people and places real to them. Others implored the Fullers to pray for them or for their loved ones enmeshed in sin or danger. Now that her husband was saved through listening to the program, confided one woman, "I am praying for the salvation of my mother and father and also my only sister and her husband. Please pray for them. I feel as if I know you personally, you and your good wife."[93] "Bro. Fuller will you and Honey join me in prayer for Don and Bob who have loved you since 3 and 4 yrs old[?]" asked a concerned grandmother who spoke as if the Fullers knew her grandsons personally.[94] The details of individual families' struggles spilled out in these letters of petition. "I should like you to pray for the salvation of my husband," wrote Ruth Shafer of Liberty, Nebraska. "He has been wandering in trouble and sin for years. He had planned to come home for Christmas, but was picked up again for drinking and is back again at the Saugus Rehabilitation Center. . . . Perhaps if more of us joined in prayer, he would accept Christ."[95] A Virginia follower shared her fears: "My Husband been out sick for 5 weeks he has heart-trouble. My daughter just come home from the Hospital. Doctor, will you all pray that my Daughter and Husband will get in good health." She signed off with a telling request, as if needing reassurance her concerns were not going unrecognized—"P.S. Please let me know if you received this."[96]

The proliferation of letters petitioning the Fullers to pray to God on their behalf seems to be the most significant aspect of the surviving collection of listeners' correspondence. A thread

Mail room of the Fuller Evangelistic Foundation, circa 1943.
Fuller Theological Seminary Archive, Pasadena, California.

of desperation runs through so many of them, a sense of the kind of "lost causes" about which faithful Catholic women in the same period were writing to the cult of Saint Jude, the patron saint of hopeless causes, in Chicago.[97] Despite the obvious theological and practical differences between conservative evangelical Protestants and pious Roman Catholics, what is similar is the giving over of spiritual burdens to those whom the sufferers feel are more qualified to intercede. So many seemed to assign to Charles and Grace special powers—as if the prayers the Fullers might offer somehow carried more weight with God. The *Revival Hour* audience was a movement in search of a leader, if we can generalize from the people who felt that their problems exceeded their abilities and that the Fullers not only cared but also could attend to those problems with divine help.

In short, the audience for the *Old Fashioned Revival Hour* was not confined to the rural margins of an urban nation; nor was it dominated by the uneducated or culturally unsophisticated. What the evidence suggests is very nearly the opposite: moderate fundamentalists were entering and reshaping the American mainstream. They were scattered among the rest of the population, no longer gathered into holy commonwealths or tightly insulated subcultures. From their perspective, they lived among the unbelievers to purify the culture. The Fullers were able to tap into the broad evangelical folk culture that persisted in American life and that had prepared evangelical Protestants to accept mass-media evangelism of the scale the Fullers mounted.

Popular support for the *Old Fashioned Revival Hour* and its blanket coverage of, as Fuller put it, "90 percent of the globe" evoked praise within the evangelical subculture but suspicion and opposition from some quarters outside it and from some militants within.[98] The program's unrelenting emphasis on moving listeners to perceive their sinfulness and make a decision for Christ struck many as narrow minded. In the 1940s several different organizations advocating different roles for evangelical broadcasting broke out into open debate over the issue, and broadcasting became one of the key issues around which evangelicals, who were determined to keep their public voice, rallied. Fuller played a key role in the formation of the National Association of Evangelicals in 1942 and the National Religious Broadcasters in 1944—organizations that were both, like the original fundamentalist alliances in the 1910s, conservative responses to a perceived attack by religious liberals. The Mutual network was the sole holdout in permitting paid-time religious programming and came under increasing pressure from the Federal Council of Churches to change its policies—which would have meant a 25 percent loss of income. Fuller had paid $1.6 million in 1943 to Mutual; he was by far its biggest customer.[99] In the fall of that year, Mutual decided to allow paid-time religious programs on Sunday mornings only. Fuller kept a Sunday morning half-hour time slot on Mutual for his *Pilgrim's Hour* program but took the more popular, hour-long *Old Fashioned Revival Hour* off the network altogether.

Neither the geographic range nor the financial stability of the *Old Fashioned Revival Hour* was adversely affected by the move from Mutual. Charles Fuller arranged for a nearly coast-to-coast group of independent radio stations to air the program, which was broadcast live from the Long Beach Municipal Auditorium.[100] It meant considerably more advertising for the Gospel Broadcasting Association, because the show was no longer billed with other Mutual radio hits and it took some time for fans to find the program at new times and on new stations.[101] But in many ways the Long Beach Auditorium's setup and the independent-station solution suited the Fullers' style. As his son put it, "While Charles Fuller found it very difficult to counsel with individuals, he came fully into his own on a platform before a large audience."[102] The auditorium was located on the waterfront, next to a boardwalk amusement park and near a military installation and the naval port. The neighborhood bustled with folks out for Sunday recreation and servicemen on shore leave; flags fluttering in the sea breeze, large signs in front of the auditorium, and the flyer-waving ushers dispersed along the sidewalk all added to the festive atmosphere building up to each *Old Fashioned Revival Hour* broadcast.[103] Some in the Long Beach audience had come long distances on a kind of pilgrimage; others wandered in from the sunny boardwalk on a whim.

The fifteen years of broadcasting from Long Beach—the later several were partially broadcast by ABC—were the height of the

Fullers' career. Charles was then in his sixties, a white-haired, grandfatherly giant of a man; Grace continued to read the letters and appear prominently in the program as the sweet-voiced matron. In the various marketing devices employed to sell the *Old Fashioned Revival Hour,* nostalgic themes still dominated. There were musical albums, including an "Old Fashioned Christmas," on which the cover art depicted Charles and Grace in a holly-bedecked living room surrounded by children. And there were at least two slickly produced souvenir booklets, marking the program's twenty-eighth and thirty-fifth anniversary years. Both booklets, recounting the couple's life stories and conversions and sketching the history of the program in providential language, looked like family scrapbooks, thick with black-and-white photos of the family at leisure.[104] The couple even starred in a short-lived version of the *Revival Hour,* called the *Old Fashioned Meeting,* on ABC television. Interestingly, the program portrayed a Sunday meeting at a simple, fictional wooden frame church, not as a grand and urbane Long Beach affair.[105]

Despite the domestic, "plain-folks" public image of the Fullers, Charles pursued a business-savvy career behind the scenes. He felt increasingly pulled into a more institutional role within evangelicalism. He founded the Fuller Evangelistic Foundation (FEF) in 1943 to help support missionization abroad. Charles was sickened by the cancer of liberalism he saw eating away at the prominent theological seminaries, including Princeton Theological, where his son had begun studying. By the mid-1940s he felt strongly that he should found a school "to accomplish great things for the cause of Christ in a time of dire world need. Certainly this old world is becoming increasingly confused and chaotic and Godless. . . . The vision and the great need have enlarged before me and been pressed upon me until it seems I could not turn away from it."[106] He and longtime friend Harold Ockenga, pastor of Park Street Church in Boston and chairman of the New England Fellowship, worked to get a new evangelical seminary off the ground in 1947.[107] Fuller Theological Seminary opened in rented quarters in the fall of that year, recruiting students for its first class almost entirely through announcements on the *Revival Hour.*[108] But the relationship between the program and the seminary was marked by tension. In August 1947, for example, Fuller hesitated even to mention the upcoming Seminary convocation on the air; listeners confused the financial functions of the GBA and the FEF, and offerings declined whenever Charles asked for funds for the seminary. He complained to Harold Ockenga, "I have found that, in announcing the Seminary, that my offerings have fallen down terribly. The public is very sensitive and there seems to be a feeling that if there are funds to start such a Seminary there isn't need for sacrificial money for the radio. . . . There is tremendous interest in the Hour and people love it and will get back of it even though eggs are 80 [cents] a dozen and shoes $15.00 a pair. I hardly feel that I can jeopardize the radio income by announcing the Seminary further over the air."[109]

A month later he again sought Ockenga's advice on how to finance the seminary's building campaign without soliciting *Revival Hour* listeners for money. "I am in a peculiar position," he explained, "in that I must keep money for the radio coming in and I can hardly divide my appeals asking for both radio and school."[110] In addition, fundamentalists on the far right—predominantly Carl McIntire and John R. Rice—who felt that even Fuller Seminary was too ecumenical for their liking sniped at Fuller in the forties and early fifties. In 1952, for example, when the seminary faculty divided over whether to reject the National Council of Churches' Revised Standard Version of the Bible, biblical literalists bitterly attacked Fuller for not defending biblical inerrancy; according to some letters, the betrayal felt deeply personal to Fuller's former supporters.[111]

Such controversies reveal two key realities of the *Old Fashioned Revival Hour:* first, the program's listenership had appealed to many stripes of fundamentalists; second, the *Hour* was sensitive to public pressure. The Fullers were perceived as responsive to their listeners, but even further, they were seen as accountable to their paying customers, who did not hesitate to make themselves heard when the "product" in which they felt they'd "invested" turned out to be not what they'd hoped for. As the man behind the scenes of the midcentury wrangling for institutions that would unite fundamentalists, Fuller tried to stretch the tent to cover everyone. Such a strategy left him open to criticism that he was sacrificing the movement's integrity, and he recognized that in some circles he was as much a liability as a godsend.

It was a relief for Fuller, then, when along came a fiery young evangelist who would simply steamroller all the minor squabbling among evangelicals with his telegenic revivals. When Billy Graham drew national media attention during his successful Los Angeles rally in the fall of 1949, Charles Fuller appeared on the stand with him and paid for part of Graham's next venue, Ockenga's hometown of Boston.[112] Fuller sent Billy Graham east, writing to Ockenga that he hoped he would "prove of blessing in Boston, too," and recommending him as a "real strategist in general as well as a fine preacher." He predicted, "God has marvelously put His hand upon Him and is going to use him in a unique way throughout our nation."[113] But if Fuller longed for evangelicals to regain their cultural standing, he said little of this from the pulpit of the *Old Fashioned Revival Hour* in the 1950s. He took a more subtle tack than outright estrangement of those who wanted to keep a healthy distance from the "Godless old world." The format of the program continued to deliver more of the same: the familiar gospel songs, the vaguely dispensationalist preaching, drawing on Cold War fears, and exhorting souls to come to God.

In 1958, ABC cut its radio shows to half an hour. The last Long Beach broadcast was 12 January of that year, and the *Old Fashioned Revival Hour* was transformed into a half-hour-long studio program. The new format had some advantages: Fuller could tape more than one week in a single session and have some time off for travel, but he deeply missed performing in front of a live audience.[114] In 1963, ABC cut the show, so the Fullers again picked up a string of independent stations to continue bringing the program to their loyal (but aging) listeners.

Fuller seemed well settled into the role of gentle fundamentalist sage in the later years of his ministry, leaving both the aggressive organizing and the relentless infighting to others. Letters from listeners that have survived from this period, peppered with references to "many years" of listening, suggest the audience had aged with the Fullers. Folks complained about their fixed incomes, described themselves as "we who have known and loved you through these many years," spoke of loved ones who had passed away, or admitted that their memory was "not very good any more."[115] Harold and Sadie Lucy, a couple from Whittier, California, echoed the sentiments of many others: "What great changes these years have brought! But through them all, that same voice has been the guiding light of our lives—a comfort in times of trial. Words just can not express what your never failing messages have meant to us. We love 'Honey's' voice and encouraging words, and the music is the best on the air."[116]

Grace Fuller's health failed in the mid-1960s; she died in 1966 after surgery for pancreatic fibroids. The man who left few personal documents of any kind tucked a note among his papers, written the day his wife passed away: "June 11, 1966. 2:30 P.M. Grace at home with the Lord. 54 years—nine months of wonderful life together. Good night, 'honey.' We will see each other in the coming eternal morning. Charles."[117] A grieving and lonely Fuller withdrew from his ministry in 1967, appearing less and less often on the *Revival Hour.* He wrote to Ockenga, apparently without irony but with a poignant choice of words, "Life seems pretty hard at times, but your prayers for me mean a great deal and I know God is answering as we remember each other before the Throne of Grace."[118] At age eighty, he died in March 1968 of congestive heart failure. The *Old Fashioned Revival Hour* was then hosted by Fuller Seminary president David Hubbard; the program ended when its name was changed to *A Joyful Sound* in 1968.[119]

The long-term success of the *Old Fashioned Revival Hour* suggests that commercial religious radio's reliance on ordinary donors was both key to its popularity and a serious weak spot. The *Old Fashioned Revival Hour* was a paradigm of success—its popularity much celebrated and envied in the world of religious broadcasting, its format much imitated. But the ministry was vulnerable in, or depending on how you look at it, accountable for, its dependence on small-change donors. The program had no sponsor, no established congregation or church behind it, no denomination's backing. This contributed to its broad appeal but also led to the Fullers' constant worry over the *Revival Hour.* It continued only so long as everyday Americans paid for it—and though they could not know this when they began, everyday Americans continued to pay for it long after radio ceased being the dominant mass medium. Here is clear evidence of agency on the part of listeners, who were not mere passive recipients of mass-media evangelism. The public shaped the Fullers' ministry with their dollars, and this fact highlights the interdependence between money and media in making and sustaining mediated religious communities.

The program also attracted listeners with the Fullers' plain-folks personas, which were conscious and astute constructions. The companionable and cozy family image projected on the *Old Fashioned Revival Hour* proved critical to the program's success in postwar America. Other programs and evangelistic ministries rose to prominence without women having a place, but Grace's involvement was more than coincidental to the skyrocketing success of the program. The show literally could not be done without both Charles and Grace at the microphones and in the Gospel Broadcasting Association office. And they certainly used the "happy family" metaphor to market the program and to draw donors.

Finally, the broad appeal of the *Revival Hour* speaks to the diversity contained within the growing evangelical coalition—there was something in it for almost everyone, and it served as a crucial umbrella to help unify Christian conservatives and land them squarely in the world of American popular culture. Charles Fuller represented among evangelicals an important voice of moderation between ecumenicists and separatists. Especially on the issue of dispensationalism and its place in evangelicalism, Fuller's voice was respected, and his influence among lay church folk—apparent to everyone because of the scale of donations to his ministry—helped unite the subculture. He played a key role in launching Billy Graham and other neo-evangelical leaders, in whom he invested his hopes for a nationally respected voice of religious conservatives. He defined the evangelical mainstream: embracing modern means but hewing to traditional doctrines.

Fuller was also traditional in the degree to which his cosmology was personalized. God was utterly real, incarnate in the world and concerned with the details of individuals' lives; likewise, Satan was a real entity. Life was a struggle between the forces of good and evil at every moment—and never more so than in the moments spent declaring the gospel. Wilbur Smith remembered

Charles saying after some of his broadcasts, "I felt the very de-
mons contending with me this afternoon as I was preaching the
gospel. They seemed to be trying to close my lips and befog my
mind."[120] He attributed little to himself but saw instead in his experiences a reflection of the ongoing triumph of good over evil;
in this he stands for many Christian conservatives who "surren-
dered" their trust to God. Hardships were not punishment but
lessons—and if that was the case, evangelicals in the middle decades of the century found many opportunities for instruction.
As Grace put it, "In every cup of bitterness that God offers us, or
that God permits Satan to offer us, there is a sweetness we could
have no other way."[121] As the nation became "increasingly and terribly chaotic," the basics of the gospel were the foundational rock
for the Fullers and their followers: fervent personal and group
prayer, daily sustenance from the biblical Word of God, the tug-
ging of the Holy Spirit, and their unshakable conviction that for
them Christ had prepared a mansion, to which he longed to bring
them.

5 We Must Not Be Muzzled
Interreligious Struggle for Radio Access in the 1940s

On a wintry Sunday morning in January 1944, the wind howled down the cavernous streets of Manhattan, scooping up a few stray leaves and swirling them into the doorway of Calvary Baptist, the "skyscraper church" on Fifty-seventh Street. Calvary's pastor, William Ward Ayer, was speaking to an estimated audience of half a million people from an ornately carved pulpit crowned with the slender stalk of a WHN radio microphone. A Canadian-born graduate of the Moody Bible Institute, converted in 1916 by Billy Sunday, Ayer had been calling New Yorkers to repentance since the mid-1930s, his sermons summarized each week in the *New York Times* and the *Herald Tribune*.[1] This morning Ayer reflected on three critical issues he saw shaping up. The first two—mounting national war debt and growing personal immorality—called for sacrifice and repentance on a nationwide scale and for the healing of deep wounds. But the third was perhaps equally worrisome: a threat to radio as "God's present-day means of getting His gospel out to the world." Ayer saw a dangerous trend in recent cases such as that of an Oklahoma fundamentalist suddenly being issued a new set of stringent controls by the station from which he bought time. Unable to ask for funds over the air or to deliver "controversial messages" of biblical prophecy and required to submit his sermons to the station for advance approval, the broadcaster had to quit altogether, and Ayer wondered who might be targeted next.[2]

Religious radio in the early forties was the "hottest" and most controversial material radio station owners had to handle. According to Ayer, the dishonest or flamboyant practices of some fundamentalist radio evangelists shamed the whole industry. "I believe most radio stations are amicable to high-type gospel broadcasts," declared Ayer, "but crackpots, racketeers, fly-by-nights, ranters, and sensationalists bring reproach upon all our programs." He called for religious broadcasters to demonstrate more sincerity and honesty, and he praised a group that had recently organized to give a voice to "recognized" evangelical broadcasters. As the first president of that new group, the National Religious Broadcasters (NRB), Ayer believed "we must not be muzzled."[3]

Radio ruled American popular culture in the forties, a reality Ayer and his contemporaries knew well. When Paul Rader and Aimee Semple McPherson launched their radio programming in the early to mid-1920s, fewer than 5 percent of all households owned a radio. But by the late 1950s, when the Fullers were still achieving soaring ratings, fewer than 5 percent of all households did *not* own a radio.[4] Because many American households became increasingly mobile, being on radio took on heightened importance in the middle decades of the century. From the 1920s forward, migration rates into cities accelerated, and communities across the nation were disrupted and transformed by the depression and the Second World War.[5] After the war, a wave of southerners went to the urban Midwest, midwesterners to the Far West.[6] Forward-looking religious conservatives saw that the strength of their movement lay in transcending region altogether and being heard anywhere a potential believer might want to listen. Evangelicals separated from their geographic roots could retain their religious identity, belonging to another kind of community through the radio. For some evangelicals, such new associations became a part of their supercharged passion to purify the world. Far from retreating from the world into their rarefied religious spaces, they were vigorously extending outward their conception of what might constitute sacred space.

The forties and fifties were decades of nourishment for the fundamentalist and evangelical subculture; in these years new and

previously unimaginable alliances were brokered as Protestantism underwent an organizational rearrangement during and immediately after the war. Where once historians saw decades of
hibernation in the middle of the century, a vibrant and contentious fundamentalist/evangelical sphere emerges when we look
at the mass media and popular culture.[7] Those who seek the roots
of the religious right's emergence in the sixties can consider the
two prior decades of determined struggle of evangelicals to maintain their secure place in the nation's broadcast media—a struggle
that went forward on organizational, legal, political, and cultural
fronts.

For the religious right, radio became a symbol of both the level
of acculturation religious broadcasters had achieved and their
hopes for revival. Being on radio announced to the world that
they had "arrived," but only barely, with a long way to go. Feeling somewhat marginalized even while being present on radio
was the irritation around which layers of evangelical organization would be deposited, the way a pearl grows. Measurements
of radio audiences and program ratings applied only to regularly scheduled programs on the three big networks (CBS, NBC
Red, and NBC Blue), with no indication of how many people listened to non-network religious programming.[8] What limited audience research there was, such as the series of statewide surveys
conducted in 1938 and 1941 by H. B. Summers at Kansas State
College for Iowa, Kansas, and other midwestern states, revealed
that religious programming (both "religious music" and "devo-
tionals") appealed to people in certain demographic categories—
more women than men, less educated rather than more, older
rather than younger. This type of programming apparently was
neither the most nor the least popular on radio, a respectably
sized niche in which radio evangelists had a substantial stake by
the forties.[9]

Interdenominational cooperation did not come naturally, especially since fundamentalists regularly castigated Protestant ecu-
menism in the form of the Federal Council of Churches. Yet new
strategies were imperative if religious radio broadcasting was to
survive in a media-saturated world that had proved itself—as fun-

Farmer in Meeker County, Minnesota, listening to the radio, 1940.
Photograph by John Vachon, Farm Security Administration; Prints and
Photographs Division, Library of Congress.

damentalists saw it—hostile to the true and biblical gospel. Hence conservative Protestants founded a variety of councils and organizations in an attempt to preserve and strengthen their presence on radio: the American Council of Churches of Christ (ACCC) in 1941, the National Association of Evangelicals (NAE) in 1942, and the National Religious Broadcasters (NRB) in 1944 as an affiliate of the NAE. These organizations hoped to self-regulate fundamentalist commercial religious programs on the production side, just as the National Association of Broadcasters self-regulated the broadcasting side.

The ACCC, the NAE, and the NRB were not a united fundamentalist front, however. Conservatives were as deeply divided among themselves in the forties as they were from liberal Protestants. As strident crusaders for truth, in Nancy Ammerman's words, fundamentalists "battle against their own imperfections, and they engage in verbal campaigns against evil wherever it may be found—even in their own ranks."[10] Separatist fundamentalists, such as Carl McIntire, the American Council's founder, busily denounced as heretics the wing of fundamentalism that was trying to define itself as progressive. For its part, this wing, represented by the NAE, became known as the "neo-evangelicals." Neo-evangelicals tried to reform fundamentalism and ended up rejecting many of its doctrines altogether by 1960, differentiating themselves by severing ties between evangelical and fundamentalist organizations.[11] Meanwhile, the gap continued to yawn between liberals and conservatives, even *within* many Protestant denominations. These were critical decades of definition and relocation for all Protestants, many of whom felt undervalued within the Federal Council or ostracized from its aims.[12]

Carl McIntire, for example, was a minister who had been defrocked for apostasy in 1936 by the Presbyterian Church (U.S.A.) after leading an unsuccessful campaign to rout modernism out of the denomination and out of Princeton Theological Seminary. Pastor of a small breakaway sect, the Bible Presbyterian Church in Collingswood, New Jersey, McIntire edited a popular, inexpensive weekly paper, the *Christian Beacon*.[13] In 1941, he called for a "militantly pro-gospel and anti-modernist" alternative to the Federal Council, to be named the American Council of Churches of

Christ in America.[14] Himself a broadcaster over Philadelphia station WPEN, McIntire felt that the current state of religious radio pointed up the need for his organization. The Federal Council's monopolistic arrangements with the major radio networks left the defenders of the old-time religion out of the media loop. "The very nature of radio calls for a central body representing the historic faith," McIntire argued.[15]

McIntire's version of the historic faith was a particularly uncompromising one, however, and while the American Council fulfilled its purpose as a thorn in the flesh of the Federal Council, other, more moderate fundamentalists viewed the American Council with considerable distaste and soon founded their own organization to promote a more "positive" and cooperative vision of fundamentalism. The group grew out of a network of Bible conferences and regional organizations, notably the New England Fellowship, led by J. Elwin Wright. In 1942, Wright and other fundamentalists in his orbit—including the pastor of Boston's Park Street Church, Harold Ockenga; Charles Fuller; Wilbur Smith; Ralph T. Davis; and leaders of Moody Bible Institute and Wheaton College—all met in Chicago to organize their loose coalition into the National Association of Evangelicals for United Action (NAE). Representatives from the American Council attended the meeting, seeking to unite the new group under the ACCC's umbrella, but they were rebuffed.[16] The NAE's scope and structure mirrored those of the Federal Council—although, significantly, it was a parachurch coalition, not a council of churches.[17] The NAE eventually far surpassed the fundamentalist American Council in numbers and in effectiveness, although Joel Carpenter points out that "for a long time yet, no one outside of conservative Protestant circles would recognize the need to distinguish between evangelicals and fundamentalists. From the vantage point of mainline Protestantism they were all antiecumenical sectarians."[18] The differences between the two organizations were highly apparent at the time, however, both to McIntire and to the core of the NAE's founders.

The NAE immediately devoted its efforts to clearing the way for evangelical broadcasting; in the spring of 1942, for example, three NAE delegates (J. Elwin Wright, Harold Ockenga, and a Mr. Lundquist representing Moody Bible Institute's WBMI station) went to Ohio State University to speak for fundamentalist broadcasters at the annual meeting of the Institute for Education by Radio. The institute's Religious Work-Study Group that year was contemplating a series of recommendations about religious radio, and the conservatives wanted to contribute their input. The meeting would prove to be an important one in shaping the direction of religious broadcasting in the forties.

In that year the institute's group focused on the role of religious radio in wartime. Its recommendations sought to deflate the negative impact of vitriolic and politicized sermons, proposing that religious broadcasts should be positive and affirmative, should not attack other faiths, should not be charged for airtime, and should not solicit donations. Walter C. Van Kirk, speaking in an early session of the conference, stressed that religious radio in wartime was obliged to "quicken the spiritual life of the American people" and that American versions of hate-mongering Hitlers should have no place on radio.[19] Of particular danger to the institute delegates in 1942 were programs "used occasionally for blunt attacks upon other faiths but more often for proselytizing and intolerance by inference or implication," reported Willard Johnson, president of the interdenominational Religious Radio Association. Broadcast rights, he argued, were coupled with duties: "Freedom of worship is not a shield behind which we are guaranteed immunity to attack the sincere faith of others."[20] Jewish representative Rabbi Applebaum felt that *all* religious life was under attack in the United States and that radio should promote religion in general, not exhibit unseemly competition among denominations. Similarly, Edward Heffron, a Roman Catholic delegate, felt that all religious broadcasts should be aired on sustaining time; commercial broadcasting encouraged racketeering by tying a program's continuation to asking for money. "Such appeals cannot be consistently excluded from commercial time; they can be, and they nearly always are, excluded from sustaining time."[21]

This high-minded and noble rhetoric, from those with uncontested access to sustaining time, appeared patently discriminatory to the evangelicals present at the meeting. The combined effect of the recommendations looked like "an attempt was being instituted to get the evangelical broadcasts off the air," since they singled out commercial broadcasts and "practically all the programs for which payment is made are sponsored by evangelicals."[22] Wright addressed the session, explaining that "fundamentalist groups felt they had been driven off the air and assumed that this code might drive them off completely. For that reason, he said, his group would not favor an all-sustaining time policy." Wright knew that "a great deal of racketeering [was] going on in religious broadcasting, and said that his group [was] desirous of giving full co-operation in curbing such programs without injury to legitimate broadcasts, but he opposed a blanket recommendation against appeals for contributions."[23] After a lively debate, the recommendations were altered as a concession to Wright, Ockenga, and Lundquist: religious doctrine need not be watered down for broadcasts, and religious programs should be aired on sustaining time "wherever possible."[24]

Securing radio time was an early goal of the NAE and a reason behind its organization; at the institute meeting Wright referred to the NAE several times as the first cohesive voice representing the 15 million to 20 million Protestants who disagreed with or who were unaffiliated with the Federal Council.[25] The NAE trumpeted the 1942 institute meeting as a decisive victory, a demonstration of the success of its cooperative strategy. The organization's historian attributed the alterations to Lundquist's and Wright's "gentlemanly but firm stand."[26] The changes made to the recommendations, according to NAE documents in 1942, showed "the vast amount of constructive work which may be accomplished by the new movement."[27]

The reality of the situation was that the NAE had a long road ahead as an advocate for evangelical broadcasters, and while the 1942 institute recommendations were modified in the NAE's favor, the early forties were still a troubled time for commercial religious broadcasters. It was, opined the NAE, a "critical and strategic hour—critical because the future of gospel broadcasting is in jeopardy, and strategic because of the great challenge of the unreached masses."[28] In 1943 the Mutual network, which had been the sole major network selling time for religious programs, changed its policies. On its paid programs, now relegated to the hours before noon on Sunday, all talk of funds was banned. Some of the network's highest-paying customers (e.g., *Voice of Prophecy, Lutheran Hour,* and *Young People's Church of the Air*) were willing to be heard earlier and to refrain from asking for funds on the air. But others, notably Charles Fuller's *Old Fashioned Revival Hour,* his *Pilgrim Hour,* and Paul ("First Mate Bob") Myers's *Haven of Rest,* went to their own jerry-rigged independent networks. Although the NBC Blue network, the predecessor of ABC, did give some sustaining time in 1943 to the American Council (as we will see, over the strenuous objection of the Federal Council), conservative access to network time was constricted even further by Mutual's move.[29]

The battleground of paid programming began to shift from the nationwide radio networks to the individual stations where evangelicals bought time at market rates. Conservatives tried to be as widely heard as possible and were willing (and for the most part able) to pay for that time. And proponents of sustaining time were worried. *Christian Century* writer Charles Crowe, in August 1944, pointed out the double risk involved in such practices: "Insincere and unauthorized 'evangelists' are making a handsome living from such programs. At the same time, the public gets a distorted and one-sided picture of current religious thinking because most of these programs follow the ultraconservative fundamentalist pattern." Crowe called for the Federal Communications Commission to take action on the problem and seize the moment to ban paid religious programming once and for all. To be fair, Crowe felt that sustaining time should be given to minority and fundamentalist groups, too, but only if they could promote "the spiritual resources of the nation by emphasizing the great faiths common to differing communions . . . and by calling people to a deeper faith in God as a basis for victorious living in troubled times."[30]

Crowe's rhetoric echoed that of the various radio departments associated with the Federal Council of Churches that, like the American Council and the NAE, were getting organized around radio in the early to mid-forties.[31] The Federal Council had an active Radio Committee, which produced the *National Radio Pulpit* and the *National Vespers Hour,* and several of the larger constituent denominations, such as the Presbyterian Church (U.S.A.) and the Northern Baptists, also had in-house radio departments. The Protestant Radio Conference (established in 1945), a cooperative religious broadcasting organization, produced radio programs mainly in the South, using the studios of the Protestant Radio Center in Atlanta. Five of the largest Protestant denominations had formed the Joint Religious Radio Commission (JRRC) to coordinate their radio work.[32] The Federal Council itself was preparing to combine with ten other organizations to form the National Council of Churches of Christ. Although the merger was not final until 1950, plans were being laid in the mid-forties, and the radio departments kept in close communication with each other, with leaders serving on one another's boards and executive committees. The Protestant Radio Commission (PRC; formally launched in March 1948) was formed by joining the Federal Council's Department of National Religious Radio with the Joint Religious Radio Commission.[33] The new PRC took over the *National Radio Pulpit* and the other programs of the Federal Council; it was not "an integral part of the Federal Council" but rather a "combined enterprise" with its offices in the same building as the Federal Council.[34] The Religious Radio Association was formed as an outgrowth of the Religious Radio Work-Study Group of the Institute for Education by Radio in 1946. The association included representatives from Protestant, Jewish, and Roman Catholic faiths and was intended to foster fellowship and share relevant data, but it did not include evangelicals in its ranks.

All these mergers looked threatening to evangelical broadcasters. The periodical of the NAE called the formation of the Protestant Radio Commission an ominous step along the road to "super radio control" by the Federal Council.[35] Some small revivalistic groups charged that the Joint Religious Radio Committee had as its ulterior goal "fighting them and their commercial religious programs."[36]

Evangelicals had built their own radio industry networks, too, primarily in the midwestern corridor including Chicago and Detroit. Two small radio networks based in Detroit, the Associated Broadcasting Company (which soon foundered) and the Wolverine Network, offered salable airtime to religious conservatives by 1945. The region also boasted the nation's only advertising agency catering exclusively to religious customers, to offer evangelical broadcasters "professional production of commercial religious programs and for outlets in the face of exclusion from independent stations."[37]

In 1944, evangelical broadcasters, especially concerned over Mutual's decision to restrict paid religious programming, moved to found a trade association of their own.[38] The result, the National Religious Broadcasters (NRB), had the unusual distinction of being the most ecumenical of the fundamentalist organizations. Glenn Tingley, one of the founders, remembered an early prayer meeting at the La Salle Hotel, with evangelical Charles Fuller (*Old Fashioned Revival Hour*), Pentecostals Charles Leaming (*Faith Gospel Broadcast*) and John Zoller (*Christ for Everyone*), and Lutheran Eugene Bertermann (*Lutheran Hour*) present among others. "Some knelt by their chairs," Tingley remembered. "Charles Leaming and John Zoller flattened themselves against the floor. It's a memory I can never forget—Lutheran, Episcopalian, Baptist, Presbyterian, Pentecostal, Free Methodist—all of us united, calling on the Lord."[39]

As this unusually interdenominational beginning suggested, the NRB wove together members of groups even on the margins of fundamentalism, including Holiness and Pentecostal churches. For example, Myron Boyd (the *Light and Life Hour* broadcaster) served at various times in his career as president of the NAE, of the NRB, and of the Christian Holiness Association.[40] Another early NRB member, Howard Ferrin, had worked on radio with Paul Rader, then became president of Barrington College in Rhode Island, and was active in J. Elwin Wright's New England Fellowship and the NAE from their inceptions.[41] Charles Leaming was ordained a Foursquare pastor in 1927 by Aimee Semple McPherson herself and had conducted radio programs on KFSG but left the church because of McPherson's marriage to David Hutton. In the early thirties Leaming helped found another Pentecostal sect, the Open Bible Standard Churches. A graduate of BIOLA like Charles Fuller, Leaming had been on the air since 1929, eventually hosting the *Faith Gospel Broadcast* from St. Petersburg, Florida.[42]

In April 1944, while a group of some 150 evangelical Protestant broadcasters were attending the meeting of the Institute for Education by Radio in Columbus, Ohio, they organized the NRB and elected its first officers. William Ward Ayer served as the first chairman of the new organization,[43] which formally convened a constitutional convention at the Moody Bible Church in Chicago in September of that same year and adopted the following statement of purpose:

> The objects of this Association shall be to foster and encourage the broadcasting of religious programs; to establish and maintain high standards with respect to content, method of presentation, speakers' qualifications and ethical practices to the end that such programs may be constantly developed and improved and that their public interest and usefulness may be enhanced; to secure for its members, and for other persons and organizations engaged in broadcasting such programs, adequate, fair and regular access to the radio listening public through the use of existing and future broadcast stations and networks, both aural and visual; to protect its members and such other persons and organizations from being barred from such access, and from being unjustly or unreasonably subjected to injury, obstacle, restriction or discrimination in obtaining and continuing to have such access; and, in every lawful and proper manner, to promote or oppose governmental laws and regulations and business customs and practices according to whether or not they further or hinder the accomplishment of these objects.[44]

Among the first tasks of the NRB's leaders and executive committee was to write and pass a code of ethics for radio evangelism. Ayer wrote much of the code's text, which encouraged "high standards," called for sponsorship of broadcasts by nonprofit organizations, and stipulated that appeals for money should be of "a bona fide character for legitimate religious purposes" presented "in a dignified Christian manner" with financial accountability, including receipts to all donors.[45] The NRB then sent this code "to all radio stations and networks," trying to undermine the Federal Council's claim to speak for all of Protestantism.[46] In 1947, the NRB was made the "official radio arm of the NAE," to "represent the radio interests of all evangelical Christians."[47] There was a division of labor between the two organizations; the NAE continued to push for more sustaining time for evangelicals, while the NRB concerned itself mainly with cleaning up the image of commercial religious time. When compared with the NAE, the NRB's broader membership base and lack of a strict doctrinal creed lent it greater legitimacy in the eyes of the radio industry.[48]

Writing retrospectively of the forties, NRB president James De-Forest Murch was convinced that "if it had not been for the [NRB] the National Council of Churches [the Federal Council's successor] would have taken over all Protestant time on the airwaves at the national level and that evangelical broadcasting would have been completely eliminated."[49] Instead of "rashly" and recklessly criticizing the Federal Council (as, they felt, was McIntire's destructive strategy), the NRB's leaders worked behind the scenes to influence the radio industry. "After many months of correspondence and conference," Murch wrote, "understandings were reached which fully protected the rights of all accredited religious broadcasters at national and local levels. The distinctively evangelical testimony was assured of a voice on the air. . . . The airlanes would be kept perpetually available for the preaching of the Gospel."[50]

The fragile rapprochement between evangelical broadcasters and radio stations with time to sell evolved in an atmosphere of continuing mutual suspicion among the NRB, the Federal Council, and McIntire's American Council. Evangelicals and fundamentalists, including McIntire, remained convinced that the Federal Council was mounting an overt pressure campaign against their broadcasts. This was anathema because the Federal Council's radio spokesmen gutted the historic faith; evangelicals saw them as "men who denied the inerrancy and inspiration of the holy scriptures as well as the cardinal doctrine of salvation by grace through faith in Christ."[51]

A typical portrayal of the evangelicals' view that the Federal Council had "sabotaged" Christian doctrine may be found in J. Elwin Wright's 1944 indictment of the Federal Council, *Death in the Pot.*[52] The fruits of the Federal Council were "the destruction of evangelical faith" and the decline of churches—Wright blamed the Federal Council's doctrinal liberalism and its social gospel politics for drops in church attendance in his own home region of New England. The planned consolidation of the Federal Council and ten other organizations into a National Council, what Wright called a "campaign for a superchurch," would create a "hydra-headed monstrosity." He called for other conservatives to support the NAE, work for revival, and prepare "against the day of regimentation of religion." The beliefs of fundamentalists such as Wright followed from an unwavering conviction in the literal truth of the Bible, and this is why Bible-based preaching on the radio took on such an importance in their minds and deserved so tenacious a fight within the industry. The real enemy, which the Federal Council only embodied, was modernism. "Modernism," explained Wright, "usually starts with doubt of the inerrancy of the Bible. Having cast aside the only reliable source of authoritative teaching there is no stopping place for unbelief this side of absolute atheism."[53] Similarly, Gerald Winrod, leader of the Defenders of the Christian Faith, published a scathing castigation of the Federal Council in 1946 that recounted the efforts of liberals to suppress radio fundamentalism.[54]

During this entire period, the Federal Council watched conservatives as closely as it was being watched by them. The council kept files on a variety of religious organizations, including both the American Council and the NAE. According to the Federal Council's files, the American Council represented "the most extreme Fundamentalist groups," constituting only half a percent of American Protestantism. The NAE was also a "Fundamentalist group" but "more moderate in spirit and policies." They noted that the American Council attacked the NAE frequently as a "compromiser" for not insisting that true Christians separate out from "apostate" churches such as Methodist, Presbyterian (U.S.A.), and Northern Baptist.[55] Elsewhere in an internal memo on the American Council, the NAE was called "a rival body of more temperate Fundamentalists," while the American Council's main interest was to "disrupt the cooperative unity in Protestantism," despite its small membership and marginal status.[56]

In 1943, the Presbyterian Church became aware that McIntire and fellow defrocked pastor H. McAllister Griffiths were seeking sustaining time from the NBC Blue radio network, and it worked to prevent this from happening. McIntire had been using time on WPEN Philadelphia to issue broadcasts that the Presbyterian hierarchy deemed "vicious" and "libelous." The clerk of the denomination wrote anxiously to Frank R. Goodman, the chairman of the Committee on Religious Radio, "I know of nothing that would disturb the religious situation quite so much as any granting of privileges to the men in question."[57] Radio station WPEN had recently refused to sell time to McIntire when the station's ownership changed hands. He had sued WPEN for breach of contract, and the case proceeded all the way up to the Federal Circuit Court of Appeals, which ruled in the favor of WPEN, to McIntire's chagrin.[58]

Goodman personally appealed to the Blue network not to grant time to Griffiths and McIntire, on behalf of either McIntire's church or the American Council, which he characterized as "not a council of Protestant denominations representing any general constituency, but of individuals who are in violent protest against what Protestantism in general is standing for," who "spend most of their time in denunciation and violent criticism of everyone who is not in their tiny fold." Goodman asked the network to air only those programs promoting "broad tolerance" and to insist on "the central and basic truths of religion as the necessary message for America," rather than "bickering and quarreling and name calling" over the air.[59] His appeal failed when the Blue network announced plans to give McIntire and Griffiths time starting in February 1944, preempting a Friday noon broadcast of the Federal Council. The Federal Council decided to word its opposition not by claiming that it should be the sole recipient of airtime but by stressing to the network that the two defrocked Presbyterians would weaken the "fine standing" of religious radio and drag down the dignity of the institution.[60]

That the institution of gospel broadcasting badly needed a shot of dignity was clear in the mid-forties; the business of religious broadcasting was, in some people's minds, nothing more than a moneymaking scheme in disguise. Liberal broadcaster Everett Parker complained that conservative broadcasting was undignified and irresponsible.[61] He argued, "Many of the religious programs are of a low quality artistically, and their religious value is doubtful. They lack dignity. Many of the ministers seem to play upon the credulity, the sentimentality, the superstitions, and the fears of their audiences. Their appeals for money are often blatant, but apparently they are sufficiently effective to bring in enough money to pay the costs of the broadcasts and perhaps even to make them profitable."[62]

The forties had made commercial religious radio a big business. Mutual—the only national network that then still sold time for religion—collected more than $2.1 million for its religious broadcasts in 1942, more than double its income from this source in 1941.[63] In 1944, this number had jumped to $3.5 million, a full quarter of its income.[64] Yet it was no secret in the radio industry that Mutual executives didn't like the fundamentalist programs; in 1943 a radio insider predicted that when the network could get the income elsewhere, commercialized religion would go. And indeed, Mutual did change its policy later that year. Network paid programming was on its way out, but as long as there were "struggling independents with plenty of time to sell and not much money in the bank," commercial religious broadcasting kept growing.[65] Within a decade, NRB members would be paying more than an estimated $10 million to broadcast over radio.[66]

While Christian benevolent organizations, such as the Gideons and the Christian Business Men's Association to name only two, made regular and sometimes substantial donations to evangelical radio efforts, most broadcasters relied heavily on individual donations to pay for airtime. And it was the nature of their verbal appeal over the air that so disconcerted liberals like Everett Parker. Even the most well respected of fundamentalists, such as Charles Fuller, were not immune to using emotionally manipulative language in on-air appeals. A Mr. Newland wrote to Charles Fuller in September 1954, after hearing one of Fuller's appeals on the air—giving us a hint as to the wording Fuller chose: "I did not realize that this inspired and inspiring program is in 'dire straits' and is about to go off the air."[67] Some broadcasters hawked free merchandise such as Bibles, tracts, or what William Martin has called "holy kitsch": calendars, blessed prayer cloths, and lapel pins.[68] Through offering items to people who wrote to the program, broadcasters could build a mailing list for direct-mail appeals instead of using airtime for financial appeals. In the case of the *Old Fashioned Revival Hour,* for instance, both the monthly *Heart to Heart Talk* and occasional direct-mailing letters reminded people of the constant need for contributions. In one such letter, sent in the spring of 1949 when the *Hour* was slated to join ABC, Fuller asked first for specific prayers for six different aspects of the radio ministry and only then noted that changes in radio schedules were "costly" and asked listeners to "stand faithfully by, doing the best you can to keep your offerings coming, and getting others, if possible, to help during this time of transition."[69]

Individuals, important as they were to the continuity of religious radio, rarely could afford to contribute substantial funds toward its support. Some, as their own financial situations limited their giving, devised creative solutions to maximize their gifts. Charles Fuller remembered that one listener "placed a little jar by her radio, and though she could never send a large amount she dropped in a dime or a quarter each time she listened just as though a collection plate had been passed. Then when a dollar or two had accumulated, she would send it." He editorialized, "She felt that a quarter was not enough to send (but it is!) and she could not spare a larger amount, but in this way she felt she was having a real part in carrying on the program which has meant so much to so many."[70] Another *Old Fashioned Revival Hour* listener sent thirty dollars earned from selling homemade aprons over a period of seven months in 1949.[71]

Many radio listeners made their radio donations part of their "tithe," or the amount of their income (usually 10 percent) they felt should be dedicated to the Lord. A woman who listened to Carl McIntire's broadcasts decided to divide her religious giving equally between her local church and McIntire's radio fund.[72] "I made a promise to the Lord to give 10% of all that I am blessed with, to him," explained a listener from Olive View, California, as she mailed a donation to the *Old Fashioned Revival Hour.*[73] Some evangelicals made the disbursement of their tithe a matter of personal revelation. For example, Horace Ricks sent ten dollars as "part of the tithe from my G.I. insurance check. I feel definitely that the Lord would have me send this money for this particular phase of His work."[74] A couple from Georgia "covenanted" to pray for particular broadcasts' "victory" and "give as our Lord has laid it upon our hearts."[75] Identical language was used by a listener in Downey, California, in her letter explaining how she used her one-dollar tithe in the "marketplace" of competing preachers: "As my husband and I listened to your last Sunday's broadcast, the Lord moved upon our hearts to send you our 'This Week's' radio ministry tithe. Each week we try to send our small tithe to some radio minister, whom we feel the Lord has laid upon our hearts."[76]

Donors to radio ministries seem to have conceived of their money as going first to the Lord and only indirectly to the broadcasters. The giving of funds to radio as a worthy cause was enmeshed in conservatives' rituals of prayer and of seeking God's will in all things, feeling "moved in the heart" to know where the Lord needed their quarters and dollars. Unfortunately, donors' letters only tell us about the segment of the population who responded to on-air pleas for funds or to the urgent-sounding mass mailings coming to their postal boxes—and remain silent on why other listeners chose *not* to send money. But the accumulation of the "small change" elicited for radio ministries was a staggering sum. By 1943, reported *Variety* magazine, an estimated $200 million was "rolling into church coffers each year from radio listeners," allowing racketeers and "religious pirates" to get rich quick without adhering to standards of accounting.[77] This is why the code of ethics was such an important prong of the NRB's efforts to promote evangelical broadcasting.

The broadcast industry itself, too, was changing in the mid-forties. On everyone's mind were two technological developments on the immediate horizon: FM radio broadcasting, and television. Even as early as 1945, FM was being called by one evangelical broadcaster "a necessary service for all the people" that "should be extended on a nationwide basis."[78] It offered better reception and minimal sound distortion. Unlike with AM, there was little interference from other household electrical appliances, and there was a "channel cushion," or what one religious broadcaster called a "strip of velvet silence," between stations. But, as a new technology, FM was more expensive to use on the broadcast end, and listeners needed a new radio to receive it. Furthermore, its coverage was not as wide, so it was ill suited to rural broadcast-ing.[79] Evangelicals saw FM as a new opportunity, which along with television might free up radio time for their purchase.[80] In fact, these changes in the industry even freed up some *sustaining* time for conservatives. The American Council was invited to broadcast on ABC and Mutual for a fifteen-minute sustaining-time broad-cast in January through March 1946; McIntire rejoiced that the Federal Council monopoly on sustaining time had been broken, opening the door "for programs in which the true Gospel could be heard."[81] The NAE also had time for a regular program on Mutual and ABC radio during the summer months in the late forties.[82]

All the same, sustaining-time handouts from the networks were not enough to offset losses in commercial time that seemed to reach epidemic proportions in the middle years of the forties. Conservatives blamed a stepped-up pressure campaign by the Federal Council, but at the same time they saw a potential chink in the Federal Council's armor. The FCC had ruled in 1945 on the case of Texas temperance evangelist Reverend Sam Morris, who had fought for time in proportion to that used by liquor interests on his local radio stations. The ruling in Morris's favor had encouraged conservative broadcasters to use fairness in radio broadcasting as their legal platform to gain time comparable to the Federal Council's.[83] Everywhere fundamentalists and evan-gelicals looked in the mid-forties, they saw their broadcasts under siege by what they believed to be undeserved and patently un-fair practices. In 1945, a writer in the *Sunday School Times,* for example, accused the Joint Religious Radio Committee of trying to "crowd off" everyone else from the airwaves and criticized lib-eral Protestants' arrangements with the national networks as a dangerous enmeshing of church and state. The author, like many other conservative Protestants, firmly believed that all religious programming should be paid for, that none should be subsidized, that the success of Fuller's *Old Fashioned Revival Hour* proved his (inflated) assertion that gospel broadcasting was "what people desire above everything else," and that Federal Council broad-casts, if forced to compete on the open market for airtime, would soon disappear. He cautioned, "Let there be no radio-supported religion, any more than a State-supported religion."[84]

Were conservatives indeed being forced off the air by the efforts of the Federal Council? Some were. Carl McIntire's elimination from the WPEN broadcast schedule in 1945 was a bitter pill for him, a signal that all of gospel broadcasting was endangered. The logical extension of the court of appeals ruling upholding WPEN's decision, McIntire thought, was that "Gospel broadcasting is pretty much at an end in the United States."[85] No region of the country seemed immune. In November of that year, the twelfth season of a noon-hour broadcast sponsored by the Christian Business Men's Committee of Chicago (CBMC) over WJJD was abruptly canceled. The CBMC attributed the change to a "pressure campaign" by the "modernistic enemies of the gospel."[86] In Minneapolis, too, in the summer of 1946, station WDGY banned all paid religious programs. A council of the city's fundamentalist ministers protested and circulated a petition asking Congress to amend the FCC legislation to require stations to sell time for religious programs.[87]

Also in 1946, a Birmingham broadcaster and founding member of the NRB, Glenn Tingley, worried for the fate of his *Radio Revival* program. He had broadcast the fifteen-minute broadcast since the late twenties and had built up his "network" to include forty-five stations across the South. But Tingley learned of a "powerfully organized and financed lobby that was determined to banish gospel radio preachers from the air," and he filed for a station license himself to stay on the air. He reported that twenty thousand people had marched "in a forceful demonstration of protest" through the streets of Knoxville, Tennessee, when that city's stations cut their commercial religious programs.[88] Tingley organized a "national Radio Emergency Committee" that soon presented fifty-four thousand letters of protest to the House Un-American Activities Committee, advocating the right of gospel radio preachers to purchase time.[89]

In Buffalo, New York, Clinton Churchill, the second president of the National Religious Broadcasters, was engaged in a similar fight to stay on the air. Churchill founded Buffalo radio station WKBW in 1925 to broadcast the gospel from his Churchill Tabernacle; he had sold the station to the Buffalo Broadcasting Commission six years later, with a stipulation in the contract that the station would always reserve time for Tabernacle broadcasts, but in April 1946, the station's owners terminated the Churchill broadcasts. Churchill tried to get a license for a nearby, more powerful station broadcasting at the same frequency, and at the same time he fought the station's interpretation of the FCC ruling through legal channels.[90] Churchill returned to the air for a triumphant All-Night New Year's Eve broadcast over WKBW on 31 December 1946; the choir took all-night requests by telegram and over the tabernacle's three phone lines, performing a tightly packed program of sacred music. Churchill's victory was praised in the NAE's periodical as an important step in the "fight to maintain the rights of evangelicals on the airwaves."[91]

By the spring of 1947, evangelicals were trying to explain "the growing attitude of major networks and stations in refusing to sell time to Gospel broadcasters." They noticed an alarming trend: "Regular broadcast channels are over-crowded and present station schedules are reducing or denying time for Gospel programs."[92] Much of their "evidence" of the Federal Council's complicity in these developments emerged that summer in a series of congressional hearings concerning a bill proposed by two Republicans, Senator Wallace White and Congressman Charles Wolverton, which would have amended the FCC legislation to require radio stations to give equal opportunities to all sides of controversial issues.[93] The bill was opposed and defeated by representatives of the radio industry, but not before conservatives had used the occasion to present what they saw as evidence for organized strong-arm tactics by the Federal Council.[94] Both the American Council and the NAE sent representatives to testify. American Council lawyer William Bennet also filed a brief with the committee, seeking an amendment that would prohibit stations from "arbitrarily and as a rule and practice" refusing to sell airtime for religion and arguing that even the existing Radio Act prevented stations from "giving away such time as another broadcaster is ready, willing and able to pay for at customary rates."[95] Basically, two separate issues related to religious broadcasting were involved in the hearings: first, whether religious broadcasters—Christian station owners in particular—were permitted to use controversial language in their broadcasts and to air editorial opinions, and second, whether conservatives were being unfairly denied access to the airwaves.

On the first question, in his testimony before the committee, Carl McIntire argued forcefully that it was in the public interest for radio stations, like newspapers, to exercise the right to hold and pronounce editorial opinions.[96] And as to the second, McIntire hoped the new law would provide some measure of legal protection for commercial radio religion, which was at the mercy of station operators' whims and the Federal Council's influence. He advocated federal protection of the open market for religious programs, arguing that faithful believers should be able to make contributions to keep on the air the programs they wanted just as others could do with programs sponsored by, say, cigarette corporations.[97] McIntire's conviction that the Federal Council was behind program cancellations was well known.[98] As he had told readers of the *Christian Beacon* in a special issue reporting on the White bill: "Station after station has been arbitrarily cutting off their paid Gospel programs and throwing out the Gospel broadcasts which bring the message of salvation. As stations have begun to discontinue paid programs they have decided to give time to religion and the Federal Council steps in claiming to represent the larger Protestant groups and its local affiliates to receive the bulk, if not all, of this time for the spreading of their diluted message of modernism."[99] Characterizing the American Council as an organization "raised up by God" to rival the Federal Council, McIntire believed that his testimony had uncovered the hypocrisy of the Federal Council in its radio work: "With feigned words it proclaims its respect for minorities and its love of freedom, but its actual conduct belies those statements."[100]

Like the American Council, the NAE and the NRB were concerned about how the legality of "editorializing" by station management might affect church-affiliated stations and sought assurances from the FCC that "the expression of religious opinions" on the air would be protected.[101] The NRB's case before the congressional committee was made by Dale Crowley, a Washington-area radio fundamentalist (spokesman of the *King's Business* broadcast) and editor of a watchdog newsletter called the *Capital Voice*.[102] Crowley made a "vigorous plea for specific legislation requiring licensees to sell time for religious broadcasting." Like McIntire, he said that after the networks eliminated paid programming, other stations "recently arbitrarily eliminated all 'commercial religious' programs from their schedules, substituting therefor[e] 'sustaining' programs." These policies Crowley labeled unfair, un-American, and opposed to the spirit of the Radio Act. "Hundreds of licensees are throttling the progress of the churches, and other religious organizations," he said. "They have crowded God into a corner."[103]

Eugene Bertermann, producer of one of the nation's largest commercial religious broadcasts, the *Lutheran Hour,* and active member of the NRB, also had his say before the committee. He acknowledged that the fair allocation of time among so many religious broadcasters was a real problem but charged that "religious broadcasting has been subjected to a series of discriminatory and unfair practices." Some stations refused to grant time at all for religion, some granted unsalable time or paltry amounts, and many discriminated in giving sustaining time to a single central agency, a practice that Bertermann claimed worked well for Catholics and Jews but not for Protestantism. Bertermann allowed that the Federal Council did not set out deliberately to establish a monopoly but nevertheless had shown "a definite disposition to maintain a monopoly." And he, like McIntire, believed that a free market for religious airtime was a national priority: "Radio time can be purchased—usually at the best hours of the broadcasting day—for the selling of hair oil, hand lotion, chicken soup, soap powder, beer, tooth paste—but simultaneously restrictive discrimination is exercised against programs dedicated to the moral and spiritual upbuilding of our country."[104]

By the end of 1947, when the White-Wolverton bill died without coming to a vote, conservative broadcasters were frustrated with the lack of protections for their programs. As James Pearson, pastor of the "Radio Mission Church" out of KFNF (Iowa), began his twenty-second year as a temperance preacher on the air, he believed that racketeering was a real problem. "Some religious broadcasters are working the money side of things hard, and in time it is going to hurt the cause," Pearson reflected. For the first time, the competition had gotten so fierce that he had radio time bought out from under him. But he despaired of finding an easy solution, "since some broadcasters are worthy and doing a real good."[105]

In 1947, one episode relating to religious broadcasting seemed for a time to capture the attention of the entire radio industry. The case, like a lens, focused the thinking of all sides and brought them to a clearer articulation of their respective positions on religious radio. It had begun in late 1944, when Robert Harold Scott, a tall and quiet retired court reporter who had been living in Palo Alto, California, approached three San Francisco–area radio stations (KPO and KFRC San Francisco and KQW San Jose) to purchase time for a broadcast. Scott was not a religious broadcaster, however; he was an atheist who felt that his beliefs were suppressed in favor of religious programs. When all three stations denied his proposals, Scott petitioned the FCC on 27 March 1945 for the licenses of all three stations to be revoked, claiming that their failure to sell him airtime violated their public responsibility to present both sides of a controversial issue.[106] The existence of God, Scott argued, was a question open to debate, and stations displayed an illegal bias in presenting direct attacks on atheism as well as "indirect arguments [against atheism] such as church services, prayers, Bible readings, and other kinds of religious programs." Scott wrote: "I do not throw stones at church windows. I do not mock at people kneeling in prayer. I respect every man's right to have and to express any religious belief whatsoever. But I abhor and denounce those who, while asserting this right, seek, in one way or another, to prevent others from expressing contrary views."[107]

The religious broadcasts heard on KPO, KQW, and KFRC in 1946 were a fairly standard lineup of the time, covering the range of mainline and evangelical Protestant faiths, Catholic programming, and even the Jewish *Israel Hour* and a Church of Jesus Christ of Latter-day Saints broadcast from Salt Lake City, as well as simulcasts of various local services.[108] Executives speaking for KQW and KFRC contended that they were, in fact, serving the public interest by denying time to Mr. Scott, saying that in any case the issue of God's existence was not "of sufficient public moment." Station KPO, the NBC affiliate, pointed to the small numbers of atheists as evidence that there was no significant controversy involved.[109] The central question was whether stations opting to air religious broadcasts to the exclusion of antireligious ones constituted a de facto establishment of religion on the public airwaves. The Federal Communications Commission recognized that the issue had long-reaching implications and took more than a year to consider the case.

When it did issue a ruling in July 1946, the commission denied Scott's petition to shut down the stations involved, even while asserting that freedom of religious disbelief was a right as equal and worthy of protection as that of religious belief. The commission left it to the discretion of individual broadcasters to determine what a particular community might find "distasteful or objectionable." The ruling's text had been authored by one of its most liberal members, Clifford Durr, who wrote that beliefs about God differed so much as to render it impossible to decide whose views were atheistic and whose were theistic.[110] Durr's ruling even ventured to suppose that Thomas Jefferson, Andrew Jackson, and Abraham Lincoln, if living in 1946, might all be legitimately barred from the airwaves on the grounds of seeking to promulgate their atheistic beliefs. He conceded that the broadcasters' position was one that lent itself to abuse. Therefore, the commissioners urged licensees to be fair in their decisions about controversial issues and not to base their judgments about the merits of a particular point of view solely on the number of people holding that view.[111]

The ruling surprised and outraged many in the religious radio industry. *Broadcasting* magazine portrayed the ruling as a "cudgel for right of expression of atheistic viewpoints."[112] Privately, F. Ernest Johnson of the Federal Council thought Scott's claim "specious" and the FCC ruling "a bit inept."[113] A Methodist periodical, *Zion's Herald,* expressing a minority view, praised the ruling as a victory safeguarding the freedom of religion through the equal protection of unbelief. Bishop Garfield Bromley Oxnam, speaking for the Federal Council, agreed—but other religious leaders such as Rabbi Solomon Metz of Washington and spokesmen for Catholic University heartily did not.

In the mainstream American press, *Time* called the whole issue a "hot potato" and reported that the ruling "entitled" atheists to "all the radio time they could get."[114] This opinion was shared by the president of the New England Fellowship, J. Elwin Wright. In an editorial for the *United Evangelical Action,* Wright warned that the ruling would unleash "a flood of propaganda against God coming out of the radio sets of the nation." Wright pointed out that the medium of radio was fundamentally different from "the press, the pulpit and the platform" because the number of possible channels was limited by the broadcast spectrum. Not everyone with an opinion, therefore, was entitled to "unlimited opportunity" to broadcast those opinions. He grandly stated "It has always been regarded as contrary to the public interest that atheism be promoted," suggesting that the FCC ruling represented a disturbing "change of national policy" that effectively elevated atheism to the same level as "reputable" religions. He called for "a national declaration of solidarity . . . and a public affirmation that we believe all anti-God propaganda to be contrary to the public interest." Wright concluded pointedly: "Isn't there a fundamental weakness in our Bill of Rights and Constitution under which attacks upon the government of the United States are punishable by severe penalties while attacks against the government of heaven are tolerated?"[115]

In November 1946, radio station KQW, the CBS affiliate in San Francisco, unexpectedly gave Robert Scott a half hour of Sunday morning time to make his broadcast, which he did on the seventeenth of that month—preempting a scheduled broadcast of the Mormon Tabernacle Choir. Scott's speech was itself unremarkable; both *Time* and *Newsweek* noted the lack of "sensationalism" as Scott "rehashed" standard arguments against the existence of God. The radio station received more than five thousand letters within a week, 75 percent of which were critical but a quarter of which supported Scott's broadcast and his right to make it.[116] Station KQW decided, however, not to air further broadcasts by Scott. He threatened to petition the FCC again.[117] The American Civil Liberties Union (ACLU) worked on his behalf behind the scenes, trying to win the support of the Federal Council to Scott's cause. In January 1947, the ACLU's national director, Roger Baldwin, wrote Samuel McCrea Cavert that the broadcast had been "entirely in good taste." Baldwin argued that it was self-evident that broadcasters should air "all sides of a question suitable for radio presentation," and he urged Cavert to lend his influence in the matter by writing to the FCC's chairman. Apparently, Cavert did not.[118]

In the summer of 1948 the controversy over Scott's case heated up again. A Christian and Jewish ecumenical radio organization, the Religious Radio Association, pressed the FCC for a clarification of the ruling. The association's president, Edward Heffron, worried that some stations could construe the ruling to mean that atheists should have the chance "to reply to almost every type of religious broadcast."[119] The FCC tried to soften the ruling's impact, issuing a follow-up statement in August 1948 reassuring religious broadcasters that its decision had not intended to say that atheists were "entitled to radio time upon request."[120] In fact, the commission's position had not wavered; the FCC throughout its history consistently had refused to arbitrate among groups of churches who sought time for the espousal of their particular doctrines. The FCC made broadcasts of religious programs a condition of station license renewal but had never specified what types of programs.[121] In the postwar years, the FCC seemed to share the opinion that would be attributed to President Dwight Eisenhower in the early fifties, that America should be anchored on the recognition of a Supreme Being and on religious faith but, as Eisenhower reportedly put it, "I don't care what kind it is."[122]

The Scott ruling came under scrutiny in early September 1948 by a special House committee investigating the FCC, chaired by Indiana Republican Forest Harness. Interestingly, the committee heard very little that directly bore on the right of atheists to be heard on the air, and although one atheist did testify, there is no evidence that it was Robert Scott.[123] Rather, the hearings were railroaded by the ongoing debate among Protestant broadcasters over access to the air. Harness acted "on the complaints of radio and religious groups" that station managers were unsure whether they could "continue to give broadcasting time to divine worship without jeopardizing their licenses."[124] Edward Heffron's Religious Radio Association complained the loudest in 1948, issuing a lengthy press release full of references to the "burden" the ruling could impose on broadcasters and making dire predictions about the elimination of religious broadcasts if broadcasters were required to "make a right of reply available to atheists every time they broadcast church service, prayer, Bible readings," and so on.[125] For one, Harness was convinced that "the continued broadcasting of religious programs had been seriously jeopardized by the Scott decision."[126]

During the hearings, a broadcast industry attorney reported that the Scott decision was the topic of discussion of many district meetings he had attended recently and that station owners frequently asked him whether they were now obligated to grant time to atheists—or even Communists—who requested airtime. Another committee witness feared that if it was left to stand, every instance of religious language under public and governmental control was threatened, including the words about God printed on currency and the chaplaincies at military and land-grant colleges. "Every media [sic] of expression where you touch the public, provided that media is under Federal control, it seems to me open to these questions," he testified.[127] Don Petty, president of the National Association of Broadcasters, accused the FCC of acting like the "thought police."[128]

Rosell Hyde, FCC commissioner, testified before the committee that religious groups had nothing in the Scott decision with which to argue. "If anything is clear," he stressed, "it is that the Commission has consistently and unequivocally stated that the broadcasting of religious programs is an important element of service in the public interest. The Commission has made this clear time and time again, in its licensing proceedings, in its public statements and in its correspondence." In his view, the FCC had neither discriminated against religious organizations nor given them a preferred status. Hyde was aware that the American Council ("representing various Evangelical denominations") felt unfairly shut out of sustaining-time broadcasts. But the FCC was not the referee for that fight, Hyde believed; rather, the commission's role was to promote the idea that religious broadcasts were in the public interest and leave the rest to the fair judgment of individual licensees.[129]

In its interim report on the hearings, Harness's committee declared the Scott ruling's language "unintelligible" and "impossible of clear and unambiguous interpretation." The report speculated on the dire consequences of atheistic broadcasts being aired in response to those from each of the three major religious groups (Catholic, Protestant, and Jewish), thus having an impact far out of proportion to the percentage of the population holding atheistic views. The committee was especially concerned for impressionable children and the elderly, "who would have their declining years punctuated with irreligious attacks on the very principles which had guided them throughout their lives." The committee's report held that, in light of recent U.S. Supreme Court rulings (NBC v. *United States* and *McCollum v. Board of Education*), the presentation of religious views alone did not constitute a public controversy.[130] Wayne Coy, chairman of the FCC, had the last word on Capitol Hill about the Scott case. In a lengthy and closely argued statement, he criticized broadcasters and others for misinterpreting the Scott decision and urged that the final test be "one of reasonableness and overall fairness," or in other words, that licensees should not prohibit from the air people with whose views they happened to disagree.[131] Robert Scott, however, was never granted time on radio again.[132]

In 1948, the NAB adopted several revisions of its code regarding religious broadcasting. Radio should not "be used for the presentation of controversial questions or for the expression of partisan opinions or discussions"[133] or to "convey attacks upon religion." The new code prohibited on-air solicitation of funds or any merchandise offer except of free copies of the message or "religious momentoes [*sic*]."[134] According to McIntire, it was the "most disastrous, the most far-reaching attack which has yet been made in this country upon the Gospel." Even the "independent man like Charles Fuller" was not safe in the climate of suppression fundamentalists perceived.[135] Yet for the first time, the mainline Religious Radio Association opposed the NAB code and tried to join forces with the Federal Council to oppose the new provision.[136] Association president Willard Johnson believed that even before its official passage the new NAB code had been "used by one network against a very popular religious radio program," and he feared that others would be attacked or suppressed with this passage as a justification. "If religion is to have a social message on the radio, this code is a threat," wrote Johnson.[137]

Conservatives' contribution to religious radio finally received some recognition from mainline Protestant groups. By the late 1940s commercial religious broadcasters successfully added their voices to the political debates concerning religion's place on radio through the influence of their new organizations. Infighting among religious conservatives hampered their effectiveness; however, the goal to preserve the profitable niche for gospel broadcasting had occasionally repressed fundamentalists' accustomed suspicion of interdenominational cooperation. Clearing the airwaves for conservative religious radio may have been the first issue of national import around which evangelicals and fundamentalists rallied in the postwar era, setting the stage for their gradual but irreversible reentry into American popular culture. The NRB in particular has become, in the sixty-odd years since its founding, the nucleus of a vibrant media subculture both serving the growing evangelical movement and popularizing its worldview—developments that were hard won by forties commercial religious broadcasters and certainly much regretted by determined nonbelievers such as Robert Scott and equally determined multidenominational Protestant groups such as the Federal Council.

6

Mainstreaming the Good News
Radio and Postwar Popular Culture

In 1950, the NAE, the ACCC, and the NRB emerged from a decade of coalition building in American fundamentalism. Self-definition had been the critical task of the forties, and while evangelicals —personified by the leaders of the NAE—had parted ways with fundamentalists such as McIntire and the American Council, religious broadcasting remained an important area of overlap between these two wings of the fundamentalist subculture. The mass medium of radio carried fundamentalism to a cultural crossroads, poised for a hoped-for revival. Yet religious radio still seemed a calculated risk for station owners in the postwar era. Admitting that unscrupulous broadcasters tainted the image of an entire industry, the NAE's 1947 annual report confessed, "Our most serious obstacles are those which we, as religious broadcasters, create for ourselves."[1] Conservatism was a movement badly in need of a hero. In 1949, the rise of a dynamic young evangelist symbolized the gains conservative Protestants were making in using media to promote their worldview, giving fundamentalism a new popular icon.[2]

A Southern Baptist born in 1918 in North Carolina, Billy Graham was a product of the fundamentalist Bible college network, educated at Bob Jones University, Florida Bible Institute, and Wheaton College. A man of boundless energy, Graham had been a door-to-door Fuller Brush salesman before attracting notice on the preaching circuits of independent Bible churches and earning the support of "powerful conservative Northern Baptist leaders in Chicago."[3] Graham traveled as a field representative for the up-beat organization Youth for Christ, led by evangelist Torrey Johnson, and at thirty had been appointed the president of a small religious college in Minneapolis, Northwestern Schools.[4] In 1949 he launched a three-week revival campaign in Los Angeles. Picking up on the announcement just prior to the campaign's opening that Russia had successfully tested an atomic bomb, Graham used Cold War uncertainty to portray stark contrasts between sinner and saved and to reinforce the sense that now was the time to make a personal decision for Christ.[5] His revival style was straightforward and unembellished, relying heavily on extemporaneous open-Bible preaching punctuated by old-time hymns and gospel solos. And his look was unforgettable, as a journalist at the time described: "His ties are bright, his clothes found in the young business men's and youth's departments of a store. Wide-brimmed hats are a favorite. Flaming argyle socks are the rule, not the exception."[6]

Graham's host for the successful revival was Christ for Greater Los Angeles, a group representing two hundred churches with several previous evangelistic campaigns under its belt. Graham set his own terms for the 1949 campaign, insisting that the group involve even more local churches, put up a larger tent, and raise the budget.[7] Like the nineteenth-century revivalist Charles Finney, Billy Graham was an ambitious and methodical planner of his revivals. As it turned out, the campaign attracted unusual attention from the local and national media and was going full steam at the end of the three weeks, so Graham extended it another month; more than 350,000 people passed through the tent during the seventy-two meetings.[8]

Graham's next two mass revivals, between January and March 1950 in Boston and South Carolina, also drew stadium- and tent-packing crowds and put Graham's name and photo in nearly every major magazine and newspaper. Though Graham could not control the way he was portrayed in the press (which, after Hearst's Los Angeles papers "puffed" him, was generally quite favorable), he did have a careful handle on almost every other aspect of his large urban revivals, from publicity and planning up to a year in advance, to prayer meetings and careful training of volunteers, to "decision cards" and other meticulous record keeping.[9] The publicity garnered by Graham's revivals in early 1950 and the sheer size of the meetings seemed a sudden and striking success for fundamentalists; Graham apparently came out of nowhere. As Robert Ellwood has put it so well, in Graham's campaigns "the billows of the evangelical renewal that rose in America in the latter decades of the twentieth century were beginning to stir. All the signs were there: countercultural message, cultural conformity in such media as sharp dress and the latest communications technology, thorough up-to-date personnel mobilization, conservative politics, mass audiences, rhetoric directed to the individual."[10]

Graham spoke to ordinary people of the power of everyday faithfulness. "Listen," he told the crowds jammed into the Los Angeles revival tent, "it's not how many souls you['ve] won; how big the meetings were that you had. It's whether you are faithful in the place where God puts you. If God puts you to selling automobile tires and you sell them faithfully as unto the Lord and witness for Christ at every opportunity . . . you'll get that crown." He spoke of Christian communities reaching for divine power through individual revival: "We are gathering for our prayer meetings, church services and Sunday school conventions. Committees meet; Bible classes are conducted; Bible schools are carried on, but we have no power because we do not have the Spirit of God in power and in fulness in our lives."[11]

Billy Graham's preaching style had been developed through listening to radio, in particular to Walter Maier's *Lutheran Hour* and the clipped cadence of highly rated newscaster Walter Winchell.[12] Graham had hoped evangelical radio would develop a "wider audience among nonbelievers" and regretted that there were so few nationally heard programs like Maier's and Charles Fuller's. Graham had some experience on radio himself, taking over for Torrey Johnson on the Chicago-area program *Songs in the Night* during his years at the Illinois fundamentalist Bible college in Wheaton and then speaking often on KTIS, the station of the Northwestern Schools.[13] In 1950, after Dr. Maier died, Theodore Elsner, a Philadelphia broadcaster and current president of the NRB, met Billy Graham while vacationing in New Jersey. Elsner believed that God had impressed on his heart that Graham should succeed Maier on national radio, and he told Graham of this conviction. Within a few weeks Elsner arranged for two radio agents, Fred Dienert (Elsner's son-in-law) and Dienert's partner, Walter Bennett, a born-again Christian himself, to contact Graham and then meet with him during his Portland campaign in August 1950.[14]

On the last night of the meeting, Graham told the agents that if he raised twenty-five thousand dollars by midnight for radio, he'd agree to do a national radio program. Incredibly, by the time that night's service ended, exactly twenty-four thousand dollars had been collected. When Graham and his evangelistic team returned to the hotel after dinner, two letters were waiting at the desk for Graham, postmarked a few days earlier, and each contained a check for five hundred dollars. Graham, believing this was God's sign, went forward with plans for a thirteen-week program on ABC, called *Hour of Decision*.[15] The title suggested the inevitable and fervently declared call at the end of each sermon for unsaved listeners to become born again, but it also evoked the times in which the program was launched—times of risk, indecision, and hope for evangelicals in American culture. It was their "hour" of decision, their time to attempt greater relevance and influence. Graham consciously avoided "folksy" sermonizing on the air, instead writing fast-paced sermons based on current events. He even installed a news Teletype machine in his home to catch the latest headlines. The program came live from places as diverse as the Hollywood Bowl and the Korean front lines. *Hour of Decision* made news, reproduced the form of radio news, and was the logical culmination of the religious conservatives' treating religion itself as "good news"—that is, as timely and important information for the country at large. Letters from listeners formed the basis of a mailing list that would become the Billy Graham Evangelistic Association (BGEA), and Graham found he could pay for *Hour of Decision* with "a minimum of comment about finances." The BGEA's statement of purpose was simple: "to spread and propagate the Gospel of the Lord Jesus Christ by any and all means."[16]

Most fundamentalists interpreted Graham's good fortune in

Billy Graham at the first broadcast of his Hour of Decision *radio program, Atlanta, Georgia, 1950. Photograph courtesy of Russ Busby, Billy Graham Evangelistic Association, Montreat, North Carolina.*

the early fifties as God's having chosen him for the work. "He was fast becoming the symbol of a rethinking of religion in America," wrote the fundamentalist historian Louis Gasper.[17] As Graham himself later reflected, "What we saw in 1950 were the early stirrings of a wide-reaching spiritual search—stirrings that helped to create an unaccustomed audience for the Gospel."[18] Indeed, religious revival seemed ubiquitous in the early fifties. In part, it was due to a postwar church construction boom; but it was something more, a palpable spiritual longing that found expression in the efflorescence of many faiths, including Protestantism. "Religion is not a hobby with the American people, nor is it a hunger felt only by a few. It is a basic force in people's lives," said the liberal Protestant broadcaster Everett Parker in 1950.[19]

Over the decade of the fifties, membership in American churches rose from 64.5 million to 114.5 million, to include more than 60 percent of the national population by 1960.[20] Americans joined more churches, paid larger offerings, built more sanctuaries, published and read more religious books and magazines than ever before. Fundamentalist faiths benefited; historian Robert Ellwood speaks of an "evangelical mood rising." The fastest-growing denomination between 1940 and 1960 was the Southern Baptist Convention; the new magazine launched by Graham and edited by a professor at Fuller Theological Seminary was the modishly titled *Christianity Today*.[21]

Even the consolidation of the Protestant mainline into the National Council of Churches of Christ, which was finalized in 1950, reflected these broader sociological changes in American religion —in other words, 1940s fundamentalist fears about the modernist "hydra" proved exaggerated.[22] Historian Henry Pratt has shown that around the time of the merger, doctrinally more conservative churches began participating in the council more actively and at higher levels.[23] Within the National Council, which was a larger and somewhat less centralized organization than the Federal Council had been, the "active minority" effecting the decisions was far more liberal than the majority of the council's members; although conservatives within the council were growing in number, they were unable to form a cohesive bloc to oppose the liberals' having their way on social questions.[24]

Evangelical organizing, urban mass revivals covered with interest in the mainstream media, and the growing tensions between liberal Protestantism and the new evangelicalism all shaped commercial religious broadcasting in the forties and fifties. It must be noted that the winds of federal regulation blew in evangelicals' general favor throughout this period. The White-Wolverton bill hearings and the controversy in Washington surrounding the Scott decision had demonstrated that the FCC, while encouraging religious programs, kept hands off decisions about what kind or how they should be sponsored. The commission maintained this stance throughout the fifties, neither favoring nor penalizing commercial religion. For example, in 1952 the FCC denied a petition brought by the Southern Baptist Convention's Radio Commission that certain FM frequencies should be set aside for religious broadcasting, as had been done for education, on the grounds that to do so would constitute "governmental support for the dissemination of sectarian beliefs."[25] But on the other hand, the FCC had also been petitioned—in cases similar to that brought by Robert Scott—by parties citing an excess of religious broadcasting on the air and claiming a kind of reverse religious discrimination. Some commissioners at midcentury believed that the FCC had overstepped its authority in promoting, even in a general way, religious programs: "The FCC rushed in where other government agencies are forbidden to tread when it, at least implicitly, requires religious programming and determines that a certain amount of religious broadcasting is or is not adequate or excessive, or that the public interest is or is not served by the broadcasting of particular views on religion or the views of particular churches or sects, or when it awards a preference or demerit on the basis of an official judgment as to the quantity, quality, or content of religious broadcasting—all of which it has done in reported cases."[26] Few evangelicals were complaining during the fifties about their treatment by government regulators. That much, at least, seemed to be in their favor.

Evangelicals' relations with the radio industry as a whole also showed improvement and the growth of a niche market for specialized religious stations.[27] In 1954, *Christian Life* magazine issued a listing of the major "Gospel radio programs" of the "larger broadcasters," which included 208 programs, all supported by direct contributions, and twenty-seven radio stations with an all-gospel format.[28] Giving may have also increased as the decade lengthened, according to historian Louis Gasper: "Becoming fearful the channels might be closed, people increased their support of their favorite programs to keep them on the air. Moreover, some people listened to and supported the various religious broadcasts because they were concerned over the seriousness of the threat of atomic warfare with Russia."[29]

Finally, evangelical broadcasters began to develop some new and more politically conscious strategies. When it was first organized, the NRB had pressed its case with good legal counsel and the momentum of a fresh coalition. In the mid-fifties, to "safeguard its achievements" the NRB rented office space in Washington, D.C., with a small full-time staff to promote "preservation, improvement and extension of evangelical biblical broadcasting."[30] It also moved its annual meeting to the nation's capital and added a "Congressional breakfast" to which the delegates invited their representatives and senators. In addition, NRB leaders became highly aware of their press coverage and wrangled for positive reporting. Then-president James DeForest Murch (editor of *United Evangelical Action*) determined to get a favorable interview in *Broadcasting* magazine, which he called the radio industry's Bible: "If we could get their endorsement of the 'sale' of time for religious broadcasting as against 'free' time controlled by the Councils, we would 'have it made.'" He used two contacts—Bob Fleming, a *Christian Hour* agent, and his friend L. B. Wilson, the owner of WCKY Cincinnati—to get an interview with the magazine's editor, Sol Taishoff. The way Murch tells the tale, Taishoff was an easy sell:

> I told the story of the NRB and of the new National Council threat to the right of evangelical broadcasters to purchase time for the broadcast of religion. I said we would appreciate a word in our behalf in the columns of the journal. Sol leaned back in his chair and said, "Why can't you Protestants settle your disagreements amicably and make some sort of compromise on your broadcasting policies?" I said, "Well, there are several

kinds of Protestants and we are unwilling to give up our differing convictions for the sake of unity. May I illustrate? There are several kinds of Jews—Orthodox, Reformed, and Conservative. . . ." With a hearty laugh Sol threw up his hands and immediately retorted, "You don't need to argue your case any further. I know what you are talking about. You certainly have equal rights before the law and the sale of time is the easiest way to guarantee those rights." He then called in two of his best reporters and said, "Hear this man's case and pepper him with questions. Then, I want you to report on the NRB convention for our next issue." When that number came out from the press it contained not only a good news story but a boxed editorial championing our cause. The finest relations between the NRB and the magazine have existed ever since.[31]

In 1956, the Broadcasting and Film Commission (BFC), a central department of the National Council of Churches, made a last, rather desperate plea in favor of sustaining time and issued a policy statement on religious broadcasting coming out strongly against the sale of airtime for broadcasting on both radio and television.[32] William Ward Ayer and other leaders of the NRB described the statement as a renewal of the council's "long-time effort to control Protestant religious broadcasting in America and to eliminate evangelical, biblical Gospel preaching from the airwaves."[33] The National Council, however, argued that its policies were simply based on common sense—and the executive director of the BFC, S. Franklin Mack, even made a point of attending the 1957 meeting of the NRB in order to meet NRB members "on a friendly personal basis, symbolizing our desire to resolve the situation rather than to impose a solution." Mack was surprised to find "many sympathetic and understanding" delegates and described himself as "perfectly at home" in most of the conference's sessions. His visit to the NRB left Mack hopeful that in its efforts the BFC might be joined by conservative broadcasters and that commercial religious radio might be stamped out.[34]

Mack was far too optimistic in this ecumenical vision; even among the liberals many felt the BFC had gone too far toward trying to exert control over all religious broadcasting. In their responses can be read a respect for conservative broadcasters' gains on radio. One member of the BFC board was "aghast at the arrogant sweep" of the policy statement, convinced it would "inhibit the Protestant witness." Its exclusive emphasis on free time, he felt, turned the church into a "mendicant, a pauper, and a beggar going around with its hand out begging for free handouts. Other respectable organizations 'pay their way' why not the family of God?"[35] Presbyterian Paul Evans, in an open letter about the "regrettable" stand the BFC had taken, considered the biblical parable of the wheat and the tares applicable to this situation: "The master of the field told the servants not to pull up the tares lest they should also pull up the wheat. If no time was sold for religious broadcasting—to eliminate the 'huckster' it would eliminate such 'wheat' as the Lutheran Hour, the Baptist Hour, Billy Graham, First Mate Bob, the Back to God Hour, the Light and Life Hour, the Radio Bible Class, and many other sound gospel ministries."[36]

The backlash against the BFC's 1956 policy statement contributed to its failure to carry the approval of even liberal Protestants, but ultimately it was rendered impotent for reasons that had as much to do with the structure of the broadcast industry as with fundamental differences in strategy between conservatives and mainline Protestants. The 1956 policy statement was hollow thunder by the National Council and was largely ignored by the radio and television broadcast industries—in part because the financial returns on paid commercial religion were so good. It was a "blunder" on the part of the liberals, but it was also an irrelevant gesture, given that broadcasting was a far more competitive field than in the 1920s when the councils could dictate terms.[37] A large station, such as WLS in Chicago, could easily generate close to half a million dollars a year from the sale of airtime for religious programs.[38]

The BFC and the National Council could see the tide shifting and began to develop alternative strategies even as they promoted the 1956 policy statement. Interestingly enough, from 1953 to the late fifties, the National Council was seriously—and secretly—circulating proposals to begin paying for time, or to solicit commercial advertisers as corporate sponsors for mainline broadcasts, as a part of the recommendations of an internal study commission on "the role of radio, television, and films in religion."[39] The National Council also sought to create a higher profile for itself in the broadcast business by renting a "hospitality suite" at the NAB annual meeting.[40] The Long-Range Planning Committee of the Presbyterian Church (U.S.A.) argued in a 1960 report on religious broadcasting, "For the Church of the 20th century not to make extensive use of television and radio would be as unthinkable as if St. Paul had refused to travel in ships or Luther and Calvin had regarded the printing press as unworthy of use."[41] But the mainline churches were several decades behind conservatives in thinking of media—for the first time—as a financial proposition for the church; the title of a recent assessment of the Presbyterian case describes the "blurred vision and missed mission" of the National Council denominations with regard to commercial radio religion.[42]

In contrast, broadcasters of the religious right never wavered in their commitment to a single, overriding goal: the conversion of the unsaved American public through the powerful—yet personal—reach of the medium of radio. The drama embedded in revivalism—the enacting of a conversion or reliving of one's own past conversion—became another kind of American entertainment form. With the same reassuring regularity with which a radio drama detective solved the crime, a radio serial hero saved the day, or a radio game show contestant won a cache of valuable prizes, all within the tidy and familiar confines of a time slot to which listeners could "tune in next time," radio revivalism unfailingly brought its listeners around to the same conclusion in every program. Just as radio advertisements were designed to awaken in consumers previously unrecognized desires ("I *do* need a new Buick!"), radio evangelism stimulated people's unspoken fears and longings ("I *am* lonely, I *do* need peace in my heart, I *am* unsure about my future"), then offering emotionally satisfying and practical solutions that rang true in the lives of millions.

The end of the fifties marked an important moment for popular religion. In 1960, the FCC ended its policy of distinguishing between sustaining-time and commercial programs in determining whether a station met FCC standards for service in the public interest.[43] Naturally this change removed any incentive stations had to air free programs, as commercial religious broadcasting could be a profitable sideline for stations looking for paying customers in otherwise unsalable time slots. It took until the mid-seventies, though, for the National Council to endorse paid programming and to "defend the right of any religious organization to purchase time from stations and networks."[44] The 1960 federal policy statement allowed radio and television stations to claim their paid religious broadcasting as public service time, permitting the year to become a cultural milestone marking the "virtual silencing" of mainline churches in mass media. Writes historian Thomas Reeves, "The failure of these churches, hardly suffering from poverty, to raise the necessary funds to keep on the air revealed a spiritual malaise that in retrospect appears tragic. Hereafter, the fundamentalists and evangelicals would have the media, growing in influence as never before, almost to themselves."[45]

Of course, much of that new media growth would be on television—a story that has been well documented elsewhere. Briefly, both mainline and conservative religious broadcasters turned their attention immediately to television and to the "televangelism" it made possible. In particular, mainline churches hoped (in vain, as it turned out) for the foothold on television that they had already lost on radio. In 1950, director of the Protestant Radio Commission C. Everett Parker told the delegates gathered at the Fifth Annual Religious Radio Workshop that religion—and *not* the religion of Christian fundamentalism—deserved a prominent place on television. "We will not bow before the demands that soap and cigarets [*sic*] be first in people's thinking," he declared, "nor will the churches allow religious programming on television to be captured by so-called Evangelists, whose sole qualification is the ability to pay for network and station time." Parker even erroneously thought that radio would soon become outmoded: "Radio is only whistling in the dark when it insists that TV will not replace it in the immediate future."[46]

Since the introduction of television into American broadcasting, four trends have marked the crossroads of American religion, media, and culture: abandonment of sustaining time, growth in

Billy Graham (Hour of Decision), Charles Fuller (Old Fashioned Revival Hour), and Oswald C. J. Hoffmann (Lutheran Hour) at the World Congress on Evangelism, Berlin, 1966. Fuller Theological Seminary Archive, Pasadena, California.

all media simultaneously (including the Internet as well as Christian book and magazine publishing), increased visibility of evangelical Christians in public discourse and popular culture, and movement of the mass media toward the center of American life. The first of these, the end of sustaining-time religious broadcasting, was already evident in the fifties for both radio and television and was nearly complete by the seventies. In 1959 53 percent of religious television programs were paid-time commercial broadcasts, but in 1977 92 percent were commercial programs.[47] At the same time that television and commercial televangelism were growing rapidly, radio was also continuing to thrive as FM frequencies and transistor radios revived the industry as a whole. Following the successful pattern laid down by golden-age religious radio preachers, many large-scale radio ministries are still structured like their 1950s predecessors. Christian-format radio stations have grown steadily since the fifties—a "dependable, relatively trouble-free source of substantial gain for their owners."[48]

These developments rode tandem with a heightened visibility for conservative Protestants: a birth of a new identity in which the media played the role of midwife. In part, their visibility was simply a matter of the rest of the country taking notice of the vital and growing conservative subculture—the 1976 "discovery" of evangelicalism sparked by Jimmy Carter's presidential campaign was long overdue.[49] In part, there seemed to be more evangelical Christians because of the way they were defined in national polls. Robert Wuthnow, writing of the seventies, pointed out that "suddenly, it could be touted that a third of the population regarded themselves as evangelicals. Or by more stringent criteria, such as holding a literal view of the Bible, proselytizing, *and* having had a born-again experience, about one person in five could be counted as an evangelical. By virtue of the capacity of opinion polling to define aspects of the culture, therefore, evangelicals came to be regarded as a force some 30 or 40 million strong."[50]

Evangelicals' new visible status in American society was therefore partially effected by changing definitions of what it meant to be a conservative. But conservatives were also becoming more aware of the muscle in their movement and astute at using that muscle toward political action. This was a distinct shift in evangelical thinking. In 1944, fundamentalist J. Elwin Wright had insisted, "Our task as the ambassadors of God is not to make the Church a political machine to run the governments of the world but to evangelize." At that time, Wright opposed churches having political lobbies: "We do not believe the world will be saved by social or political reform." The one ameliorative tool Christians possessed, according to Wright, was the regeneration of human hearts through revival.[51] Such views had come to a nearly complete turnaround within the space of only two decades, and conservative Protestants began mobilizing in more politicized ways for less strictly otherworldly causes—in particular, to oppose the legalizing of abortion in 1973 and the proposed Equal Rights Amendment in 1979.[52] American media (print and broadcast) both *reported* the formation of this outspoken and visible wing of the movement and *facilitated* its coherence. The appearance of conservative political content in televangelist ministries offered evangelicals a new "framework of intelligibility" for their being in the world and "brought along" the ministries' followers in a way that was relevant to their religious outlook.[53]

Finally, the second half of the twentieth century was notable for broadcast media's becoming increasingly important, if not central, as the site of American discourse. Religious groups in the fifties were already anticipating this reality, for better or worse: liberal Protestant Dallas Smythe in 1958 reported that the mass media had usurped the educative role of the family, church, and school in a single generation.[54] Smythe's assessment seems even more apropos as the century neared its end—when the mass media conveyed (and, just as frequently, purveyed) our national myths, symbols, and narratives. Those media, of course, were not monolithic but riddled with internal contradictions and ambiguous messages. They nonetheless defined the boundaries of the common national culture, and no religion survives long that does not recognize, accommodate to, or help shape this reality.

James Hudnut-Beumler, Robert Wuthnow, and others have defined the middle ground in recent American religion as a pragmatic, "anti-intellectual" practice of faith devoid of controversy—what will "play in Peoria," so to speak—well suited to the relativistic and diverse landscape of the broadcast media.[55] The radio ministries I have addressed in this work, and media-infused Protestant religion since 1960, enmeshed evangelicals in an inextricable relationship with the mass media—defining them by it, for better or worse. Contemporary evangelicals recognize this in many ways; I have even seen advertised in an Assemblies of God publications catalog a book titled *Preaching to Programmed People,* offering suggestions to ministers about "maintaining the attention of a TV-conditioned congregation."[56] The radio and television "conditioning" of American Christians is not, however, a lamentable example of raging worldliness. Rather, it followed from the (by no means predictable) decisions made by 1920s fundamentalists to adapt religion to broadcast media and of their listeners to adapt the broadcast media into personal worship rituals. The popularity of American revival religion owes much to the inseparable combination of religious and secular elements—this is the source of its relevance to so many people and also the seed of its ambivalence toward social change.

Religious radio sought to counter the social fragmentation of American life by using the very tool—the mass media—being portrayed as the culprit in the breakdown of American community. Communication, after all, lies at the heart of religious experience and at the soul of media institutions. In both realms, the goal is to control the channels of communication and thereby control the messages transmitted and the behavior elicited.[57] Radio evangelism prefigured the ways in which other forms of mass media would be employed to cement an evangelical "community" that would be, Protestant conservatives hoped, less circumscribed by region, race, or class than physical communities across the United States. Media ministries offered their listeners and viewers a model of the world they hoped to create and a model for that world through the translocal links they fostered.[58] Evangelicals in this study, like those active in media ministries today, claimed the status of gatekeepers to what Stewart Hoover has called a "lost America of social and cultural connectedness."[59] The resulting coalitions and shifts in the American religious landscape were not predetermined by the mediated messages conservatives broadcast, but evangelical broadcasting helped its committed listeners envision a national community and helped increase visibility for the revivalist cause. Religious radio changed the evangelical movement's self-perception and strategic position in American life from marginalized outsider to ubiquitous cultural presence, preparing the way for an aggressive assault on moral and political fronts in the latter half of the twentieth century.

For the broadcasters during radio's golden age, however, the distant goal was not domination of the nation's political agenda but the fulfillment of biblical prophecy and the return of their Lord—hastened, they hoped, by proselytizing on worldwide radio. Dr. Charles Leaming, one of the original founders of the National Religious Broadcasters, pastor of Faith Temple in St. Petersburg, Florida, and radio pastor of a program called *Waves of Truth,* celebrated fifty years of broadcasting the gospel by radio in 1980. Congratulating his colleague and friend, William Ward Ayer reflected back on the years trying to pull together a coalition of evangelical broadcasters. Those had been "blessed but oftimes hectic days," strengthening radio as a chosen medium for God's purposes. "Of course you can't have another fifty years," Ayer told the seventy-five-year-old Leaming, "and I hope it won't be needed, because with millions of others I feel that Our Lord may soon appear in the Glory and we will be given another nature and another medium for serving our Saviour forever."[60] The irrepressible evangelical spirit that had carried religious radio so far can be illustrated best by Ayer's advice to Pastor Leaming, as one radio man to another, expressing hope that the future will always hold out the promise of the passing of this present world into another, finer realm.

Notes

ABBREVIATIONS
BGCA
    Archives of the Billy Graham Center, Wheaton College, Wheaton,
    Illinois
BNM
    Board of National Missions, General Department of Mission,
    Interpretation and Mass Communication/Mass Media, Department/
    Division of Radio and Television/Mass Media, Records 1926–71
    (Record Group 303.2), Presbyterian Church (U.S.A.) Department
    of History, Philadelphia, Pennsylvania
FRC
    Federal Radio Commission Records, Federal Records Center,
    Suitland, Maryland
FTS
    Charles and Grace Fuller Collection, David du Plessis Archive, Fuller
    Theological Seminary, Pasadena, California
HTH
    Heart to Heart Talk
IER
    Institute for Education by Radio/TV Collection, Ohio State University
    Archive, Columbus, Ohio
NCC
    Records of the National Council of Churches and Federal Council of
    Churches, archived at the Presbyterian Church (U.S.A.) Department
    of History, Philadelphia, Pennsylvania
NRB
    Collection of the National Religious Broadcasters, Manassas, Virginia
OIGC
    Collection of the Ockenga Institute, Gordon-Conwell Theological
    Seminary, Hamilton, Massachusetts
WWCC
    World Wide Christian Courier

INTRODUCTION
    1. Mrs. Phoebe Huffman to Rev. Charles Fuller and Family, 21 January
[1954], FTS.
    2. Martín-Barbero, *Communication, Culture, and Hegemony;* Hoover
and Wagner, "History and Policy in American Broadcast Treatment of
Religion"; Cruz and Lewis, *Viewing, Reading, Listening;* Jameson, "Reification and Utopia in Mass Culture." Much of this new scholarship is informed by semiotics and literary criticism, building on reader-response

theory. See, for example, Lyon, *Intentions;* Morley, "Changing Paradigms in Audience Research"; Holub, *Reception Theory;* Tompkins, *Reader-Response Criticism;* Freund, *Return of the Reader;* Eco, *Role of the Reader;* and Allen, *Channels of Discourse.*

3. Hulsether, "Evangelical Popular Religion as a Source for North American Liberation Theology?," 75.

4. Long, "Textual Interpretation as Collective Action," 194.

5. W. C. Allen, quoted in Nelson, *Prairie Winnows Out Its Own,* 112.

6. Forbes and Mahan, *Religion and Popular Culture in America;* Berger, *Far Glory;* Binion, *After Christianity;* Bounds, *Coming Together/Coming Apart;* Casanova, *Public Religions in the Modern World;* Dekker, Luidens, and Rice, *Rethinking Secularization;* Smith, *American Evangelicalism;* Swatos and Olson, *Secularization Debate;* Beckford, "Start Together and Finish Together"; Warner, "Work in Progress"; Yamane, "Secularization on Trial."

7. Hoover, *Mass Media Religion,* 36; Schultze, "Mythos of the Electronic Church"; Ong, *Presence of the Word.*

8. Ong, *Presence of the Word,* 148, 161, 257–58, 288; Eliade, *Sacred and the Profane.*

9. Smith, *Voice for God,* 110.

10. Franklin, *Autobiography of Benjamin Franklin,* 119–20.

11. Raymond Gram Swing, "Radio and the Future," in Tyson and MacLatchy, *Education on the Air,* 4–5.

12. "Here Are Ten Facts That Everyone Should Know about Radio," from Greenville, Tex., local newspaper, clipping in Fuller scrapbook 3, FTS.

13. "Twisting the Devil's Tail."

14. Meister, "Presbyterians and Mass Media," 185.

15. Rader, *Life's Greatest Adventure,* 79.

16. Hatch, *Democratization of American Christianity;* Stout, *New England Soul;* Moore, *Selling God;* Lambert, *"Pedlar in Divinity";* Kamensky, *Governing the Tongue.*

17. Fox and Lears, *Culture of Consumption,* xi–xii.

18. King, "Reform Establishment and the Ambiguities of Influence," 122; Smith, *American Evangelicalism,* 4–9; McLoughlin, *Revivals, Awakenings, and Reform,* 150–62; Marty, "Sacred and Secular in American History."

19. The five "fundamentals" were biblical authority, virgin birth of Jesus Christ, Christ's physical resurrection, his substitutionary atonement, and his literal second coming. See Ammerman, *Bible Believers,* 18–24; also Marsden, *Fundamentalism and American Culture;* Marsden, "Preachers of Paradox"; Boone, *Bible Tells Them So;* Lawrence, *Defenders of God;* and Hunter, *American Evangelicalism.*

20. Watt, *Transforming Faith.*

21. Weber, *Protestant Ethic and the Spirit of Capitalism,* in Lawrence, *Defenders of God,* 252 n. 3; also Blau, Land, and Redding, "Expansion of Religious Affiliation."

22. For the older version, see Ginger, *Six Days of Forever?,* and Levine, *Defender of the Faith;* also Harding, "Representing Fundamentalism." For revised perspectives, see Cornelius, "Their Stage Drew All the World"; Gilbert, *Redeeming Culture;* Larson, *Summer for the Gods;* and Hangen, "Fundamentalism's Unseen Victory."

23. Carpenter, *Revive Us Again;* Carpenter, "From Fundamentalism to the New Evangelical Coalition"; Carpenter, "Fundamentalist Institutions and the Rise of Evangelical Protestantism"; Martin, *With God on Our Side,* 16–17.

24. Wuthnow, *Restructuring of American Religion,* 137.

25. Carpenter, *Revive Us Again,* 85–86.

26. Berger, "Sociological View of the Secularization of Theology"; Covert, *Mass Media between the Wars,* xii.

27. Bennet, "Bible School Lesson," 7.

28. Douglas, "Effects of Modernization on Religious Change"; Berger, "From the Crisis of Religion to the Crisis of Secularity."

29. Lawrence, *Defenders of God,* 1; Berman, *All That Is Solid Melts into Air.*

30. Alexander, *Televangelism Reconsidered,* 46.

31. Lawrence, *Defenders of God,* 1–3; Singal, *War Within;* Kolakowski, *Modernity on Endless Trial;* Hutchinson, *Modernist Impulse in American Protestantism.*

32. Leach, *Land of Desire;* Lears, *Fables of Abundance;* Ewen and Ewen, *Channels of Desire;* Strasser, *Satisfaction Guaranteed;* Sobel, *Manipulators.*

33. Susman, "Communication and Culture," xxxi–xxxii; Goethals, *Electronic Golden Calf;* Carl Williams, "Acoustic Space," *Explorations,* February 1955, quoted in Marchand, *Marshall McLuhan,* 123–24; see also Lazere, *American Media and Mass Culture;* Snow, *Creating Media Culture;* and Stanton, *Mass Media and Mass Culture.*

34. Religious broadcasting receives little more than passing mention in the aging seminal work on the field, Barnouw, *Tower in Babel* and *Golden Web;* religion receives scant or no treatment in general texts such as Sterling and Kittross, *Stay Tuned;* Hilmes, *Radio Voices;* Czitrom, *Media and the American Mind;* Meyrowitz, *No Sense of Place;* and Smulyan, *Selling Radio.* See also Hangen, "Man of the Hour."

35. Cohen, *Making a New Deal,* 133–36, 142–43, 325.

36. Neth, *Preserving the Family Farm;* Jellison, *Entitled to Power;* Kirby, *Rural Worlds Lost;* Danbom, *Born in the Country;* Zunz, *Making America Corporate;* Barron, *Mixed Harvest.*

37. Nelson, *Prairie Winnows Out Its Own,* ix.

38. Lynd and Lynd, *Middletown,* 269; Nye, *Electrifying America,* 21–22.

39. Schwarzlose, "Technology and the Individual," 100–101; Sterling and Kittross, *Stay Tuned,* 656.

40. Summers, "Kansas Radio Listener," 5–6; Summers, "Iowa Rural Radio Listener," 5.

41. Sustaining time is defined as "any program which is neither paid for by a sponsor nor interrupted by spot announcements." Edelman, *Licensing of Radio Services,* 78.

42. Covert, "We May Hear Too Much," 199–220.

43. Morgan, *Rising in the West,* 226.

44. McQuail, "Mass Media," 511–12.

45. Religious radio is disappointingly absent from works such as MacDonald, *Don't Touch That Dial;* Marquis, "Written on the Wind"; Rosen, *Modern Stentors;* Mander, "Public Debate about Broadcasting in the Twenties"; and McChesney, *Telecommunications, Mass Media, and Democracy.*

46. For overviews, see Armstrong, *Electric Church;* Siedell, *Gospel Radio;* Ward, *Air of Salvation;* Erickson, *Religious Radio and Television;* Hill, *Airwaves to the Soul;* and Ellens, *Models of Religious Broadcasting.* For individual biographies, see Hood, "New Old-Time Religion"; Adair, *M. R. De Haan;* Webb, *About My Father's Business;* Stanley, *Feminist Pillar of Fire;* Miller, *Harry Emerson Fosdick;* and Davis, "Radio Priest."

47. Schultze, "Evangelical Radio and the Rise of the Electronic Church"; Schultze, "Invisible Medium"; Martin, "Mass Communications"; and Voskuil, "Power of the Air." See also Sweet, "Communication and Change."

48. Dorgan, *Airwaves of Zion;* Brinkley, *Voices of Protest;* Apostolidis, *Stations of the Cross;* see also Warner, *New Wine in Old Wineskins,* for another example of a religious community study with an eye to how churches use media to grow.

49. Morgan, *Visual Piety,* 12–13.

50. "Radio Log of Evangelical Broadcasts," *Christian Life,* August 1948, 17, quoted in Gasper, *Fundamentalist Movement,* 77.

51. Voskuil, "Power of the Air"; Finke and Stark, *Churching of America.*

52. Eskridge, "Evangelical Broadcasting," 129.

53. Schultze, "Evangelical Radio and the Rise of the Electronic Church," 302.

54. This point was nicely conveyed in Grundy, "'We Always Tried to Be Good People.'"

55. Mitchell, "Radio Religion"; Clements, "Rhetoric of the Radio Ministry."

56. Fosdick's sermon was preached in the First Presbyterian Church, New York City, on 21 May 1922 and was subsequently published in *Christian Century,* 8 June 1922.

57. McIntire, *Twentieth Century Reformation,* 205.

58. Carpenter, *Revive Us Again,* 233; Sittser, *Cautious Patriotism,* 105.

59. Reeves, *Empty Church;* Meister, "Presbyterians and Mass Media"; Voskuil, "Reaching Out"; Jacobsen and Trollinger, *Re-forming the Center;* Smith, *American Evangelicalism;* Gaustad, *"Did* the Fundamentalists Win?"

60. Smith, Sikkink, and Bailey, "Devotion in Dixie and Beyond"; Yamane, "Secularization on Trial"; Bounds, *Coming Together/Coming Apart.*

CHAPTER ONE

1. Voskuil, "Power of the Air," 71.

2. Berkman, "Long before Falwell," 1–11; Bendroth, "Fundamentalism and the Mass Media," 76–79; Eskridge, "Evangelical Broadcasting," 128–29.

3. Berkman, "Long before Falwell"; Bendroth, "Fundamentalism and the Media"; Loveless, *Manual of Gospel Broadcasting,* 15–16.

4. Schultze, "Evangelical Radio and the Rise of the Electronic Church," 291.

5. Martin, "Mass Communications," 1711; Sweet, "Communication and Change," 56.

6. Ayer, "Will Americans Be Allowed to Broadcast the Gospel?," 3.

7. Barnouw, *Tower in Babel;* Hilmes, *Radio Voices;* Sterling and Kittross, *Stay Tuned;* McChesney, *Telecommunications, Mass Media, and Democracy.*

8. Owen Young to Macfarland, 6 November 1926, NCC 18-17-24.

9. M. H. Aylesworth to Macfarland, 21 February 1927, NCC 18-17-24. Macfarland declined Aylesworth's offer to send over a radio from NBC.

10. Macfarland to Julius Rosenwald, 7 May 1927, NCC 18-17-24.

11. Charles S. Macfarland, "Radio and Religion," radio address, n.d., NCC 18-18-2.

12. Erickson, *Religious Radio and Television,* 80–81, 135; Miller, *Harry Emerson Fosdick.*

13. Sweet, "Communication and Change," 61; Schultze, "Evangelical Radio and the Rise of the Electronic Church."

14. "Minutes of the Executive Committee of the National Religious Radio Committee," 6 February 1928, NCC 18-17-24.

15. Sterling and Kittross, *Stay Tuned,* 575–80.

16. Edelman, *Licensing of Radio Services,* 77.

17. Hawkins, "Diamond Days," 14.

18. Additionally, religious groups were able to obtain licenses from the FRC and the FCC if they were able to demonstrate that they could produce balanced programming. Contrary to the view taken by most evangelical scholars (for example, Quentin Schultze) not only did some key religious stations retain their licenses in the late twenties and the thirties, but the FRC and FCC licensed many other religious groups and

claimed, at least, that applications from religious groups were treated fairly. See Schultze, "Evangelical Radio and the Rise of the Electronic Church"; "Minutes of the Executive Committee of the National Religious Radio Committee"; Sterling and Kittross, *Stay Tuned,* 575–80; and Cox, "FCC, the Constitution, and Religious Broadcast Programming." For a list of religious groups licensed as station owners by the FCC, see Rosell Hyde, "Statement of Commissioner Rosell H. Hyde," 1 September 1948, BNM 303.2-11-64; Saunders, "National Religious Broadcasters"; and Brown, "Survey of the Programming."

19. "Religion and the Radio," *Federal Council Bulletin,* March 1928, 19, BNM 303.2-1-2.

20. Reeves, *Empty Church,* 120, 116; Moore, *Religious Outsiders,* 150–72.

21. Cantril and Allport, *Psychology of Radio,* 11.

22. Federal Radio Commission, *Third Annual Report* (Washington, D.C.: U.S. Government Printing Office, 1929), 24, quoted in Schultze, "Evangelical Radio and the Rise of the Electronic Church," 293.

23. "Religious Radio, Greater New York Federation of Churches," 1931, BNM 303.2-1-2.

24. "Resolution," 23 April 1928, Greater New York Federation of Churches, BNM 303.2-1-2.

25. Charles S. Macfarland, "Radio and Religion," radio address, n.d., NCC 18-18-2.

26. Stone, *On the Boundaries of American Evangelicalism,* 77–79.

27. The station licensed to Robert Schuler's Trinity Methodist Church in Los Angeles was denied renewal after his "zealous and at times loose-tongued" attacks on "Catholics, local officials, and judges sitting on current cases." Cantril and Allport, *Psychology of Radio,* 51; Edelman, *Licensing of Radio Services,* 81.

28. Murch, *Adventuring for Christ in Changing Times,* 173.

29. Quotation from Saunders, "National Religious Broadcasters," 203.

30. "For the Information of Editors," typescript two-page report, n.d., NCC 18-17-24. It was just this document that Lowell Sperry Saunders recognized was the key to proving whether fundamentalists' claims against the Federal Council were true and to which he did not have access when he wrote his dissertation—he said the NRB was unwilling or unable to produce it ("National Religious Broadcasters," 203). It can be viewed in the records of the Federal Council.

31. Charles Macfarland to L. W. Boe, 1 May 1929, NCC 18-17-24.

32. "A Memorandum from Charles S. Macfarland to the Members of the Conference on Religious Publicity," 7 May 1929, NCC 18-17-24.

33. Samuel McCrea Cavert to Rev. E. A. E. Palmquist, 22 November 1929, NCC 18-17-24.

34. Ibid.

35. Brinkley, *Voices of Protest;* Brown, "Selling Airtime for Controversy"; Fishwick, "Father Coughlin Time"; Schlesinger, *Age of Roosevelt;* Stegner, "Radio Priest and His Flock."

36. Cited in Fishwick, "Father Coughlin Time," 33.

37. Brinkley, *Voices of Protest,* 94–95.

38. Schlesinger, *Age of Roosevelt,* 20.

39. Brinkley, *Voices of Protest,* 100. After CBS changed its policy, it inaugurated the sustaining-time program *Church of the Air,* influenced by a "delegation of bishops," according to Brown, "Selling Airtime for Controversy," 201.

40. Brinkley, *Voices of Protest,* 119.

41. Schlesinger, *Age of Roosevelt,* 20.

42. Fishwick, "Father Coughlin Time," 46; Stegner, "Radio Priest and His Flock," 237–38; Brinkley, *Voices of Protest,* 83.

43. Stegner, "Radio Priest and His Flock," 238; Schlesinger, *Age of Roosevelt,* 20.

44. Stegner, "Radio Priest and His Flock," 239–40.

45. Tyson and MacLatchy, *Education on the Air,* 5.

46. Ibid., 4.

47. MacLatchy, *Education on the Air: Tenth Yearbook,* 45–46.

48. Quoted in Brown, "Selling Airtime for Controversy," 203.

49. Maier, *Fourth Lutheran Hour,* 128.

50. Stegner, "Radio Priest and His Flock," 250; see also Baldwin, *Henry Ford and the Jews,* 293–308.

51. "Proceedings, Fifth Annual Convention of the National Association of Broadcasters," 19–21 September 1927, Hotel Astor, New York City, p. 19, FCC file 89-6: "National Association of Broadcasters prior to 1928, New York City/March 17, 1927–December 31, 1927," quoted in Brown, "Selling Airtime for Controversy," 208.

52. Brown, "Selling Airtime for Controversy," 214.

53. Ibid., 209–10.

54. "The Code of the National Association of Broadcasters/ Adopted by the 17th Annual Convention of the NAB/July 11, 1939," National Association of Broadcasters, Washington, D.C., 1939, 5, FCC file 89-6: "National Association of Broadcasters, June 28, 1939–October 20, 1939," quoted in Brown, "Selling Airtime for Controversy," 211.

55. Sol Taiahoff, "NAB Adopts Code, Demands, ASCAP Action," *Broadcasting and Broadcast Advertising,* 15 July 1939, 7–8, 13–14, quoted in Brown, "Selling Airtime for Controversy," 212; Stegner, "Radio Priest and His Flock," 253; Brinkley, *Voices of Protest,* 267.

56. MacLatchy, *Education on the Air: Tenth Yearbook,* 54.

57. Quoted in Brown, "Selling Airtime for Controversy," 212.

58. Stegner, "Radio Priest and His Flock," 253; Brinkley, *Voices of Protest,* 267.

59. Fishwick, "Father Coughlin Time," 45.

60. Ibid., 34.

61. MacLatchy, *Education on the Air: Tenth Yearbook,* 67.

62. Jack Gould, "Clergymen Assail Radio Chain Curb," *New York Times,* 12 June 1941, L8.

CHAPTER TWO

1. Interview with Andrew Wyzenbeek conducted by Robert Shuster, 1978, BGCA 40, tape 1.

2. Rader's biography has been meticulously written in Eskridge, "Only Believe." For Rader's dissatisfaction with theologically liberal churches of his day, see pp. 17–18.

3. Ibid., 8–25.

4. Ibid., 26; Wacker, *Heaven Below,* 256; Blumhofer, *Aimee Semple Mc-Pherson,* 191.

5. Rader, *Life's Greatest Adventure,* 77.

6. Rader, *Paul Rader's Stories of His Early Life,* 53–54.

7. Notes from taped interviews with Pauline (Rader) Noll and Harriet (Rader) Kisler, conducted by Larry Eskridge in August 1984, Collection of Larry Eskridge, Institute for the Study of American Evangelicals, Wheaton, Ill.

8. Tucker, *Redemption of Paul Rader,* 94.

9. Marsden, *Fundamentalism and American Culture,* 32–39, 141.

10. Reverend William A. Ashby (Glasgow, Scotland) to Paul Rader, BGCA 30-45-1.

11. Eskridge, "Only Believe," 36–42.

12. Mrs. Ruth Boyer Anderson to H. D. Campbell, n.d., BGCA 330-45-1.

13. Carpenter, *Revive Us Again,* 79.

14. "How to Make the Christmas Bells Ring at the Chicago Gospel Tabernacle," 1922 pamphlet, collection of the Chicago Historical Society, used by permission from the Paul Rader Papers, BGCA 38.

15. *WWCC,* March 1927, back page.

16. Despite Rader's sometimes heavy-handed male slant on the gospel, the tabernacle attracted both men and women and embraced a fairly broad congregation, including blacks from the city's South Side as well as Swedes from the immediate neighborhood and a cross section of recent European immigrants from around the city. Rader, *Paul Rader's Stories of His Early Life,* 38; Eskridge, "Only Believe," 84–85.

17. Eskridge, "Only Believe," 38; promotional materials in "Paul Rader —Ephemera," BGCA 38.

18. Clarence W. Jones, "Paul Rader: Pioneer of Gospel Broadcasting," unpublished article sent to Mrs. Lyell Rader, 23 July 1960, 1–2, BGCA 38-1-14. In his reminiscence, Jones claimed that Rader's first broadcast from the rooftop was over WHT, not WBU.

19. Eskridge, "Only Believe," 116–17; Ward, *Air of Salvation,* 28–29; "First Radio Revival," *Chicago Daily News,* 3 June 1922, 3, cited in Eskridge, "Only Believe," 117.

20. Jones, "Paul Rader"; Neely, *Come Up to This Mountain,* 32–35.

21. Latham, "National Radio Chapel WHT 400," 18. The most generous supporter of the Chicago Gospel Tabernacle efforts over the years was Albert M. Johnson, the wealthy head of the National Life Insurance Company, whose wife, Bessie, had been converted by Rader. Johnson bankrolled the tabernacle when donations did not meet expenses and was a financial safety net for some of Rader's more risky proposals. Eskridge, "Only Believe," 69–71, 122.

22. Eskridge, "Only Believe," 121.

23. Oral history of Merrill Dunlop, BGCA 50, tape 1; Eskridge, "Only Believe," 129.

24. Johnson, "National Radio Chapel: What It Is," *National Radio Chapel Announcer,* December 1925, 2.

25. Rader, *Radio Messages by Paul Rader,* 14, 17.

26. Ibid., 28–31.

27. "Hi-Ways and By-Ways," *National Radio Chapel Announcer,* February 1926, 27.

28. Latham, "National Radio Chapel WHT 400," *National Radio Chapel Announcer,* December 1926, 18.

29. Johnson, "National Radio Chapel WHT Chicago 400," *National Radio Chapel Announcer,* March 1926, 22.

30. Johnson, "National Radio Chapel Topics," *National Radio Chapel Announcer,* March 1927, 9.

31. Ibid., 14.

32. Rader, *Paul Rader's Stories of His Early Life,* 4.

33. "Profiles of Great Preachers," fifty-first anniversary souvenir pamphlet for the *Heaven and Home Hour* (ca. 1984), 33. NRB file on Paul Rader, National Religious Broadcasters, Manassas, Va.

34. Jones, "Paul Rader," 2.

35. Eskridge, "Only Believe," 66–67.

36. "Hi-Ways and By-Ways," *National Radio Chapel Announcer,* February 1926, 27.

37. "Extracts from Radio Letters," 33.

38. Johnson, "National Radio Chapel Topics," *National Radio Chapel Announcer,* April 1927, 11.

39. "Tuning In," 8.

40. "Radio Ranger Watch Tower," 13.

41. "Hi-Ways and By-Ways," *National Radio Chapel Announcer,* March 1926, 29, 36.

42. Introducing a "Family Tree" segment on the *Back Home Hour,* Floyd Johnson would sing, "There's a blossom that's blooming for you /

On the old family tree. / For each relative loyal and true, / On the old family tree. / On the old family tree, / On the old family tree, / And may none of its wonderful blossoms e'er fade, / From the old family tree." Johnson, "National Radio Chapel Chicago WHT 400," 10.

43. Ibid., 26.

44. Ibid., 27.

45. *WWCC,* June 1927, 14; Johnson, "National Radio Chapel Topics," *National Radio Chapel Announcer,* July 1927, 17–18.

46. Johnson, "National Radio Chapel Topics," July 1927, 18.

47. Contract between Paul Rader and J. S. Boyd, 13 September 1927, WBBM Records, Accession #173-58-A-42, box 119, FRC.

48. Eskridge, "Only Believe," 141.

49. For example, see the half-page ad in the *WWCC,* December 1927, 32.

50. Rader, *Radio Messages by Paul Rader,* 23.

51. J. S. Boyd, addendum 12(C) to FRC application dated 11 April 1927, WBBM Records, Accession #173-58-A-42, box 119, FRC.

52. WBBM Air Theatre program, December 1930 and February 1931, in WBBM Records, Accession #173-58-A-42, box 119, FRC.

53. "Broadcasters' Radio Programs," 22 June 1930, included in WBBM Records, Accession #173-58-A-42, box 119, FRC.

54. Frizen, "Radio Message," 12; "A Radio Message," *WWCC,* January 1928, 8.

55. "A Radio Message," *WWCC,* February 1928, 38.

56. Eskridge, "Only Believe," 84; Interestingly enough, Rader had some ties to Pentecostals through more than his belief in faith healing. In 1926 he substituted at Aimee Semple McPherson's Angelus Temple while she took a trip to the Holy Land, and during the time of her disappearance there was some speculation that he might assume her pulpit. See, for example, "Rader Believes Missing Woman Suffering Mental Lapse," clipping in Paul Rader Papers, collection 38, box 1, folder 2, BGCA.

57. Interview with Merrill Dunlop by Robert Shuster, 21 November 1978, collection 50, tape 1; see also the "Knapsack for 'Reveille Hour': Souvenirs of the Breakfast Brigade," collection 38, box 1, folder 13, both in BGCA.

58. Paul Rader, "Spit and Whittle Club," reprint of undated *Reveille Hour* broadcast over WJBT, collection 38, box 1, folder 13, BGCA.

59. Paul Rader, "Hello by Radio," undated poem (ca. 1929), collection 38, box 1, folder 13, BGCA.

60. "Radio Relatives Review," 2, 16.

61. During part of this period the host of the *Reveille Hour* was William B. Hogg, who later went to California and started the *Country Church of Hollywood* broadcast, a kind of religious predecessor of the television show *Hee-Haw.*

62. Eskridge, "Only Believe," 145–46.

63. Ibid., 190.

64. "Our Musical Evangelists," 116.

65. "Souvenir and Remembrance of Eight Wonderful Years of Gospel Broadcasting," Fort Wayne Gospel Temple pamphlet, 1936. collection 38, BGCA.

66. Undated clipping from the Fort Wayne Gospel Temple radio album, collection 38, BGCA.

67. Notes on taped interview with Harriet (Rader) Kisler, conducted in August 1984 by Larry Eskridge.

68. Smith, *Voice for God,* 80.

69. Carpenter, *Revive Us Again,* 10–12.

CHAPTER THREE

1. McWilliams, "Aimee Semple McPherson," 77–78.

2. McPherson, *This Is That,* 16, 22, 27.

3. Ibid., 46.

4. Ibid., 80–81. After a brief period during which Harold joined Aimee on her tours as "the preacher's husband," their divorce was finalized in 1921.

5. Ibid., 88, 99, 104, 125; Blumhofer, *Aimee Semple McPherson,* 116.

6. The name referred to her fourfold statement of faith, based on the vision of the Old Testament prophet Ezekiel, identifying the four "corners" of the gospel as Christ's roles: Savior, Baptizer, Healer, and Coming King. Blumhofer, *Aimee Semple McPherson,* 153.

7. Getting her hair bobbed in 1927 outraged some of her followers and confirmed the opinion of hard-line fundamentalists that Sister Aimee was misguided to begin with. See "Aimee's Bob Foe Seeks Church," 27 April 1927 (date uncertain), McPherson clipping file at Los Angeles Public Library; also Rice, *Bobbed Hair, Bossy Wives, and Women Preachers,* 38.

8. Hood, "New Old-Time Religion," 28.

9. Blumhofer, *Aimee Semple McPherson,* 322.

10. McPherson, *Story of My Life,* 240–41; Hood, "New Old-Time Religion," 29; *There Is a God! Debate between Aimee Semple McPherson, Fundamentalist, and Charles Lee Smith, Atheist* (Los Angeles: Foursquare Publications, n.d.).

11. Epstein, *Sister Aimee,* 438–39; Blumhofer, *Aimee Semple McPherson,* 379; Hood, "New Old-Time Religion," 30.

12. "Aimee Semple McPherson: Thousands Mourn at Famed Evangelist's Funeral," 85–88.

13. McPherson, *Story of My Life,* 128; McPherson, *This Is That,* 543.

14. "A Brief History of Angelus Temple," n.d., Foursquare Church typescript in author's possession.

15. Clark, "Miracles for a Dime," 355; Epstein, *Sister Aimee,* 247–59; Hood, "New Old-Time Religion," 48–58; Blumhofer, *Aimee Semple McPherson,* 50–52.

16. Blumhofer, *Aimee Semple McPherson,* 260–61; Clark, "Miracles for a Dime," 355; Lothrop, "West of Eden."

17. Epstein, *Sister Aimee,* 256.

18. The Rockridge Radio Station is now radio station KNEW.

19. McPherson, *This Is That,* 423–24.

20. *Bridal Call,* August 1923.

21. Ibid., December 1923/January 1924, inside back cover. McPherson was one of a number of southern California Pentecostals taking over the airwaves, such as Pastor Roy Ogan of Bakersfield, radio preacher to the Okies in Bakersfield. Morgan, *Rising in the West,* 129.

22. *Bridal Call,* July 1923, 15.

23. Ibid.

24. Ibid.

25. Lothrop, "West of Eden," 50, 56.

26. McPherson, *Story of My Life,* 127–28.

27. *Bridal Call,* March 1926, 26.

28. Ibid., April 1924, 19, quoted in Neeb, "Historical Study," 130.

29. Ibid.

30. Bliven, "Sister Aimee," 289–91.

31. Comstock, "Aimee Semple McPherson," 12.

32. See, for example, K. G. Ormiston, "Listening In Radio K.F.S.G.," *Bridal Call,* October 1924, 30, and "What Radio Means to Me," *Bridal Call,* January 1925, 18.

33. Interview with Raymond Becker, 23 October 1965, in Neeb, "Historical Study," 128.

34. *Bridal Call,* April 1924, 18.

35. Ibid.

36. Neeb, "Historical Study," 153–55.

37. McPherson, *This Is That,* 250.

38. Biery, "Starring Aimee Semple McPherson," 99.

39. Neeb, "Historical Study," 156.

40. Dacre, "Aimee Semple McPherson," 79.

41. Hilmes, *Radio Voices,* 62–96; Sterling and Kittross, *Stay Tuned,* 72–79, 115–23.

42. Neeb, "Historical Study," 157–58; unfortunately, it seems that scripts from these radio dramas have not survived.

43. "Evangelistic Campaign Aids," collection 103, BGCA.

44. Erickson, *Religious Radio and Television,* 127.

45. Sterling and Kittross, *Stay Tuned,* 130.

46. Hood, "New Old-Time Religion," 72–73; Neeb, "Historical Study," 143.

47. Hood, "New Old-Time Religion," 75; Ellens, *Models of Religious Broadcasting,* 73.

48. Aimee Semple McPherson, "Dedication of Radio Tower: Sermon Transcript," 30 November 1939, collection 103, reel 12, p. 3, BGCA.

49. Comstock, "Aimee Semple McPherson"; Julia Budlong, "Aimee Semple McPherson," *The Nation,* 19 June 1929, 737–39, cited in Shanks, "Historical and Critical Study," 34, 37–39.

50. Comstock, "Aimee Semple McPherson," 15. A concurring opinion is "Christ in Vaudeville," *New Statesman and Nation,* 6 October 1928: 785–86, quoted in Shanks, "Historical and Critical Study," 42: "[The California coast] includes a large and continually growing element made up of the simplest folk from the prairie States: men and women from the farms and small towns of Kansas and Iowa, who have got on well enough to abandon the plough and the store before approaching old age. In the atmosphere of prosperous America they have lapsed from the sternness of their lives in the toil that, so long as the pioneer conditions lasted, claimed every dweller in the Middle West until the last days of his earthly pilgrimage. They tend, accordingly, to retire in good time, and the golden climate of California makes an irresistible call to them. They answer it, and carry their Middle Western habits and conscience with them to Los Angeles or San Diego, where boredom too frequently swallows them up. The morals of Hollywood naturally horrify them; but they understand the Four-square Gospel, and when it is proclaimed by an enchantress such as Aimee Semple McPherson, they are as wax in her hands."

51. Dacre, "Aimee Semple McPherson," 79.

52. McWilliams, "Aimee Semple McPherson," 59; Lothrop, "West of Eden," 52.

53. Smith, *Voice for God,* 31; McWilliams, "Aimee Semple McPherson," 59.

54. Singleton, "Popular Culture or the Culture of the Populace?," 260; Singleton, *Religion in the City of Angels,* 119–84.

55. McWilliams, "Aimee Semple McPherson," 59.

56. Murrow Mayo, "Aimee Rises from the Sea," *New Republic,* 25 December 1929, 137, quoted in Shanks, "Historical and Critical Study," 35–40.

57. Mencken, "Two Enterprising Ladies," 506–8.

58. Budlong, "Aimee Semple McPherson," 737; McWilliams, *Southern California Country,* 260; *Los Angeles: A Guide to the City and Its Environs,* 2d ed. (New York: Hastings House, 1951), 72.

59. Hood, "New Old-Time Religion," 68.

60. McWilliams, *Southern California Country,* 263; Anderson, in his *Vision of the Disinherited,* observes that Aimee Semple McPherson's constituency changed over time. Between 1917 and 1919 she frequently preached to field workers both black and white in integrated Florida

tent meetings and to working-class laborers in Los Angeles and West Virginia. When she later limited the distinctly charismatic Pentecostal aspects of her work to "tarrying places" and back rooms, she was more successful among the middle classes. For example, "Once established in Los Angeles, her following was drawn more from the lower middle classes of rural white migrants than from those humbler classes who frequented the smaller Pentecostal missions of the city" (25). See also McPherson, *This Is That,* 169–84, 219–39, 324–48.

61. Quoted in McLoughlin, "Aimee Semple McPherson," 208.

62. Bliven, "Sister Aimee," 289.

63. Hood, "New Old-Time Religion," 86–87; Wacker, "Travail of a Broken Family."

64. Anderson, *Vision of the Disinherited,* 7.

65. McLoughlin, "Aimee Semple McPherson," 207.

66. My argument here agrees with that made for late-twentieth-century televangelism by Alexander, "Televangelism." On fundamentalist criticism of Sister Aimee's fashionable appearance, see, for example, Rice, *Bobbed Hair, Bossy Wives, and Women Preachers.*

67. "Evangelistic Campaign Aids," collection 103, BGCA.

CHAPTER FOUR

1. Charles Fuller to Harold Ockenga, 30 January 1963, OIGC.

2. Smith, *Voice for God,* 39.

3. Fuller, *Give the Winds a Mighty Voice,* 10–20; Smith, *Voice for God,* 33–50.

4. Quoted in Smith, *Voice for God,* 46.

5. Fuller, *Give the Winds a Mighty Voice,* 20–26.

6. Ibid., 30–32. The text that both Grace and Charles found so convincing was *The Mysteries of the Kingdom of Heaven,* written by F. W. Grant, a Plymouth Brethren teacher; it was lent by Mrs. Barnhill. See Smith, *Voice for God,* 75–78.

7. Fuller, *Give the Winds a Mighty Voice,* 33–34. Charles himself wrongly recalled the year as 1917 in a letter to Paul Rader's family; Charles E. Fuller to Mrs. Lyell Rader, 2 February 1961, collection 38, box 1, folder 14, BGCA.

8. Fuller, *Give the Winds a Mighty Voice,* 33–34.

9. *Placentia Courier* quoted in ibid., 35–38, 51–59; Smith, *Voice for God,* 89–91.

10. Fuller, *Give the Winds a Mighty Voice,* 17–18.

11. Ibid., 75. The tabernacle's founder, E. Howard Cadle, was a successful businessman who had built the ten-thousand-seat arena in Indianapolis in the early 1920s. He was bankrupt by the late 1920s, and the tabernacle was available for rent by other groups, such as the Defenders conference. In 1931, Cadle would stage a dramatic comeback, and

through his own radio ministry on the "superpower" 500,000-watt Cincinnati station WLW and his aggressive business marketing he made himself a rich man. Cadle, like Fuller, made big business out of fundamentalist radio; but there is no evidence the two men knew each other or imitated each other's styles. See "Cash and Cadle," 39; "Cadle of Indianapolis Streamlines Evangelism," 73–77; and Ted Slutz, "Selling Christ: E. Howard Cadle's Big Business for God," unpublished paper, 1995, in author's possession.

12. There is some question over the date of this fateful decision in the Pullman car. Daniel P. Fuller attaches it to the Cadle conference in 1929 (*Give the Winds a Mighty Voice*, 74–75); Wilbur Smith gives the meeting's date as 1927 (*Voice for God*, 117), as does J. Elwin Wright (*Old Fashioned Revival Hour*, 84).

13. Fuller, *Give the Winds a Mighty Voice*, 77–79; Smith, *Voice for God*, 118; and Wright, *Old Fashioned Revival Hour*, 86, set the date of initial KREG broadcasting from Calvary in February 1928, rather than February 1930, although both sources provide identical quotes from the local newspaper in Fullerton. Fuller seems to have been interested in assigning as early a date as possible to his broadcasting debut in order to be able to claim that the *Old Fashioned Revival Hour* was the longest-running religious radio broadcast. Smith and Wright, close friends of Charles's and authors of worshipful hagiographies written in years when anything written about the Fullers was calculated to elicit donations, may have taken Fuller's word on the start of Calvary broadcasts. Daniel P. Fuller, writing after his father's death and with, I surmise, more complete access to sources, sets the date later.

14. Fuller, *Give the Winds a Mighty Voice*, 79–80.

15. Ibid., 81.

16. Ibid., 83.

17. Ibid., 85–86.

18. Ibid., 90–93, 96.

19. Ibid., 99.

20. Ibid., 104.

21. *HTH*, November (?) 1933, quoted in ibid., 101. Charles seems to have deferred to Grace on correspondence in general; he penned brief messages for the *HTH* mailings, but they were written by Grace, who used "we" to refer to herself and Charles together. In their private correspondence, Grace frequently took Charles's dictation and wrote letters for him to his colleagues. Examples are letters such as the ones from Charles/Grace to Harold Ockenga, dated 5 April 1947 and 23 May 1947, OIGC.

22. Wright, *Old Fashioned Revival Hour*, 25; the entire collection may be found in the David du Plessis Archive at Fuller Theological Seminary, Pasadena, Calif.

23. Charles Fuller recounted that by the fall of 1935 he had received "palatial home letters written on monogrammed note paper, and [a letter] from the miner's cabin written on a smudgy piece of a paper bag," and had heard "from black and white, from doctors and lawyers, laundresses and laborers, from sick beds in hospitals, sanitoriums, asylums, from ships on the sea, from the floor of the Grand Canyon, from lonely sheep herders on the Canadian plains, from beacon light keepers, from the Bible Institute boys who pick up our program while spinning along in their car on the Florida highways . . . from prisoners in San Quentin, from families snowbound during the long winters of the North, from lonely prairie farm homes, and many other places." Quoted in Fuller, *Give the Winds a Mighty Voice,* 110.

24. Wright, *Old Fashioned Revival Hour,* 88; Fuller, *Give the Winds a Mighty Voice,* 146, 158.

25. Fuller, *Give the Winds a Mighty Voice,* 113.

26. See Chapter 1.

27. Fuller, *Give the Winds a Mighty Voice,* 115; emphasis in Charles Fuller's original.

28. Ibid., 116.

29. Ibid., 122–23.

30. *HTH,* October 1937, quoted in ibid., 123–24.

31. Quoted in Fuller, *Give the Winds a Mighty Voice,* 125.

32. Quotation from ibid., 127.

33. Ibid., 129, 131.

34. Charles G. Trumbull, "The Miracle Gospel Broadcast of America," *Sunday School Times,* 22 October 1938; reprinted as a tract by the Gospel Broadcasting Association, FTS; Fuller, *Give the Winds a Mighty Voice,* 136.

35. Trumbull, "Miracle Gospel Broadcast of America," 15.

36. "WCTT Carries 'Revival Hour' Each Sunday," *Corbin (Kentucky) Daily Tribune,* 30 December 1953, 5, reprinted in the *Chattanooga News–Free Press,* 2 January 1954.

37. Smith, *Voice for God,* 138–39.

38. Message delivered in September 1948 or 1949, quoted in ibid., 211.

39. Fuller, *Give the Winds a Mighty Voice,* 127.

40. "Big Churches Learn Radio 'Savvy,'" 74.

41. Quoted in Wright, *Old Fashioned Revival Hour,* 241.

42. Boyer, *When Time Shall Be No More,* 90–112; Ahlstrom, *Religious History of the American People,* 808–12; Marsden, *Reforming Fundamentalism;* Sandeen, *Roots of Fundamentalism.*

43. Marsden, *Reforming Fundamentalism,* 38–39; Harold Ockenga to Charles Fuller, 12 March 1947, OIGC.

44. Marsden, *Reforming Fundamentalism.*

45. Charles Fuller, "The First Resurrection—Three Stages," radio notes for 10 April 1955, collection 100, box 1, folder 8, BGCA.

46. Charles Fuller to Harold Ockenga, 20 December 1956, OIGC.

47. Harold Ockenga to Charles Fuller, 29 March 1960, OIGC.

48. Marsden, *Reforming Fundamentalism,* 162–66, 189–91, 200–202; see also Weber, *Living in the Shadow of the Second Coming,* and Stone, *Guide to the End of the World.*

49. In Marsden, *Reforming Fundamentalism,* 222–23.

50. See, for example, the glowing praise in "Old Fashioned Revival Hour Has Carved Its Niche in U.S.," *Dodge City (Kans.) Daily Globe,* 2 January 1954: "The secret of Dr. Fuller's ministry is said to be his unusual ability for those of his listeners who are already saved[,] together with an evangelistic message to the unsaved. His delivery is devoid of any attempt at dramatic projection or any of the usual theatrical histrionics sometimes employed by evangelists. This simplicity and sincerity provide the combination which conclusively shows any analyst the secret of Dr. Fuller's success is that the people believe him and trust him to give them a spiritual 'feast' each Sunday. This trust is an accolade that has been shown only to very few ministers in the past century."

51. Mr. and Mrs. T. J. Drayton to Brother and Sister Fuller, 3 April 1936, FTS.

52. Trumbull, "Miracle Gospel Broadcast of America," 9.

53. Mr. and Mrs. Joseph Penicaro to Dr. Fuller, n.d. (in Letters 1963), FTS.

54. Rev. Thomas E. Howse to Dr. and Mrs. Fuller, 17 July 1954, FTS.

55. L. C. Winkler to Brother Fuller, 13 April 1942, FTS.

56. Wright, *Old Fashioned Revival Hour,* 21–22.

57. Publicity material for "Revival Hour Night," BGCA 20-33-27.

58. "Wife, Mother, Soulwinner," *Christian Herald and Signs of Our Times,* 10 January 1953.

59. Leibman, *Living Room Lectures,* 174–75, 198–207; Taylor, *Prime-Time Families,* chap. 2; May, *Homeward Bound;* Hudnut-Beumler, *Looking for God in the Suburbs.*

60. Charles Fuller to Harold Ockenga, 14 April 1947, OIGC.

61. Goff, "We Have Heard the Joyful Sound"; also Fuller, *Give the Winds a Mighty Voice,* 142–44, 167.

62. *HTH,* June 1942, quoted in Fuller, *Give the Winds a Mighty Voice,* 145.

63. Fuller, *Give the Winds a Mighty Voice,* 141, 149.

64. Grace Fuller to Harold Ockenga, 15 April 1948, OIGC.

65. Charles Fuller to Harold Ockenga, 2 June 1948, OIGC.

66. *HTH,* June 1948, 4.

67. Grace Fuller to Harold Ockenga, 1 October 1953, OIGC.

68. *HTH,* December 1963.

69. Since I've already alluded to the *Pilgrim Hour,* about whose audience less is known and which was not promoted as widely (or cost as

much for airtime) as the *Old Fashioned Revival Hour,* I am focusing in this section only on the latter.

70. Grace Fuller to Harold Ockenga, 23 January 1947, OIGC.

71. "Big Churches Learn Radio 'Savvy,'" 74.

72. Erickson, *Religious Radio and Television,* 83.

73. In a 1962 lecture to Fuller Theological Seminary evangelism class, quoted in Fuller, *Give the Winds a Mighty Voice,* 46–47.

74. Scrapbooks sampled were those for 1945–54 and 1950–52, compiled by Dispatch Photo News Service, New York City, in FTS. States for which there were no scrapbook clippings were Connecticut, Delaware, District of Columbia, Georgia, Hawaii, Maine, Maryland, New Hampshire, New Jersey, New Mexico, Rhode Island, Utah, Vermont, West Virginia, and Wyoming. This does not necessarily mean the *Old Fashioned Revival Hour* was not listed or mentioned in newspapers in these states.

75. Parker, Barry, and Smythe, *Television-Radio Audience and Religion,* 207–10, 220, 356–62.

76. Radio Log celebrating thirty-eight years on the radio (ca. 1963), mailed with undated letter addressed "For You, a Friend of the Gospel," BGCA 100, folder 1–4.

77. Wright, *Old Fashioned Revival Hour;* Smith, *Voice for God.*

78. Fuller, *Heavenly Sunshine.* Any conclusions about audience demographics drawn from the collection of letters available today must be qualified; there is simply no way to be systematic about knowing which letters were preserved and which were discarded. There may be a bias toward what the staff, or the Fullers themselves, thought (or hoped) the audience looked like. On the other hand, the letters could be fairly representative of the kinds of letters they were getting (including some hostile mail). There is no evidence the Fullers developed any explicit policy about which letters were saved; absent such a policy, I tend to believe that what was winnowed out over several decades would approximate a fair sample of letters received; my conclusions below reflect this assumption.

79. For example, "A Lonely Serviceman Palmer" (Tucson, Ariz.) to the Fullers, n.d.; William Emery (Salem, Oreg.) to Rev. Chas E. Fuller and Mrs. Fuller, 5 January 1936; Wesley Kosin (pastor of Au Sable Grove Presbyterian in Yorkville, Ill.) to Brother Fuller, 21 October 1937; E. Eagle (Harlan, Ky.) to Rev. Chas E. Fuller, 9 January 1939; Gordon Gunderson to the Fullers, 8 March 1952, FTS.

80. Mrs. O. A. Slack to Brother Fuller and Honey, 23 January 1955, FTS.

81. Beverley Ruth McNalley (Joyce, Wash.) to Reveran [*sic*] Fuller, 15 March 1936, FTS.

82. F. J. Funk to Mr. Charles E. Fuller, 27 August 1950, FTS.

83. Unsigned to Mr. and Mrs. Fuller, 12 May 1942, FTS. See also the

letter from a twenty-six-year-old unnamed Grundy Center, Iowa, farmer mentioning his prosperous farm, which was edited for broadcast and read on the air by Grace Fuller on 20 February 1949 (program #595FD, audiotape copy from sixteen-inch transcription disk, personal collection of Daniel P. Fuller, courtesy of Read G. Burgan and Christian Heritage Media, Long Beach, Calif.).

84. Martha Abrell to the Fullers, 22 August 1957, FTS.

85. Unsigned to the Fullers, 15 September 1954; Jessie Innvers to Mrs. Fuller and family, 9 November 1937; Helen Hunt to Dr. Fuller, 20 December 1937, FTS.

86. Fuller, *Heavenly Sunshine,* 61–62.

87. Ibid., 53–55.

88. Boston letter in "1955 August–December" folder, FTS; Fuller, *Heavenly Sunshine,* 36; Mrs. Otto Nelson to Sister and Brother Fuller, 4 November 1935, FTS.

89. In "Letters 1942 June–December" folder, FTS.

90. For example, a navy ensign's letter: "Even tho they don't write, you can count on a good million service men and former service men who can testify that 'The Old Fashioned Revival Hour' means more to them than any other program on the air," Burke Combs to Dr. and Mrs. Fuller, n.d. (1954), FTS. Philip K. Goff has written about correspondence from soldiers in "We Have Heard the Joyful Sound" and "'Mothers, Write Your Boys "Over There" to Be Listening!': Charles Fuller's Radio Ministry and the American Military, 1940–1955," unpublished paper, 1996. This research is part of Goff's forthcoming biography of Fuller, *Heavenly Sunshine: Charles Fuller and the Southern California Roots of Twentieth-Century Evangelicalism.*

91. In "1953 Letters-March" folder, FTS.

92. Charles Fuller to Harold Ockenga, 4 August 1955, OIGC; Fuller, *Heavenly Sunshine,* 110–14.

93. Mrs. Awald Baumann to the Fullers, 7 June 1942, FTS.

94. Mrs. O. A. Slack to Brother Fuller and Honey, 23 January 1955, FTS.

95. Ruth Shafer to Friends at the Hour, 9 February 1963, FTS.

96. Ms. O. Presson to Dr. Fuller, 9 October 1950, FTS.

97. Orsi, *Thank You St. Jude.*

98. Quotation from *HTH,* June 1951. Surviving letters show that the staff penciled on each letter the amount of money enclosed, if any, and marked letters "Read" if they wanted Grace to read them. Of the ones Grace read, Charles probably himself read even a smaller subgroup; and a still smaller number of letters were chosen by Grace for the weekly readings on the air. In the papers of the *Old Fashioned Revival Hour* are some five hundred letters dating from 1935 to 1968. Most, though not all, of the letters now extant were marked "Read" by a staff member. Some

have Grace's notations: "Save" or "Keep for files." The collection is more complete for the late 1940s and early 1950s.

99. "Big Churches Learn Radio 'Savvy,'" 74. Fuller paid $929,698 for his airtime on Mutual in 1942; P. R. Rieber, "Religion for Sale at a Profit," *Magazine Digest,* December 1943, reprint in BNM 303.2-1-8.

100. Fuller, *Give the Winds a Mighty Voice,* 158–59; Smith, *Voice for God,* 135.

101. See the scrapbooks for this period in FTS.

102. Fuller, *Give the Winds a Mighty Voice,* 162.

103. Ibid., 162–63; also the film "How Firm a Foundation" (Missions Visualized, 1953), FTS.

104. The booklets and the album cover are in FTS.

105. The twenty episodes—kinescopes transferred to videotape—are in FTS.

106. Charles Fuller to Harold Ockenga, 18 April 1946, OIGC.

107. Smith, *Voice for God,* 157, 184–99. The story of Fuller Theological Seminary is well told in Marsden, *Reforming Fundamentalism.*

108. Marsden, *Reforming Fundamentalism,* 26, 56, 88.

109. Charles Fuller to Harold Ockenga, 2 August 1947, OIGC.

110. Charles Fuller to Harold Ockenga, 8 September 1947, 2, OIGC.

111. Marsden, *Reforming Fundamentalism,* 66, 98–116, 227; Grace Fuller to Harold Ockenga, 12 March 1959, OIGC.

112. Charles Fuller to Harold Ockenga, 20 December 1949, OIGC.

113. Charles Fuller to Harold Ockenga, 17 November 1949; Charles Fuller to Harold Ockenga, 13 January 1950, OIGC.

114. Fuller, *Give the Winds a Mighty Voice,* 184–85.

115. Ruth A. MacPherson to Dr. Charles E. Fuller, 3 September 1958; Martha Abrell to the Fullers, 22 August 1957; Ray L. Parker to Rev. Charles Fuller, 3 May 1965, all in FTS.

116. Harold and Sadie Lucy to "Dear Friends," 14 January 1960, FTS.

117. Fuller, *Give the Winds a Mighty Voice,* 236.

118. Charles Fuller to Harold Ockenga, 9 November 1967, OIGC.

119. Erickson, *Religious Radio and Television,* 84.

120. Smith, *Voice for God,* 222.

121. *HTH,* April 1949.

CHAPTER FIVE

1. "William Ward Ayer, Pioneer Gospel Broadcaster," *St. Petersburg Times,* 19 November 1985; "Memorial Service" for William Ward Ayer, Fifth Avenue Baptist Church, St. Petersburg, Florida; "Background and Information on Radio Ministry of William Ward Ayer, compiled by Barbara S. Ayer," all in NRB files; see also Larson, *God's Man in Manhattan.*

2. Ayer, "Will Americans Be Allowed to Broadcast the Gospel?" 3, 5.

3. Ibid., 6–8.

4. Sterling and Kittross, *Stay Tuned,* 656; see also Rose, *National Policy for Radio Broadcasting,* 123–39.

5. For example, Kirby, *Rural Worlds Lost;* Jackson, *Crabgrass Frontier.*

6. Jones, *Dispossessed;* Morgan, *Rising in the West.*

7. Carpenter, *Revive Us Again;* Stone, *On the Boundaries of American Evangelicalism.*

8. "How Radio Measures Its Audiences: Four Discussions by Research Authorities, 1939," reprinted by the Columbia Broadcasting System, Ohio State University Archives, Institute for Education by Radio/TV Collection, RG 8/d–8/3.

9. See, for example, Summers, "Iowa Rural Radio Listener," 12–14, 19, 35; Summers, "Kansas Radio Listener," 12–15; and Summers and Whan, "Study of Radio Listening Habits," 46–47.

10. Ammerman, *Bible Believers,* 99.

11. For example, Stone, *On the Boundaries of American Evangelicalism,* 75–78, 110–16.

12. See ibid.; Ellwood, *Fifties Spiritual Marketplace;* Gilbert, *Redeeming Culture.*

13. "Information about the American Council of Christian Churches," NCC 17-6-2.

14. Martin, *With God on Our Side,* 22; Marsden, "Preachers of Paradox," 154–55.

15. McIntire, *Twentieth Century Reformation,* 24.

16. "Evangelical Action!," 5–8.

17. Carpenter, *Revive Us Again,* 154.

18. Schneider, "Voice of Many Waters," 111; Carpenter, *Revive Us Again,* 152.

19. Van Kirk, "Duty of Religious Radio in Time of War."

20. Johnson, "Intolerance by Radio."

21. Minsky, "Religious Broadcasts."

22. Wright, "Radio Problems Reviewed," 1.

23. Minsky, "Religious Broadcasts."

24. Ibid.; Wright, "Radio Problems Reviewed," 1.

25. "Evangelical Action!," 120–24.

26. Murch, *Cooperation without Compromise,* 75.

27. "Evangelical Action!," 125.

28. "United We Stand," 37.

29. Crowe, "Religion on the Air," 974; "Big Churches Learn Radio 'Savvy,'" 74–76.

30. Crowe, "Religion on the Air," 973–75.

31. "New Organization in Religious Radio," 14.

32. The JRRC was composed of radio representatives from Congregational Christian, Evangelical Reformed, Methodist, Presbyterian (U.S.A.), and United Church of Canada denominations. The president was Ronald

Bridges, but the real powerhouse in the JRRC was the young director of communications for the Congregational Christian Church, Everett C. Parker, who would later become the chairman of the Protestant Radio Commission and be a vocal exponent of greater liberal Protestant involvement in the mass media in the fifties. In 1946, he had even called for a new radio department in the Federal Council for those who differed with the major denominations that ran the radio program, bringing "out into the open a major Protestant radio controversy"; "Criticize Council's Suppression Policy," 11.

33. "Protestant Radio Commission," report of third meeting, 17 March 1948, NCC 18-17-14.

34. Unsigned letter to "Norman," 4 January 1949, NCC 18-17-14.

35. "Move toward FCCCA Super Radio Control," 14.

36. "Big Churches Learn Radio 'Savvy,'" 74–76.

37. Ibid.

38. Gasper, *Fundamentalist Movement,* 82.

39. Glenn Tingley, in *Waves of Truth,* Fiftieth Anniversary Edition, 1930–80, 1980, 11, NRB.

40. "Myron F. Boyd, in Memoriam," *Light and Life Hour Transmitter,* September–October 1978, 2, NRB.

41. Bret Senft, "Ferrin: Man of the 'Golden Days,'" *NRB Convention Daily,* 28 January 1981, NRB.

42. William Simbro, "Leaming's Half-Century in Pentecostal Ministry," *Des Moines Tribune,* 30 June 1979; "Pastor Charles M. Leaming Presents 'Waves of Truth' Broadcasts Continuously since January 26, 1947," *Waves of Truth,* Fiftieth Anniversary Edition, 1930–80, 1980, 5; Charles M. Leaming, "Go Ye into All the World, and Preach the Gospel," *Waves of Truth,* Spring 1978, 2–3; Dr. W. T. Watson, "Faith Temple Founder's Day Rally, 17 September 1978," *Waves of Truth,* Holiday Edition, 1978–79, 4; "Leaming Sets New Traditions While Continuing the Old," *Religious Broadcasting,* April–May 1979, A7; Charles M. Leaming, "Fifty Years of Radio Ministry . . . across the Airways," *Waves of Truth,* Fiftieth Anniversary Edition, 1930–80, 1980, 14, NRB.

43. Early chairmen of the NRB were William Ward Ayer (1944–45), Clinton Churchill (1945–47), Theodore Elsner (1948–52), Myron Boyd (1952–54), Thomas Zimmerman (1954–56), James DeForest Murch (1956–57), and Eugene Bertermann (1957–75); dates from 1950 to 1954 are not certain.

44. Signed, William Ward Ayer, David J. Fant, and Dale Crowley, "Certificate of Incorporation," 18 December 1944, NRB.

45. *National Religious Broadcasters: Constitution and By-laws with Statement of Faith and Code of Ethics* (Buffalo, N.Y.: Office of the President, National Religious Broadcasters, 1945); William Ward Ayer, "Pioneer Gospel Broadcaster," *St. Petersburg Times,* 19 November 1985;

"Memorial Service" for William Ward Ayer, Fifth Ave. Baptist Church, St. Petersburg, Florida; "Background and Information on Radio Ministry of William Ward Ayer, compiled by Barbara S. Ayer," all in NRB; see also Larson, *God's Man in Manhattan.*

46. Gasper, *Fundamentalist Movement,* 82–83.

47. *National Religious Broadcasters: Constitution and By-laws,* 3–8.

48. Murch, *Cooperation without Compromise,* 73–81.

49. Murch, *Adventuring for Christ in Changing Times,* 177.

50. Murch, *Cooperation without Compromise,* 73–81.

51. Ibid.

52. Wright, *Death in the Pot,* 4, 34–41.

53. Ibid., 42, 22.

54. Winrod, *Persecuted Preachers,* 6–7.

55. Samuel McCrea Cavert, "Information about the American Council of Churches," n.d., NCC 17-6-2.

56. "What Is This American Council?," n.d., NCC 17-6-2.

57. Letter of William Barrow Pugh to Frank Goodman, 12 February 1943, BNM 303.2-1-8.

58. "Federal Court Upholds Radio Station," 26; Moser and Lavine, *Radio and the Law,* 118.

59. Frank Goodman (unsigned) to Phillips Carlin, 15 February 1943, BNM 303.2-1-8.

60. Ted Savage to William Barrow Pugh, 2 December 1943, BNM 303.2-1-8. To look ahead a bit, the council was still fighting McIntire's radio programming in 1960, drawing up sample letters threatening legal action against radio stations (primarily in the South) airing his *Twentieth Century Reformation* program and monitoring the show's content from week to week; memo from Carl Cannon to James Wine, "Subject: McIntire programs," 3 March 1960; letter of Charles Brackbill to James Wine, 11 March 1960; memo of S. Franklin Mack to Roy G. Ross, 7 April 1960; and undated letter drafts, NCC 17-7-8.

61. Parker was the director of the Religious Broadcasters Association, formed in 1946, and had long been the director of communication for the Congregational Christian Church and the head of the Joint Religious Radio Committee. He and Frank Goodman, a Presbyterian active in Federal Council radio circles, differed in their approach to radio. Parker, the younger of the two, was pushing the Federal Council to give more money and attention to innovative radio programs, especially drama, in an attempt to expand their share of the religious audience. See "Religious Showmanship Feud." On Parker's complaint, see Parker, "Big Business in Religious Radio," 20–23.

62. Parker and Eastman, "Religion on the Air in Chicago," 21.

63. P. R. Rieber, "Religion for Sale at a Profit," *Magazine Digest,* December 1943, reprint in BNM 303.2-1-8.

64. Crowe, "Religion on the Air," 973–75.

65. Rieber, "Religion for Sale at a Profit."

66. Murch, *Cooperation without Compromise,* 80; Gasper, *Fundamentalist Movement,* 77; Even into the 1970s, a weekly fifteen-minute time slot on a low-power station cost $200 or as much as $600 on a super-powered station; Martin, "God-Hucksters of Radio." In 1979, collectively ministers spent an estimated $100 million to purchase airtime on both radio and television; Hill, *Airwaves to the Soul,* 85.

67. Bill Newland to Dr. Fuller, 13 September 1954, FTS.

68. Martin, "God-Hucksters of Radio."

69. Fund-raising letter, circa 1949, BGCA 20-33-20.

70. Charles and Grace Fuller, *HTH,* June 1951, 4, FTS.

71. Letter from Anderson, South Carolina, dated circa October–December 1949, FTS.

72. "Echoes from Our Radio Audience," 6.

73. L. C. Winkler to Brother Fuller, 13 April 1942, FTS.

74. Horace Ricks to Brother Fuller, 12 June 1950, FTS.

75. Clyde Huntzbery to "Fellow-Christians," 18 July 1954, FTS.

76. Ivan and Carolyn Lamb to Rev. Fuller, 1 October 1953, FTS.

77. Hunt, "Church Big Biz for Radio."

78. "National Religious Radio, Annual Report, 1945," Federal Council of the Churches of Christ in America, 1, NCC 18-17-25.

79. Young, "Gospel Broadcasters and Frequency Modulation," 6.

80. Ibid.; Gasper, *Fundamentalist Movement,* 83.

81. "American Council to Broadcast on American Broadcasting Network"; "Memorandum on Policies of Religious Radio," 2 April 1947, NCC 18-18-1.

82. *United Evangelical Action,* 1 May 1948, 5; "Memorandum on Policies of Religious Radio," 2 April 1947, NCC 18-18-1.

83. The ruling would, thought a *United Evangelical Action* writer, have "an important bearing on the whole question of free speech on the air especially as it affects the right of church, temperance, and civic groups to secure equal and adequate time for patriotic, moral and religious purposes. . . . While the cases are not quite similar, the way is also open for National Religious Broadcasters, Inc., to institute proceedings demanding equal rights for true-to-the-Bible broadcasts to match the time being given to 'liberals.'" Blackmore, "American Business Men's Research Foundation Wins a Radio Victory," 7.

84. Arms, "Freedom of Religion on the Air," 5.

85. "Adverse Radio Decision."

86. "Christian Business Men's Magazine Discusses Radio," 6.

87. "Minneapolis Pastors Protesting Radio Ban."

88. What a fascinating image: a protest of that size—presumably all white people?—over radio programs, in the same region where two de-

cades later civil rights marchers would find stubborn opposition to their street protests.

89. Excerpt from *Against the Gates of Hell: The Story of Glenn V. Tingley as Told to Judith Adams* (Harrisburg, Pa.: Christian Publications, 1977), reprinted in *NRB Convention Daily,* 22 January 1980, 15–18, NRB.

90. "Tabernacle Fights for Its Broadcasting Rights."

91. Boris, "When WKBW Came Home."

92. Young, "Gospel Broadcasters and Frequency Modulation."

93. "New Bills Revise Radio Act Sharply."

94. "Witnesses Score White's Radio Bill"; "White Asks Shelving for His Radio Bill."

95. "Mr. Bennet's Brief Presented to Senate Committee."

96. Mallon, "Radio Editorials Opposed by the CIO."

97. "Mr. McIntire's Testimony before the Senate Committee."

98. "Radio 'Soap Opera' Defended as Boon."

99. "Hearing on Senate Bill."

100. "Cavert's Radio Letter, an Editorial."

101. "'Editorializing' Is New Radio Issue."

102. Crowley served as the NRB's founding secretary and was, as seen in newsletters from the early 1970s on file with the NRB, a highly anti-Semitic dispensationalist. Source: NRB personnel files.

103. "Crowley Makes a Plea for Gospel Broadcasts."

104. Bertermann, "Plea for More Time for Gospel Broadcasts."

105. James Pearson to Federal Council of Churches, 4 October 1947, NCC 18-18-1.

106. Loevinger, "Religious Liberty and Broadcasting," 649.

107. "Memorandum Opinion and Order, before the Federal Communications Commission, In re Petition of Robert Harold Scott for Revocation of Licenses of Radio Stations KQW, KPO and KFRC," 19 July 1946, 2, NCC 18-18-1.

108. For example, "Radio Programs" listings in the *Palo Alto Times,* 7 February to 10 March 1945; *San Francisco Chronicle,* March 1945; and *San Jose Mercury News* and *Herald,* November 1946.

109. "Memorandum Opinion and Order, before the Federal Communications Commission, In re Petition of Robert Harold Scott," 1.

110. "FCC Upholds Atheists' Rights to Time on Air," 97; Salmond, "Clifford Judkins Durr."

111. "Memorandum Opinion and Order, Before the Federal Communications Commission, In re Petition of Robert Harold Scott," 4–5; Edelman, *The Licensing of Radio Services,* 87.

112. "FCC Upholds Atheists' Rights to Time on Air," 4.

113. Memorandum, F. Ernest Johnson to Dr. Barnes, 24 July 1946, NCC 18-17-25.

114. "Air for Atheists," 58; "Free Air for Atheists," 70.

115. Wright, "Radio Freedom of Speech."

116. "Time for Atheism"; "Air Time for Atheism."

117. "Atheist to Sue for Radio Time?"

118. Roger M. Baldwin to Samuel McCrea Cavert, 7 January 1947, NCC 18-18-1.

119. "Radio and Television."

120. Loevinger, "Religious Liberty and Broadcasting," 649–50.

121. Ibid., 651.

122. Whitfield, *Culture of the Cold War,* 88.

123. "FCC Says Stations May Deny Time to Atheists."

124. "Atheists Get Inquiry."

125. "Clarify Stand on Atheist Programs, FCC Petitioned," Edward J. Heffron, Religious Radio Association, for release August 4, 1948; Everett C. Parker to FCC chairman Wayne Coy, 31 August 1948, both in BNM 303.2-11-64.

126. "FCC Likened to 'Thought Police.'"

127. "Investigation of Port Huron Decision," 3.

128. "FCC Likened to 'Thought Police.'"

129. Rosel H. Hyde, "Statement of Commissioner Rosel H. Hyde," 1 September 1948, BNM 303.2-11-64.

130. "Investigation of Port Huron Decision," 2–5.

131. Wayne Coy, "Personal Statement of Wayne Coy, Chairman, FCC," for release 19 September 1948, BNM 303.2-11-64. For Protestant responses to the hearing, see "FCC Says Stations May Deny Time to Atheists"; C. T. Griswold to the members of the Protestant Radio Commission, 8 October 1948, NCC 18-17-14; "The Scott Decision: From the Minutes of the Protestant Radio Commission, meeting in New York City, October 14, 1948"; F. Eppling Reinhartz to Clayton T. Griswold, 28 October 1948; Gustav K. Brandborg to Clayton T. Griswold, 1 December 1948; and Joseph E. Boyle to Clayton T. Griswold, 16 December 1948, all in BNM 303.2-11-64.

132. "Atheist Air Plea Fails"; "Pastor Invites P. A. Atheist to Hear Answer to Broadcast."

133. Letter of Willard Johnson to Samuel McCrea Cavert, 20 October 1947, NCC 18-18-1.

134. "New NAB Code Bars Attacks on Religion"; "NAB Adopts Religious Broadcasting Standards."

135. McIntire, "Radio's New Code."

136. Letter of Willard Johnson to Samuel McCrea Cavert, 20 October 1947, NCC 18-18-1.

137. Letter of Willard Johnson to Samuel McCrea Cavert, 11 November 1947, NCC 18-18-1.

CHAPTER SIX

1. "National Religious Broadcasters, Annual Report, September 1947," 7, 9, NRB.

2. Carpenter, *Revive Us Again,* 212.

3. Wuthnow, *Restructuring of American Religion,* 176.

4. Martin, *With God on Our Side,* 26.

5. McLoughlin, *Revivals, Awakenings, and Reform,* 186–90.

6. Martin, *With God on Our Side,* 24.

7. Graham, *Just As I Am,* 144.

8. Martin, *With God on Our Side,* 9–11.

9. Ellwood, *Fifties Spiritual Marketplace,* 49; Carpenter, *Early Billy Graham,* 31, 43.

10. Ellwood, *Fifties Spiritual Marketplace,* 48–49.

11. Carpenter, *Early Billy Graham,* 131, 81.

12. Carpenter, *Revive Us Again,* 217; Graham, *Just As I Am,* 176.

13. Ward, *Air of Salvation,* 78–82.

14. The Walter F. Bennett Advertising Agency had also promoted the *Lutheran Hour* and other evangelical radio programs; ibid., 78–81.

15. Graham, *Just As I Am,* 176–77. *Hour of Decision* was also heard on NBC radio, an exception to the network's policy against paid religious programming that was a result of an unplanned meeting of Graham and NBC president David Sarnoff in Hawaii in 1954. Two years later, NBC also aired one of the radio's longest-running Bible programs, Donald Barnhouse's *Bible Study Hour,* as a paid religious program. Gasper, *Fundamentalist Movement,* 83.

16. Graham, *Just As I Am,* 176–82.

17. Gasper, *Fundamentalist Movement,* 136.

18. Graham, *Just As I Am,* 170.

19. "Parker Says Church Won't Yield to Soaps, Cigarets for Place in the TV Sun," *Variety,* 9 August 1950, NCC 18-17-14.

20. Hudnut-Beumler, *Looking for God in the Suburbs,* 31–64; Wuthnow, *Restructuring of American Religion,* 35–37.

21. Ellwood, *Fifties Spiritual Marketplace,* 134–36; see also Harrell, *All Things Are Possible* and "People More Religious-Minded Than in 20's, Fuller Thinks," *Anderson (S.C.) Independent,* 6 January 1952, and "Dr. Fuller Says World Is More Religion-Minded," newspaper clipping from North Platte, Nebr., February 1952, both in Fuller scrapbooks, FTS.

22. The National Council, formed in December 1950, was made up of the Federal Council, the Protestant Radio Commission, and ten other organizations. With regard to radio, the merger brought together the Protestant Radio Commission and the Protestant Film Commission into a new central department, the Broadcasting and Film Commission (BFC).

23. Pratt, *Liberalization of American Protestantism,* 33.

24. Ibid., 82–83.

25. Cox, "FCC, the Constitution, and Religious Broadcast Programming," 210–11.

26. Loevinger, "Religious Liberty and Broadcasting," 657.

27. "Bold Attempt to Silence Gospel Broadcasting," *Marching Truth,* n.d. (ca. 1956), NRB files; Blackmore, "Shall the NCC Control Religious Broadcasting?"

28. "How Big Is Gospel Radio?" 24, 57, 86.

29. Gasper, *Fundamentalist Movement,* 84.

30. "Bold Attempt to Silence Gospel Broadcasting"; Blackmore, "Shall the NCC Control Religious Broadcasting?"

31. Murch, *Adventuring for Christ in Changing Times,* 180.

32. "Advisory Policy Statement on Religious Broadcasting," adopted by the Board of Managers of the BFC on 6 March 1956 and endorsed by the General Board of the National Council of Churches of Christ in the U.S.A. on 6 June 1956, NCC 16-1-15.

33. "Bold Attempt to Silence Gospel Broadcasting"; Blackmore, "Shall the NCC Control Religious Broadcasting?"

34. Confidential letter of S. Franklin Mack to "BFC colleagues," 1 February 1957, BNM 303.2-2-7; Clayton T. Griswold, "Broadcasting Policy Comments," n.d. (1956?), BNM 303.2-2-13.

35. "Louis" to Herman Morse, enclosing a draft of a letter to S. Franklin Mack, 6 February 1956, BNM 303.2-9-30.

36. Paul A. Evans to "Friends in the Presbyterian Church," n.d., BNM 303.2-2-7.

37. Peter Horsfield, *Religious Television,* 13, quoted in Voskuil, "Power of the Air," 89–90; Cox, "FCC, the Constitution, and Religious Broadcast Programming."

38. Daves, "Bible Belt Broadcasting."

39. For example, Study Commission on the Role of Radio, Television, and Films in Religion, "A Statement of Issues," n.d. (ca. 1958), NCC 16-4-14; see also "Should Religious Broadcasts Be Sponsored by Commercial Advertisers?," n.d., NCC 16-2-28.

40. "Should Religious Broadcasts Be Sponsored by Commercial Advertisers?"; Charles Brackbill to James Wine, 11 March 1960, NCC 17-7-8.

41. The statement was originally written by Clayton T. Griswold, in his article "New Methods in a Power Age."

42. In 1960 the National Council created a public relations position, the "Associate General Secretary for Interpretation," and named James W. Wine to the position; among other issues Wine considered in his first year or two in office was trying to improve mainliners' credibility with the radio industry, which seemed thoroughly tired of giving away free time. Wine, for example, spoke as Protestantism's representative before the FCC in 1960 on the subject of increased television advertising and violence on children's programming and what he called a "general slack-

ening of the will to enforce and the will to obey existing regulations." James Wine, "Federal Communications Commission, Washington D.C., Public Hearing, December 7, 1959, Statement on Behalf of NCCCUSA," 4, NCC 16-3-3. On the assessment of the Presbyterian case, see Meister, "Presbyterians and Mass Media," 178.

43. Horsfield, *Religious Television,* 13; Hadden and Shupe, *Televangelism,* 50–52; Lacey, "Electric Church."

44. "Radio News in Brief," *Light and Life Hour Transmitter,* September–October 1978, 5, NRB.

45. Reeves, *Empty Church,* 126; see also Wuthnow, *Struggle for America's Soul.*

46. "Parker Says Church Won't Yield to Soaps, Cigarets for Place in the TV Sun"; "Church Urged to Use TV," *New York Times,* 8 August 1950; "Urge More Religious Programs: Protestant Leader Emphasizes Force of TV Programs," *Radio Daily,* 8 August 1950, all in NCC 18-17-14.

47. Federal Communications Commission, Submission by the Communications Committee of the United States Catholic Conference and others in the matter of *Amendment of the Commission's Rules Concerning Program Definitions for Commercial Broadcast Stations, etc.* (BC Docket No. 78–355, RM-2709, 1979), table 11, cited in Horsfield, *Religious Television,* 89.

48. Martin, "Mass Communications," 1715; Schultze, "Invisible Medium"; Eskridge and Noll, *More Money, More Ministry.*

49. Maus, "Believers as Behavers."

50. Wuthnow, *Restructuring of American Religion,* 193.

51. Wright, *Death in the Pot,* 35, 52–53.

52. McGirr, *Suburban Warriors;* Kintz and Lesage, *Media, Culture, and the Religious Right;* Martin, *With God on Our Side;* Harding, *Book of Jerry Falwell;* Forbes and Mahan, *Religion and Popular Culture in America;* Apostolidis, *Stations of the Cross.*

53. Wilson, *Public Religion in American Culture,* 23–27, 97, 104, 172–75; Hoover, *Mass Media Religion,* 234.

54. Smythe, "Meaning of the Communications Revolution."

55. Hudnut-Beumler, *Looking for God in the Suburbs,* 83.

56. Timothy A. Turner, *Preaching to Programmed People,* advertised in *Gospel Publishing House Catalog* (Springfield, Mo.: Gospel Publishing House, 1998), 58.

57. Tomaselli and Shepperson, "Resistance through Mediated Orality," 221.

58. Alexander, "Televangelism" and *Televangelism Reconsidered.*

59. Hoover, *Mass Media Religion,* 243.

60. "Fifty Years," 11.

Bibliography

ARCHIVES
Columbus, Ohio
　　Institute for Education by Radio/TV Collection, Ohio State
　　University Archive
Hamilton, Massachusetts
　　Collection of the Ockenga Institute, Gordon-Conwell Theological
　　Seminary
Manassas, Virginia
　　Collection of the National Religious Broadcasters
Pasadena, California
　　Charles and Grace Fuller Collection, David du Plessis Archive, Fuller
　　Theological Seminary
Philadelphia, Pennsylvania
　　Presbyterian Church (U.S.A.) Department of History
　　　　Board of National Missions, General Department of Mission,
　　　　Interpretation and Mass Communication/Mass Media,
　　　　Department/Division of Radio and Television/Mass Media,
　　　　Records 1926–1971 (Record Group 303.2)
　　　　Records of the National Council of Churches and Federal Council
　　　　of Churches
Suitland, Maryland
　　Federal Radio Commission Records, Federal Records Center
Wheaton, Illinois
　　Archives of the Billy Graham Center, Wheaton College

BOOKS, ARTICLES, DISSERTATIONS, AND THESES
Adair, James R. *M. R. De Haan: The Man and His Ministry.* Grand
　　Rapids, Mich.: Zondervan, 1969.
"Adverse Radio Decision." *Christian Beacon,* 18 October 1945, 1, 8.
Ahlstrom, Sydney E. *A Religious History of the American People.* New
　　Haven: Yale University Press, 1972.
"Aimee Semple McPherson: Thousands Mourn at Famed Evangelist's
　　Funeral." *Life,* 30 October 1944, 85–88.
"Air for Atheists." *Time,* 5 August 1946, 58.
"Air Time for Atheism." *Newsweek,* 2 December 1946, 71.
Alexander, Bobby C. "Televangelism: Redressive Ritual within a Larger
　　Social Drama." In *Rethinking Media, Religion, and Culture,* edited by
　　Stewart M. Hoover and Knut Lundby, 194–208. Thousand Oaks,
　　Calif.: Sage Publications, 1997.
———. *Televangelism Reconsidered: Ritual in the Search for Human
　　Community.* Atlanta: Scholars Press, 1994.

Allen, Robert C. *Channels of Discourse: Television and Contemporary Criticism.* Chapel Hill: University of North Carolina Press, 1987.

"American Council to Broadcast on American Broadcasting Network January, February, March." *Christian Beacon,* 6 December 1945, 1.

Ammerman, Nancy. *Bible Believers: Fundamentalists in a Modern World.* New Brunswick, N.J.: Rutgers University Press, 1987.

Anderson, Robert Mapes. *Vision of the Disinherited: The Making of American Pentecostalism.* New York: Oxford University Press, 1979.

Apostolidis, Paul. *Stations of the Cross: Adorno and Christian Right Radio.* Durham, N.C.: Duke University Press, 2000.

Arms, George Wells. "Freedom of Religion on the Air." *Sunday School Times,* 22 April 1945, 5.

Armstrong, Ben. *The Electric Church.* Nashville: Thomas Nelson, 1979.

"Atheist Air Plea Fails." *New York Times,* 29 October 1949, 28.

"Atheists Get Inquiry." *New York Times,* 28 August 1948, 28.

"Atheist to Sue for Radio Time?" *United Evangelical Action,* 1 April 1947, 1.

Ayer, William Ward. "Will Americans Be Allowed to Broadcast the Gospel?" *Calvary Pulpit and Monthly Messenger,* ser. 6, no. 2 (January 1944): 3–8.

Baldwin, Neil. *Henry Ford and the Jews: The Mass Production of Hate.* New York: Public Affairs, 2001.

Barnouw, Erik. *A History of Broadcasting in the United States.* Vol. 2, *A Tower in Babel.* New York: Oxford University Press, 1966.

———. *A History of Broadcasting in the United States.* Vol. 3, *The Golden Web.* New York: Oxford University Press, 1966.

Barron, Hal S. *Mixed Harvest: The Second Great Transformation in the Rural North, 1870–1930.* Studies in Rural Culture, edited by Jack Temple Kirby. Chapel Hill: University of North Carolina Press, 1997.

Beckford, James A. "'Start Together and Finish Together': Shifts in the Premises and Paradigms Underlying the Scientific Study of Religion." *Journal of the Scientific Study of Religion* 39, no. 4 (2000): 481–96.

Bendroth, Margaret Lamberts. "Fundamentalism and the Mass Media, 1930–1990." In *Religion and the Mass Media: Audiences and Adaptations,* edited by Daniel A. Stout and Judith M. Buddenbaum, 74–84. Thousand Oaks, Calif.: Sage Publications, 1996.

Bennet, James E. "Bible School Lesson: Revival under Samuel." *Christian Beacon,* 3 July 1947, 7.

Berger, Peter. *A Far Glory: The Quest for Faith in an Age of Credulity.* New York: Free Press, 1992.

———. "From the Crisis of Religion to the Crisis of Secularity." In *Religion and America: Spiritual Life in a Secular Age,* edited by Mary Douglas and Steven Tipton, 14–24. Boston: Beacon Press, 1983.

————. "A Sociological View of the Secularization of Theology." *Journal of the Scientific Study of Religion* 8, no. 1 (1967): 11–12.

Berkman, Dave. "Long before Falwell: Early Radio and Religion—As Reported by the Nation's Periodical Press." *Journal of Popular Culture* 21 (Spring 1988): 1–11.

Berman, Marshall. *All That Is Solid Melts into Air: The Experience of Modernity.* New York: Simon and Shuster, 1982.

Bertermann, Eugene R. "Plea for More Time for Gospel Broadcasts." *United Evangelical Action,* 15 August 1947, 5–6.

Biery, Ruth. "Starring Aimee Semple McPherson: The Priestess Is Going in the Talkies; Will She Some Day Tell Her Love-Life?" *Motion Picture,* April 1929, 28–29, 96–99.

"Big Churches Learn Radio 'Savvy' to Counter Revivalist Air Racket." *Newsweek,* 22 January 1945, 74.

Binion, Rudolph. *After Christianity: Christian Survivals in Post-Christian Culture.* Durango, Colo.: Logbridge-Rhodes, 1986.

Blackmore, Glenwood. "The American Business Men's Research Foundation Wins a Radio Victory of Tremendous Significance to Church and Civic Groups." *United Evangelical Action,* 15 September 1945, 7, 17.

————. "Shall the NCC Control Religious Broadcasting?" *United Evangelical Action,* 1 July 1956, 5–6.

Blau, Judith R., Kenneth C. Land, and Kent Redding. "The Expansion of Religious Affiliation: An Explanation of the Growth of Church Participation in the United States, 1850–1930." *Social Science Research* 21 (December 1992): 329–52.

Bliven, Bruce. "Sister Aimee." *New Republic,* 3 November 1926, 289–91.

Blumhofer, Edith. *Aimee Semple McPherson: Everybody's Sister.* Grand Rapids, Mich.: Eerdmans, 1993.

Boone, Kathleen. *The Bible Tells Them So: The Discourse of Protestant Fundamentalism.* Albany: State University of New York Press, 1989.

Boris, Thomas A. "When WKBW Came Home." *United Evangelical Action,* 1 February 1946, 7–8.

Bounds, Elizabeth M. *Coming Together/Coming Apart: Religion, Community, and Modernity.* New York: Routledge, 1997.

Boyer, Paul. *When Time Shall Be No More: Prophecy Belief in Modern American Culture.* Cambridge: Harvard University Press, 1992.

Brinkley, Alan. *Voices of Protest: Huey Long, Father Coughlin, and the Great Depression.* New York: Vintage Books, 1982.

Brown, James A. "Selling Airtime for Controversy: NAB Self-Regulation and Father Coughlin." *Journal of Broadcasting* 24 (Spring 1980): 199–224.

Brown, Lloyd R. "A Survey of the Programming in Full-Time Religious

Broadcasting Stations in the United States." M.R.E. thesis, Biblical Seminary (New York City), 1952.

"Cadle of Indianapolis Streamlines Evangelism with Radio, Airplane, Glass-Fronted Baptismal Tank." *Life,* 27 March 1939, 73–77.

Cantril, Hadley, and Gordon W. Allport. *The Psychology of Radio.* New York: Peter Smith, 1941.

Carpenter, Joel A. "From Fundamentalism to the New Evangelical Coalition." In *Evangelicalism and Modern America,* edited by George Marsden, 3–16. Grand Rapids, Mich.: Eerdmans, 1984.

———. "Fundamentalist Institutions and the Rise of Evangelical Protestantism, 1929–1942." *Church History* 49 (1980): 62–75.

———. *Revive Us Again: The Reawakening of American Fundamentalism.* New York: Oxford University Press, 1997.

———, ed. *The Early Billy Graham: Sermon and Revival Accounts.* Fundamentalism in American Religion, 1880–1950. New York: Garland Publishing, 1988.

Casanova, José. *Public Religions in the Modern World.* Chicago: University of Chicago Press, 1994.

"Cash and Cadle." *Time,* 11 March 1939, 39.

"Cavert's Radio Letter, an Editorial." *Christian Beacon,* 3 July 1947, 1, 4–5.

"Christian Business Men's Magazine Discusses Radio." *Christian Beacon,* 22 November 1945, 6.

Clark, David L. "Miracles for a Dime: From Chautauqua Tent to Radio Station with Sister Aimee." *California History* 57 (Winter 1978/79): 354–63.

Clements, William M. "The Rhetoric of the Radio Ministry." *Journal of American Folklore* 87 (October–December 1974): 318–27.

Cohen, Lizbeth. *Making a New Deal: Industrial Workers in Chicago, 1919–1939.* Cambridge: Cambridge University Press, 1990.

Comstock, Sarah. "Aimee Semple McPherson; Prima Donna of Revivalism." *Harper's Monthly,* December 1927, 11–19.

Cornelius, R. M. "Their Stage Drew All the World: A New Look at the Scopes Evolution Trial." *Tennessee Historical Quarterly* 40 (Summer 1981): 129–43.

Covert, Catherine L. "'We May Hear Too Much': American Sensibility and the Response to Radio, 1919–1924." In *Mass Media between the Wars: Perceptions of Cultural Tensions, 1918–1941,* edited by Catherine L. Covert and John D. Stevens, 199–220. Syracuse, N.Y.: Syracuse University Press, 1984.

Covert, Catherine L., and John D. Stevens, eds. *Mass Media between the Wars: Perceptions of Cultural Tensions, 1918–1941.* Syracuse, N.Y.: Syracuse University Press, 1984.

Cox, Kenneth. "The FCC, the Constitution, and Religious Broadcast

Programming." *George Washington Law Review* 34 (December 1965): 196–218.

"Criticize Council's Suppression Policy." *United Evangelical Action,* 1 October 1946, 11.

Crowe, Charles. "Religion on the Air." *Christian Century,* 23 August 1944, 973–75.

"Crowley Makes a Plea for Gospel Broadcasts." *United Evangelical Action,* 1 August 1947, 9.

Cruz, Jon, and Justin Lewis, eds. *Viewing, Reading, Listening: Audiences and Cultural Reception.* Boulder, Colo.: Westview Press, 1994.

Czitrom, Daniel J. *Media and the American Mind: From Morse to McLuhan.* Chapel Hill: University of North Carolina Press, 1982.

Dacre, Douglas. "Aimee Semple McPherson: High Priestess of the Jazz Age." *Macleans,* November 1951, 12–82.

Danbom, David B. *Born in the Country: A History of Rural America.* Baltimore: Johns Hopkins University Press, 1995.

Daves, Michael. "Bible Belt Broadcasting." *Christian Century,* 28 June 1961, 800–801.

Davis, Richard Akin. "Radio Priest: The Public Career of Father Charles Edward Coughlin." Ph.D. diss., University of North Carolina, 1974.

Dekker, Gerard, Donald A. Luidens, and Rodger R. Rice, eds. *Rethinking Secularization: Reformed Reactions to Modernity.* Lanham, Md.: University Press of America, 1997.

Dorgan, Howard. *The Airwaves of Zion: Radio and Religion in Appalachia.* Knoxville: University of Tennessee Press, 1993.

Douglas, Mary. "The Effects of Modernization on Religious Change." In *Religion and America: Spiritual Life in a Secular Age,* edited by Mary Douglas and Steven Tipton, 25–42. Boston: Beacon Press, 1983.

"Echoes from Our Radio Audience." *Christian Beacon,* 13 February 1936, 6.

Eco, Umberto. *The Role of the Reader.* London: Hutchinson, 1981.

Edelman, Murray. *The Licensing of Radio Services in the United States, 1927 to 1947: A Study in Administrative Formulation of Policy.* Illinois Studies in the Social Sciences, vol. 31, no. 4. Urbana: University of Illinois Press, 1950.

"'Editorializing' Is New Radio Issue." *United Evangelical Action,* 1 October 1947, 9.

Eliade, Mircea. *The Sacred and the Profane: The Nature of Religion,* translated by Willard R. Trask. New York: Harcourt Brace, 1959.

Ellens, J. Harold. *Models of Religious Broadcasting.* Grand Rapids, Mich.: Eerdmans, 1974.

Ellwood, Robert S. *The Fifties Spiritual Marketplace: American Religion in a Decade of Conflict.* New Brunswick, N.J.: Rutgers University Press, 1997.

Epstein, Daniel Mark. *Sister Aimee: The Life of Aimee Semple McPherson.* San Diego: Harvest, Harcourt Brace and Company, 1993.

Erickson, Hal. *Religious Radio and Television in the United States, 1921–1991: Programs and Personalities.* Jefferson, N.C.: McFarland, 1992.

Eskridge, Larry K. "Evangelical Broadcasting: Its Meaning for Evangelicals." In *Transforming Faith: The Sacred and Secular in Modern American History,* edited by M. L. Bradbury and James B. Gilbert, 127–39. Westport, Conn.: Greenwood Press, 1989.

———. "Only Believe: Paul Rader and the Chicago Gospel Tabernacle, 1922–1933." M.A. thesis, University of Maryland, 1985.

Eskridge, Larry K., and Mark A. Noll. *More Money, More Ministry: Money and Evangelicals in Recent North American History.* Grand Rapids, Mich.: Eerdmans, 2000.

"Evangelical Action! A Report of the Organization of the National Association of Evangelicals for United Action" (1942). In *A New Evangelical Coalition: Early Documents of the National Association of Evangelicals,* edited by Joel A. Carpenter. Fundamentalism in American Religion, 1880–1950. New York: Garland Publishing, 1988.

Ewen, Stuart, and Elizabeth Ewen. *Channels of Desire: Mass Images and the Shaping of American Consciousness.* Minneapolis: University of Minnesota Press, 1992.

"Extracts from Radio Letters." *World Wide Christian Courier* September 1926, 33.

"FCC Likened to 'Thought Police.'" *New York Times,* 1 September 1948, 21.

"FCC Says Stations May Deny Time to Atheists." *United Evangelical Action,* 1 October 1948, 15.

"FCC Upholds Atheists' Rights to Time on Air." *Broadcasting and Telecasting,* 22 July 1946, 4, 97.

"Federal Court Upholds Radio Station in Refusal of Time to Religious Groups." *New York Times,* 13 October 1945, 26.

"Fifty Years of Proclaiming the 'Old, Old, Story of Jesus and His Wonderful Love': Waves of Truth from the Open Bible Fiftieth Anniversary Edition, 1930–1980." National Religious Broadcasters file on Charles Leaming. Faith Temple, St. Petersburg, Fla., 1980.

Finke, Roger, and Rodney Stark. *The Churching of America: Winners and Losers in Our Religious Economy.* New Brunswick, N.J.: Rutgers University Press, 1992.

Fishwick, Marshall W. "Father Coughlin Time: The Radio and Redemption." *Journal of Popular Culture* 22 (Fall 1988): 33–47.

Forbes, Bruce David, and Jeffrey H. Mahan, eds. *Religion and Popular Culture in America.* Berkeley: University of California Press, 2000.

Fox, Richard Wightman, and T. J. Jackson Lears. *The Culture of*

Consumption: Critical Essays in American History, 1880–1980. New York: Pantheon Books, 1983.

Franklin, Benjamin. *The Autobiography of Benjamin Franklin,* edited by Kenneth Silverman. New York: Penguin Books, 1986.

"Free Air for Atheists." *Newsweek,* 12 August 1946, 70.

Freund, Elizabeth. *The Return of the Reader: Reader-Response Criticism.* New York: Methuen, 1987.

Frizen, Edwin L. "A Radio Message." *World Wide Christian Courier* February 1928, 12.

Fuller, Daniel P. *Give the Winds a Mighty Voice: The Story of Charles E. Fuller.* Waco, Tex.: Word Books, 1972.

Fuller, Mrs. Charles E. [Grace], comp. *Heavenly Sunshine: Letters to the "Old-Fashioned Revival Hour."* Westwood, N.J.: Fleming H. Revell Co., 1956.

Gasper, Louis. *The Fundamentalist Movement, 1930–1956.* 1963. Reprint, Grand Rapids, Mich.: Baker Book House, 1981.

Gaustad, Edwin Scott. *"Did* the Fundamentalists Win?" In *Religion and America: Spiritual Life in a Secular Age,* edited by Mary Douglas and Steven Tipton, 169–78. Boston: Beacon Press, 1983.

Gilbert, James. *Redeeming Culture: American Religion in an Age of Science.* Chicago: University of Chicago Press, 1997.

Ginger, Ray. *Six Days of Forever? Tennessee v. John Thomas Scopes.* London: Oxford University Press, 1958.

Goethals, Gregor. *The Electronic Golden Calf: Images, Religion, and the Making of Meaning.* Cambridge, Mass.: Cowley Publications, 1990.

Goff, Philip K. "'We Have Heard the Joyful Sound': Charles E. Fuller's Radio Broadcast and the Rise of Modern Evangelicalism." *Religion and American Culture* 9, no. 1 (1999): 67–96.

Gould, Jack. "Clergymen Assail Radio Chain Curb." *New York Times,* 12 June 1941, L8.

Graham, Billy. *Just As I Am: The Autobiography of Billy Graham.* San Francisco: Zondervan/HarperSan Francisco, 1997.

Griswold, Clayton T. "New Methods in a Power Age." *Outreach: The Women's Magazine of the Boards of National and Foreign Missions and Christian Education,* March 1951, 1–2.

Grundy, Pamela. "'We Always Tried to Be Good People': Respectability, Crazy Water Crystals, and Hillbilly Music on the Air, 1933–1935." *Journal of American History* 81 (March 1995): 1591–1620.

Hadden, Jeffrey K., and Anson Shupe. *Televangelism: Power and Politics on God's Frontier.* New York: Henry Holt, 1988.

Hangen, Tona. "Fundamentalism's Unseen Victory in the Twenties." In *History in Dispute,* Vol. 3, *American Political and Social Movements, 1900–1945: Pursuit of Progress,* edited by Robert Allison, 36–39. Detroit: St. James Press, 2000.

———. "Man of the Hour: Walter A. Maier and Religion by Radio on the *Lutheran Hour.*" In *Radio Reader: Essays in the Cultural History of Radio,* edited by Michele Hilmes and Jason Loviglio, 113–34. New York: Routledge, 2001.

Harding, Susan. *The Book of Jerry Falwell: Fundamentalist Language and Politics.* Princeton, N.J.: Princeton University Press, 2001.

———. "Representing Fundamentalism: The Problem of the Repugnant Cultural Other." *Social Research* 58 (Summer 1991): 373–93.

Harrell, David Edwin, Jr. *All Things Are Possible: The Healing and Charismatic Revivals in Modern America.* Bloomington: Indiana University Press, 1975.

Hatch, Nathan O. *The Democratization of American Christianity.* New Haven: Yale University Press, 1989.

Hawkins, Karen M. "Diamond Days: Facets from the First 75 Years." *Religious Broadcasting* 28 (January 1996): 12–26.

"Hearing on Senate Bill." *Christian Beacon,* 3 July 1947, 1.

Hill, George H. *Airwaves to the Soul: The Influence and Growth of Religious Broadcasting.* Saratoga, Calif.: R&E Publishers, 1983.

Hilmes, Michele. *Radio Voices: American Broadcasting, 1922–1952.* Minneapolis: University of Minnesota Press, 1997.

Holub, Robert. *Reception Theory: A Critical Introduction.* London: Methuen, 1984.

Hood, John Lathan. "The New Old-Time Religion: Aimee Semple McPherson and the Original Electric Church." M.A. thesis, Wheaton College, 1981.

Hoover, Stewart M. *Mass Media Religion: The Social Sources of the Electronic Church.* Newbury Park, Calif.: Sage Publications, 1988.

Hoover, Stewart M., and Douglas K. Wagner. "History and Policy in American Broadcast Treatment of Religion." *Media, Culture and Society* 19, no. 1 (1997): 7–27.

Horsfield, Peter G. *Religious Television: The American Experience.* New York: Longman Publishing, 1984.

"How Big Is Gospel Radio?" *Christian Life,* January 1954, 24, 57, 86.

Hudnut-Beumler, James. *Looking for God in the Suburbs: The Religion of the American Dream and Its Critics, 1945–1965.* New Brunswick, N.J.: Rutgers University Press, 1994.

Hulsether, Mark. "Evangelical Popular Religion as a Source for North American Liberation Theology? Insights from Postmodern Popular Culture Theory." *American Studies* 33 (Spring 992): 63–81.

Hunt, Bill. "Church Big Biz for Radio." *Variety,* 1 December 1943; reprint in BNM 303.2-1-8.

Hunter, James Davison. *American Evangelicalism: Conservative Religion and the Quandary of Modernity.* New Brunswick, N.J.: Rutgers University Press, 1983.

Hutchinson, William R., ed. *Between the Times: The Travail of the Protestant Establishment, 1900–1960.* Cambridge: Cambridge University Press, 1989.

———. *The Modernist Impulse in American Protestantism.* Cambridge: Harvard University Press, 1976.

Jackson, Kenneth T. *Crabgrass Frontier: The Suburbanization of the United States.* New York: Oxford University Press, 1985.

Jacobsen, Douglas, and Vance Trollinger Jr., eds. *Re-forming the Center: American Protestantism, 1900 to the Present.* Grand Rapids, Mich.: Eerdmans, 1998.

Jameson, Frederic. "Reification and Utopia in Mass Culture." *Social Text* 1 (December 1979): 130–48.

Jellison, Katherine. *Entitled to Power: Farm Women and Technology, 1913–1963.* Chapel Hill: University of North Carolina Press, 1993.

Johnson, Willard. "Intolerance by Radio." In *Education on the Air: Thirteenth Yearbook of the Institute for Education by Radio,* edited by Josephine H. MacLatchy, 233–36. Columbus: Ohio State University, 1942.

Jones, Jacqueline. *The Dispossessed: America's Underclasses from the Civil War to the Present.* New York: Basic Books, 1992.

Kamensky, Jane. *Governing the Tongue: The Politics of Speech in Early New England.* New York: Oxford University Press, 1997.

King, William Maguire. "The Reform Establishment and the Ambiguities of Influence." In *Between the Times: The Travail of the Protestant Establishment, 1900–1960,* edited by William R. Hutchinson, 122–40. New York: Cambridge University Press, 1989.

Kintz, Linda, and Julia Lesage, eds. *Media, Culture, and the Religious Right.* Minneapolis: University of Minnesota Press, 1998.

Kirby, Jack Temple. *Rural Worlds Lost: The American South, 1920–1960.* Baton Rouge: Louisiana State University Press, 1987.

Kolakowski, Leszek. *Modernity on Endless Trial.* Chicago: University of Chicago Press, 1990.

Lacey, Linda-Jo. "The Electric Church: An FCC 'Established' Institution?" *Federal Communications Law Journal* 31, no. 2 (1978): 252–62

Lambert, Frank. *"Pedlar in Divinity": George Whitefield and the Transatlantic Revivals, 1737–1770.* Princeton, N.J.: Princeton University Press, 1994.

Larson, Edward J. *Summer for the Gods: The Scopes Trial and America's Continuing Debate over Science and Religion.* New York: Basic Books, 1997.

Larson, Mel. *God's Man in Manhattan* (1950). In *Enterprising Fundamentalism: Two Second-Generation Leaders,* edited by Joel A.

Carpenter. Fundamentalism in American Religion, 1880–1950. New York: Garland Publishing, 1988.

Lawrence, Bruce B. *Defenders of God: The Fundamentalist Revolt against the Modern Age.* San Francisco: Harper and Row, 1989.

Lazere, Donald, ed. *American Media and Mass Culture: Left Perspectives.* Berkeley: University of California Press, 1987.

Leach, William. *Land of Desire: Merchants, Power, and the Rise of a New American Culture.* New York: Pantheon Books, 1993.

Lears, T. J. Jackson. *Fables of Abundance: A Cultural History of Advertising in America.* New York: Basic Books, 1994.

Leibman, Nina C. *Living Room Lectures: The Fifties Family in Film and Television.* Austin: University of Texas, 1995.

Levine, Lawrence W. *Defender of the Faith: William Jennings Bryan: The Last Decade, 1915–1925.* New York: Oxford University Press, 1965.

Loevinger, Lee. "Religious Liberty and Broadcasting." *George Washington Law Review* 33 (March 1965): 631–59.

Long, Elizabeth. "Textual Interpretation as Collective Action." In *Viewing, Reading, Listening: Audiences and Cultural Reception,* edited by Jon Cruz and Justin Lewis, 181–211. Boulder, Colo.: Westview Press, 1994

Lothrop, Gloria Ricci. "West of Eden: Pioneer Media Evangelist Aimee Semple McPherson in Los Angeles." *Journal of the West* 27 (April 1988): 50–59.

Loveless, W. P. *Manual of Gospel Broadcasting.* Chicago: Moody, 1946.

Lynd, Robert S., and Helen Merrell Lynd. *Middletown: A Study in Modern American Culture.* New York: Harcourt Brace Jovanovich, 1929.

Lyon, Arabella. *Intentions: Negotiated, Contested, Ignored.* University Park: Pennsylvania State University Press, 1998.

MacDonald, J. Fred. *Don't Touch That Dial: Radio Programming in American Life, 1920–1960.* Chicago: Nelson-Hall, 1979.

MacLatchy, Josephine H., ed. *Education on the Air: Tenth Yearbook of the Institute for Education by Radio.* Columbus: Ohio State University, 1939.

Maier, Walter A. *Fourth Lutheran Hour: Winged Words for Christ.* St. Louis, Miss.: Concordia Publishing House, 1937.

Mallon, Winifred. "Radio Editorials Opposed by the CIO." *New York Times,* 5 March 1948, 20.

Mander, Mary S. "The Public Debate about Broadcasting in the Twenties: An Interpretive History." *Journal of Broadcasting* 28 (Spring 1984): 167–85.

Marchand, Philip. *Marshall McLuhan: The Medium and the Messenger.* New York: Ticknor and Fields, 1989.

Marquis, Alice Goldfarb. "Written on the Wind: The Impact of Radio during the 1930s." *Journal of Contemporary History* 19 (July 1984): 384–415.

Marsden, George. *Fundamentalism and American Culture: The Shaping of Twentieth-Century Evangelicalism, 1870-1925.* New York: Oxford University Press, 1980.

———. "Preachers of Paradox: The Religious New Right in Historical Perspective." In *Religion and America: Spiritual Life in a Secular Age,* edited by Mary Douglas and Steven Tipton, 150–68. Boston: Beacon Press, 1983.

———. *Reforming Fundamentalism: Fuller Seminary and the New Evangelicalism.* Grand Rapids, Mich.: Eerdmans, 1987.

Martin, William. "The God-Hucksters of Radio." *Atlantic,* June 1970, 51–56.

———. "Mass Communications." In *Encyclopedia of the American Religious Experience,* Vol. 3, *Studies of Traditions and Movements,* edited by Charles H. Lippy and Peter W. Williams, 1711–26. New York: Charles Scribner's Sons, 1988.

———. *With God on Our Side: The Rise of the Religious Right.* New York: Broadway Books, 1996.

Martín-Barbero, Jesús. *Communication, Culture, and Hegemony: From the Media to Mediations,* translated by Elizabeth Fox and Robert A. White. Newbury Park, Calif.: Sage Publications, 1993.

Marty, Martin E. "The Sacred and Secular in American History." In *Transforming Faith: The Sacred and Secular in Modern American History,* edited by M. L. Bradbury and James B. Gilbert, 1–10. Westport, Conn.: Greenwood Press, 1989.

Maus, Mike. "Believers as Behavers: News Coverage of Evangelicals by the Secular Media." In *American Evangelicals and the Mass Media: Perspectives on the Relationship between American Evangelicals and the Mass Media,* edited by Quentin J. Schultze, 253–73. Grand Rapids, Mich.: Academie Books, 1990.

May, Elaine Tyler. *Homeward Bound: American Families in the Cold War Era.* New York: Basic Books, 1988.

McChesney, Robert. *Telecommunications, Mass Media, and Democracy.* New York: Oxford University Press, 1993.

McGirr, Lisa. *Suburban Warriors: The Origins of the New American Right.* Princeton, N.J.: Princeton University Press, 2001.

McIntire, Carl. "Radio's New Code." *Christian Beacon,* 25 September 1947, 1–6.

———. *Twentieth Century Reformation* (1944). Fundamentalism in American Religion, 1880–1950. New York: Garland Publishing, 1988.

McLoughlin, William G. "Aimee Semple McPherson: 'Your Sister in the King's Glad Service.'" *Journal of Popular Culture* 1 (Winter 1967): 193–217.

———. *Revivals, Awakenings, and Reform: An Essay on Religion and Social Change in America, 1607–1977.* Chicago History of American Religion Series, edited by Martin Marty. Chicago: University of Chicago Press, 1978.

McPherson, Aimee Semple. *The Story of My Life.* Waco, Tex.: Word Books, 1973.

———. *This Is That: Personal Experiences, Sermons, and Writings.* Los Angeles: Echo Park Evangelistic Association, 1923.

McQuail, Denis. "Mass Media." In *The Social Science Encyclopedia,* 2d ed., edited by Adam Kuper and Jessica Kuper, 511–12. New York: Routledge, 1996.

McWilliams, Carey. "Aimee Semple McPherson: 'Sunlight in My Soul.'" In *The Aspirin Age, 1919–1941,* edited by Isabel Leighton, 50–80. New York: Simon and Schuster, 1949.

———. *Southern California Country: An Island on the Land.* New York: Duell, Sloan and Pearce, 1946.

Meister, J. W. Gregg. "Presbyterians and Mass Media: A Case of Blurred Vision and Missed Mission." In *The Diversity of Discipleship: The Presbyterians and Twentieth-Century Christian Witness,* edited by Milton J. Coalter, John M. Mulder, and Louis B. Weeks, 170–86. Louisville, Ky.: Westminster/John Knox Press, 1991.

Mencken, H. L. "Two Enterprising Ladies." *American Mercury,* April 1928, 506–8.

Meyrowitz, Joshua. *No Sense of Place: The Impact of Electronic Media on Social Behavior.* New York: Oxford University Press, 1985.

Miller, Robert Moats. *Harry Emerson Fosdick: Preacher, Pastor, Prophet.* New York: Oxford University Press, 1985.

"Minneapolis Pastors Protesting Radio Ban." *United Evangelical Action,* 1 July 1946, 10.

Minsky, Louis. "Religious Broadcasts: Report of a Work-Study Group." In *Education on the Air: Thirteenth Yearbook of the Institute for Education by Radio,* edited by Josephine H. MacLatchy, 243–56. Columbus: Ohio State University, 1942.

Mitchell, Jolyon. "Radio Religion: Radio Preachers in the USA, an Analysis of the Pictorial Language Used by Selected American Radio Preachers Broadcasting in a Visual Culture." Paper presented at the Conference on Media, Religion, and Culture, University of Colorado (Boulder), 1996.

Moore, R. Laurence. *Religious Outsiders and the Making of Americans.* New York: Oxford University Press, 1986.

———. *Selling God: American Religion in the Marketplace of Culture.* New York: Oxford University Press, 1994.

Morgan, Dan. *Rising in the West: The True Story of an "Okie" Family in Search of the American Dream.* New York: Vintage Books, 1992.

Morgan, David. *Visual Piety: A History and Theory of Popular Religious Images*. Berkeley: University of California Press, 1998.

Morley, David. "Changing Paradigms in Audience Research." In *Remote Control: Television, Audiences, and Cultural Power,* edited by Ellen Seiter et al., 16–43. London: Routledge, 1989.

Moser, J. G., and Richard A. Lavine. *Radio and the Law.* Los Angeles: Parker and Co., 1947.

"Move toward FCCCA Super Radio Control." *United Evangelical Action,* 1 April 1948, 14.

"Mr. Bennet's Brief Presented to Senate Committee." *Christian Beacon,* 3 July 1947, 5–6.

"Mr. McIntire's Testimony before the Senate Committee." *Christian Beacon,* 3 July 1947, 2.

Murch, James DeForest. *Adventuring for Christ in Changing Times: An Autobiography.* Louisville, Ky.: Restoration Press, 1973.

———. *Cooperation without Compromise.* Grand Rapids, Mich.: Eerdmans, 1956.

"NAB Adopts Religious Broadcasting Standards." *United Evangelical Action,* 1 April 1948, 14.

Neeb, Martin J., Jr. "An Historical Study of American Non-Commercial AM Broadcast Stations Owned and Operated by Religious Groups, 1920–1966." Ph.D. diss., Northwestern University, 1967.

Neely, Lois. *Come Up to This Mountain: The Miracle of Clarence W. Jones and HCJB.* Wheaton, Ill.: Tyndale House, 1980.

Nelson, Paula M. *The Prairie Winnows Out Its Own: The West River Country of South Dakota in the Years of Depression and Dust.* Iowa City: University of Iowa Press, 1996.

Neth, Mary. *Preserving the Family Farm: Women, Community, and the Foundations of Agribusiness in the Midwest, 1900–1940.* Baltimore: Johns Hopkins University Press, 1995.

"New Bills Revise Radio Act Sharply." *New York Times,* 24 May 1947, 30.

"New NAB Code Bars Attacks on Religion." *United Evangelical Action,* 1 October 1947, 9.

"New Organization in Religious Radio." *United Evangelical Action,* 1 June 1946, 14.

Nye, David E. *Electrifying America: Social Meanings of a New Technology, 1880–1940.* Cambridge: MIT Press, 1990.

Ong, Walter J. *The Presence of the Word: Some Prolegomena for Cultural and Religious History.* Minneapolis: University of Minnesota Press, 1981.

Orsi, Robert A. *Thank You St. Jude: Women's Devotion to the Patron Saint of Hopeless Causes.* New Haven: Yale University Press, 1996.

"Our Musical Evangelists: Their Life and Work." *Sacred Choralist,* August 1938, 116.

Parker, Everett C. "Big Business in Religious Radio." *Chicago Theological Seminary Register,* Winter 1944, 20–23.

Parker, Everett C., and Fred Eastman. "Religion on the Air in Chicago: A Study of Religious Programs on the Commercial Radio Stations of Chicago." *Chicago Theological Seminary Register,* Winter 1942, 12–22.

Parker, Everett C., David W. Barry, and Dallas W. Smythe. *The Television-Radio Audience and Religion.* New York: Harper and Brothers, 1955.

"Pastor Invites P. A. Atheist to Hear Answer to Broadcast." *Palo Alto Times,* 18 November 1946, 8.

Pratt, Henry J. *The Liberalization of American Protestantism: A Case Study in Complex Organizations.* Detroit: Wayne State University Press, 1972.

Rader, Paul. *Life's Greatest Adventure.* London: Victory Press, 1938.

———. *Paul Rader's Stories of His Early Life: Interspersed by Spiritual Messages of Priceless Value.* Chicago: Chicago Gospel Tabernacle, n.d.

———. *Radio Messages by Paul Rader.* Chicago: Chicago Gospel Tabernacle, 1928.

"Radio and Television." *New York Times,* 4 August 1948, 42.

"Radio Ranger Watch Tower." *National Radio Chapel Announcer,* December 1925, 13.

"Radio 'Soap Opera' Defended as Boon." *New York Times,* 21 June 1947, 28.

Reeves, Thomas C. *The Empty Church: The Suicide of Liberal Christianity.* New York: Free Press, 1996.

"Religious Showmanship Feud: Sermons 'Waste of Good Time.'" *Variety,* 20 August 1947, 25.

Rice, John R. *Bobbed Hair, Bossy Wives, and Women Preachers: Significant Questions for Honest Christian Women Settled by the Word of God.* Wheaton, Ill.: Sword of the Lord Publishers, 1941.

Rose, C. B., Jr. *National Policy for Radio Broadcasting: Report of a Committee of the National Economic and Social Planning Association.* New York: Harper and Brothers, 1940.

Rosen, Philip T. *The Modern Stentors: Radio Broadcasters and the Federal Government, 1920-1934.* Westport, Conn.: Greenwood Press, 1980.

Salmond, John A. "Clifford Judkins Durr." In *American National Biography,* edited by John A. Garraty and Mark C. Carnes, 7:158–59. New York: Oxford University Press, 1999.

Sandeen, Ernest R. *The Roots of Fundamentalism: British and American Millenarianism, 1800-1930.* Chicago: University of Chicago Press, 1970.

Saunders, Lowell Sperry. "The National Religious Broadcasters and the Availability of Commercial Radio Time." Ph.D. diss., University of Illinois, 1968.

Schlesinger, Arthur M., Jr. *The Age of Roosevelt: The Politics of Upheaval.* Boston: Houghton Mifflin, 1960.

Schneider, Robert A. "Voice of Many Waters: Church Federation in the Twentieth Century." In *Between the Times: The Travail of the Protestant Establishment, 1900–1960,* edited by William R. Hutchinson, 95–121. New York: Cambridge University Press, 1989.

Schultze, Quentin J. "Evangelical Radio and the Rise of the Electronic Church, 1921–1948." *Journal of Broadcasting and Electronic Media* 32 (Summer 1988): 289–306.

———. "The Invisible Medium: Evangelical Radio." In *American Evangelicals and the Mass Media: Perspectives on the Relationship between American Evangelicals and the Mass Media,* edited by Quentin J. Schultze, 171–95. Grand Rapids, Mich.: Academie Books, 1990.

———. "The Mythos of the Electronic Church." *Critical Studies in Mass Communication* 4 (September 1987): 245–61.

Schwarzlose, Richard A. "Technology and the Individual: The Impact of Innovation on Communication." In *Mass Media between the Wars: Perceptions of Cultural Tensions, 1918–1941,* edited by Catherine L. Covert and John D. Stevens, 87–106. Syracuse, N.Y.: Syracuse University Press, 1984.

Shanks, Kenneth Howard. "An Historical and Critical Study of the Preaching Career of Aimee Semple McPherson." Ph.D. diss., University of Southern California, 1960.

Siedell, Barry. *Gospel Radio.* Lincoln, Nebr.: Back to the Bible Broadcast, 1971.

Singal, Daniel Joseph. *The War Within: From Victorian to Modernist Thought in the South, 1919–1945.* Chapel Hill: University of North Carolina Press, 1982.

Singleton, Gregory H. "Popular Culture or the Culture of the Populace?" *Journal of Popular Culture* 11 (Summer 1977): 254–65.

———. *Religion in the City of Angels: American Protestant Culture and Urbanization, Los Angeles, 1850–1930.* Ann Arbor, Mich.: UMI Research Press, 1979.

Sittser, Gerald. *A Cautious Patriotism: The American Churches and the Second World War.* Chapel Hill: University of North Carolina Press, 1997.

Smith, Christian. *American Evangelicalism: Embattled and Thriving.* Chicago: University of Chicago Press, 1998.

Smith, Christian, David Sikkink, and Jason Bailey. "Devotion in Dixie and Beyond: A Test of the 'Shibley Thesis' on the Effects of Regional Origin and Migration on Individual Religiosity." *Journal of the Scientific Study of Religion* 37, no. 3 (1998): 494–506.

Smith, Wilbur M. *A Voice for God: The Life of Charles E. Fuller,*

Originator of the Old Fashioned Revival Hour. Boston: W. A. Wilde Co., 1949.

Smulyan, Susan. *Selling Radio: The Commercialization of American Broadcasting, 1920-1934.* Washington, D.C.: Smithsonian Institution Press, 1994.

Smythe, Dallas W. "The Meaning of the Communications Revolution." *Social Action* 23 (April 1958): 16–23.

Snow, Robert P. *Creating Media Culture.* Beverly Hills, Calif.: Sage Publishing, 1983.

Sobel, Robert. *The Manipulators: America in the Media Age.* Garden City, N.Y.: Anchor Press, 1976.

Stanley, Susie Cunningham. *Feminist Pillar of Fire: The Life of Alma White.* Cleveland, Ohio: Pilgrim Press, 1993.

Stanton, Frank. *Mass Media and Mass Culture.* Great Issues Lecture at the Hopkins Center, Dartmouth College, 26 November 1962. New York: Columbia Broadcasting System, 1963.

Stegner, Wallace. "The Radio Priest and His Flock." In *The Aspirin Age, 1919-1941,* edited by Isabel Leighton, 232–57. New York: Simon and Schuster, 1949.

Sterling, Christopher H., and John M. Kittross. *Stay Tuned: A Concise History of Broadcasting,* 2d ed. Belmont, Calif.: Wadsworth Publishing Co., 1990.

Stevens, John D. "Small Town Editors and the 'Modernized' Agrarian Myth." In *Mass Media between the Wars: Perceptions of Cultural Tensions, 1918-1941,* edited by Catherine L. Covert and John D. Stevens, 21–38. Syracuse, N.Y.: Syracuse University Press, 1984.

Stone, Jon R. *A Guide to the End of the World: Popular Eschatology in America.* New York: Garland Publishing, 1993.

———. *On the Boundaries of American Evangelicalism: The Postwar Evangelical Coalition.* New York: St. Martin's Press, 1997.

Stout, Harry S. *The New England Soul: Preaching and Religious Culture in Colonial New England.* New York: Oxford University Press, 1986.

Strasser, Susan. *Satisfaction Guaranteed: The Making of the American Mass Market.* Washington, D.C.: Smithsonian Institution Press, 1995.

Summers, H. B. "Iowa Rural Radio Listener: Survey: 1938." Kansas State College, Manhattan, Kans., 1938. Record Group 8/d–8/3, IER.

———. "Kansas Radio Listener: Survey: 1938." Kansas State College, Manhattan, Kans., 1938. Record Group 8/d–8/3, IER.

Summers, H. B., and F. L. Whan. "A Study of Radio Listening Habits in the State of Iowa, March, 1941." Central Broadcasting Company, Des Moines, Iowa, 1941. Record Group 8/d–8/3, IER.

Susman, Warren. "Communication and Culture: Keynote Essay." In *Mass Media between the Wars: Perceptions of Cultural Tensions, 1918-*

1941, edited by Catherine L. Covert and John D. Stevens, xvii–xxxii. Syracuse, N.Y.: Syracuse University Press, 1984.

Swatos, William H., Jr., and Daniel V. A. Olson, eds. *The Secularization Debate.* Lanham, Md.: Rowman and Littlefield, co-published with the Association of Sociology of Religion, 2000.

Sweet, Leonard I. "Communication and Change in American Religious History: A Historiographical Probe." In *Communication and Change in American Religious History,* edited by Leonard I. Sweet, 1–90. Grand Rapids, Mich.: Eerdmans, 1993.

"Tabernacle Fights for Its Broadcasting Rights." *United Evangelical Action,* 15 April 1946, 22.

Taylor, Ella. *Prime-Time Families: Television Culture in Postwar America.* Berkeley: University of California Press, 1989.

"Time for Atheism." *Time,* 2 December 1946, 75.

Tomaselli, Keyan G., and Arnold Shepperson. "Resistance through Mediated Orality." In *Rethinking Media, Religion, and Culture,* edited by Stewart M. Hoover and Knut Lundby, 209–26. Thousand Oaks, Calif.: Sage Publications, 1997.

Tompkins, Jane P., ed. *Reader-Response Criticism: From Formalism to Post-Structuralism.* Baltimore: Johns Hopkins University Press, 1980.

Tucker, W. Leon. *The Redemption of Paul Rader.* New York: Book Stall, 1918.

"Tuning In: The Story of a Convalescent Girl Who 'Tuned In' and Found Happiness." *National Radio Chapel Announcer,* December 1925, 8.

Turner, Timothy A. *Preaching to Programmed People: Effective Communication in a Media-Saturated Society.* Grand Rapids, Mich.: Kregel Publications, 1995.

"Twisting the Devil's Tail." *Time,* 16 March 1953, 82.

Tyson, Levering, and Josephine MacLatchy, eds. *Education on the Air and Radio and Education, 1935.* Chicago: University of Chicago Press, 1935.

"United We Stand: A Report of the Constitutional Convention of the National Association of Evangelicals, May 3–6, 1943" (1943). In *A New Evangelical Coalition: Early Documents of the National Association of Evangelicals,* edited by Joel A. Carpenter. Fundamentalism in American Religion, 1880–1950. New York: Garland Publishing, 1988.

U.S. House. *Investigation of Port Huron Decision and Scott Decision: First Interim Report of the Select Committee to Investigate the Federal Communications Commission Pursuant to H. Res. 691,* issued 24 September 1948, Miscellaneous House Reports, 80th Cong., 2d sess., H. Rept. 2461. CIS US Serial Set, Fiche 11213–19.

Van Kirk, Walter W. "The Duty of Religious Radio in Time of War."

In *Education on the Air: Thirteenth Yearbook of the Institute for Education by Radio,* edited by Josephine H. MacLatchy, 223–28. Columbus: Ohio State University, 1942.

Voskuil, Dennis N. "The Power of the Air: Evangelicals and the Rise of Religious Broadcasting." In *American Evangelicals and the Mass Media: Perspectives on the Relationship between American Evangelicals and the Mass Media,* edited by Quentin J. Schultze, 69–95. Grand Rapids, Mich.: Academie Books, 1990.

———. "Reaching Out: Mainline Protestantism and the Media." In *Between the Times: The Travail of the Protestant Establishment in America, 1900-1960,* edited by William R. Hutchinson, 72–92. New York: Cambridge University Press, 1989.

Wacker, Grant. *Heaven Below: Early Pentecostals and American Culture.* Cambridge: Harvard University Press, 2001.

———. "Travail of a Broken Family: Evangelical Responses to Pentecostalism." *Journal of Ecclesiastical History* 47 (July 1996): 505–28.

Ward, Mark, Sr. *Air of Salvation: The Story of Christian Broadcasting.* Grand Rapids, Mich.: Baker Book House, 1994.

Warner, R. Stephen. *New Wine in Old Wineskins: Evangelicals and Liberals in a Small-Town Church.* Berkeley: University of California Press, 1988.

———. "Work in Progress toward a New Paradigm for the Sociological Study of Religion in the United States." *American Journal of Sociology* 98 (1993): 1044–93.

Watt, David Harrington. *A Transforming Faith: Explorations of Twentieth-Century American Evangelicalism.* New Brunswick, N.J.: Rutgers University Press, 1991.

Webb, Lillian Ashcraft. *About My Father's Business: The Life of Elder Michaux.* Westport, Conn.: Greenwood Press, 1981.

Weber, Max. *The Protestant Ethic and the Spirit of Capitalism,* translated by Talcott Parsons. New York: Charles Scribner's Sons, 1959.

Weber, Timothy. *Living in the Shadow of the Second Coming: American Premillennialism, 1875-1925.* Chicago: University of Chicago Press, 1987.

"White Asks Shelving for His Radio Bill." *New York Times,* 28 June 1947, 16.

Whitfield, Stephen J. *The Culture of the Cold War.* Baltimore: Johns Hopkins University Press, 1991.

Wilson, John F. *Public Religion in American Culture.* Philadelphia: Temple University Press, 1979.

Winrod, Gerald B. *Persecuted Preachers.* Wichita, Kans.: Defender Publishers, 1946.

"Witnesses Score White's Radio Bill." *New York Times,* 26 June 1947, 46.

Wright, J. Elwin. *Death in the Pot: An Appraisal of the Federal Council of the Churches of Christ in America.* Boston: Fellowship Press, 1944.

———. *The Old Fashioned Revival Hour and the Broadcasters.* Boston: Fellowship Press, 1942.

———. "Radio Freedom of Speech." *United Evangelical Action,* 1 September 1946, 13.

———. "Radio Problems Reviewed." *United Evangelical Action,* 1 August 1942, 1.

Wuthnow, Robert. *The Restructuring of American Religion: Society and Faith since World War II.* Princeton, N.J.: Princeton University Press, 1988.

———. *The Struggle for America's Soul: Evangelicals, Liberals, and Secularism.* Grand Rapids, Mich.: Eerdmans, 1989.

Yamane, David. "Secularization on Trial: In Defense of a Neosecularization Paradigm." *Journal of the Scientific Study of Religion* 36, no. 1 (1997): 109–22.

Young, Lloyd E. "Gospel Broadcasters and Frequency Modulation." *United Evangelical Action,* 1 March 1947, 5–8.

Zunz, Olivier. *Making America Corporate, 1880–1920.* Chicago: University of Chicago Press, 1990.

Index